The Comics World

The Comics World

COMIC BOOKS, GRAPHIC NOVELS, AND THEIR PUBLICS

Edited by Benjamin Woo and Jeremy Stoll

University Press of Mississippi / Jackson

The University Press of Mississippi is the scholarly publishing agency of
the Mississippi Institutions of Higher Learning: Alcorn State University,
Delta State University, Jackson State University, Mississippi State University,
Mississippi University for Women, Mississippi Valley State University,
University of Mississippi, and University of Southern Mississippi.

www.upress.state.ms.us

Designed by Peter D. Halverson

The University Press of Mississippi is a member
of the Association of University Presses.
Copyright © 2021 by University Press of Mississippi

First printing 2021

∞

Library of Congress Cataloging-in-Publication Data

Names: Woo, Benjamin, editor. | Stoll, Jeremy, editor.
Title: The comics world: comic books, graphic novels, and their publics /
Benjamin Woo, Jeremy Stoll.
Description: Jackson: University Press of Mississippi, 2021. | Includes
bibliographical references and index.
Identifiers: LCCN 2021008783 (print) | LCCN 2021008784 (ebook) | ISBN
978-1-4968-3464-5 (hardback) | ISBN 978-1-4968-3465-2 (trade paperback) | ISBN
978-1-4968-3466-9 (epub) | ISBN 978-1-4968-3467-6 (epub) | ISBN 978-1-4968-
3468-3
(pdf) | ISBN 978-1-4968-3469-0 (pdf)
Subjects: LCSH: Comic books, strips, etc.—Social aspects. | Graphic
novels—Social aspects. | Comic books, strips, etc.—History and
criticism. | Graphic novels—History and criticism.
Classification: LCC PN6710 .C6676 2021 (print) | LCC PN6710 (ebook) | DDC
741.5/9—dc23
LC record available at https://lccn.loc.gov/2021008783
LC ebook record available at https://lccn.loc.gov/2021008784

British Library Cataloging-in-Publication Data available

Contents

Part 2. Circulation
89

Part 3. Reception
165

"Comics and Commerce in Canada" © 2015 Jesse Jacobs. Originally published as "The Path to TCAF: Jesse Jacobs" in the *National Post*, May 6, 2015. Reproduced with permission of the artist.

Comic Books, Graphic Novels, and Their Publics

INTRODUCING THE COMICS WORLD

Benjamin Woo and Jeremy Stoll

Imagine, if you will, a world with comic books and graphic novels at its center.

In a one-page strip commissioned by Canada's *National Post* to promote the 2015 Toronto Comic Arts Festival, the London, Ontario-based cartoonist Jesse Jacobs depicts a parallel universe where, owing to a "distinct climate and fertile soil," Canada is the heart of the comics world. This Canada is blessed with rare and valuable deposits of raw pigment and has pioneered an approach to paper production that involves growing maple trees under water and then slicing the logs like bologna. "Such an abundance of materials, in combination with generous tax breaks and government incentives," Jacobs's narrator intones, mimicking the voice of educational filmstrips of yesteryear, "have given Canada a competitive edge," and, consequently, "most of the multinational comic publishing corporations have relocated their headquarters to Toronto and the surrounding area." In this reality, the Toronto Comic Arts Festival isn't an annual convention of art comics aficionados held in the main branch of the Toronto Public Library but a Davos-like conclave of "wealthy executives and investors" who gather to celebrate their dominance of the global comic book industry.

This, of course, is not our world. Even if we aren't fooled by the clearly counterfactual claim that comics publishing is a "billion dollar a year industry" that buttresses the Canadian economy with thousands of "good union jobs," even if we know there's no such thing as the Assiniboine volcano range, there is something *uncanny* about Jacobs's art—even the geometry is different, as forms that we know ought to be circular stretch into oblongs. And what are we to make of the strange figure that floats cross-legged against a cosmic background, reading a comic book with its third eye open? Perhaps it is an artifact of the artist's interest in psychedelic imagery (Jacobs 2017; Denney 2018), yet it is hard to dismiss the panel as a merely decorative embellishment. Beyond its size—taking up more than a quarter of the entire strip—its placement in the lower *left* corner of the page, rather than the right, invites readers to return to the image over and over again as they scan down the page. Moreover, the figure pops against the teal and dark blue that dominate the page; its glossy, balloon-animal body is instead colored with the intense hues that are used as highlights throughout but are especially associated with comics. Should we envision this figure as some kind of Uatu-like alien observer who flips between universes as easily as we turn a page, or might it represent a more mundane presence like the reader themself?

Although Jacobs's visual style is most reminiscent of contemporaries like Michael DeForge or Marc Bell in its noodly grotesquerie, the strip's content evokes another tradition, the phony comic book history. But, where Seth's (2011) *Great Northern Brotherhood of Canadian Cartoonists* and Dylan Horrocks's (2001) *Hicksville* spin alternative aesthetic histories of the comics form itself and Sonny Liew's (2016) *The Art of Charlie Chan Hock Chye* uses his imaginary cartoonist to deconstruct the narrative of Singapore's political history, Jacobs implicitly raises questions about the conditions of his own work: If ink doesn't bubble up from the earth and get imprinted on thin slices of underwater maple, how *are* comics made? If comic books are not really the fastest growing sector of the economy, how *do* their creators make ends meet? The strip's conceit is only funny because it is patently false, so Jacobs's strip is one of the rare texts that demands we acknowledge its political economy. In doing so, it reminds the reader that comics and graphic novels are not simply entertaining fantasies or artful depictions of another's experience but that they are also and always already objects with a "social life" of their own (Woo 2013; Appadurai 1986). At a minimum, they are made by someone, they circulate through specific institutions in order to find their way to readers and audiences, and they have real effects in the world. For those who make their livings around comics or who claim comics reading and fandom as important parts of their identity, comics already lie at the center of our subjectively meaningful worlds.

Few questions in comics studies' short history have proven as vexing as the search for what Thierry Groensteen (2007, 12) has called "the impossible definition." Defining what comics are and how they work was a pressing concern for the generation of writers who struggled to have comics and graphic novels seen as a medium complex and rich enough to warrant the same scholarly attention as prose, poetry, visual art, or film and television. Consequently, the "attempt at definition" became a "distinct rhetorical convention" of comics scholarship (Hatfield 2010, 10)—the scholarly equivalent of "Bang! Pow! Comics aren't just for kids anymore" newspaper headlines. But, as a flurry of recent work reflecting on the past and future of comics studies suggests (Duncan and Smith 2017; Gordon 2019; Jacobs 2019; Misemer 2019; Woo 2019; "On Hillary Chute's *Why Comics?*" 2019), the field has reached something of an inflection point. Comics scholarship is thriving, and the teaching of comics and graphic novels has a presence at every level from elementary schools to graduate programs. As a result, this is an opportune moment to question the project of comics studies itself. Freed from the imperative to justify our own existence, then, where do we want to go next as a field? Instead of definitional questions like "*What* are comics?" (Hayman and Pratt 2005) or justificatory ones like "*Why* comics?" (Chute 2017), comics studies might begin asking how comics move through the socially and culturally constituted worlds in which we live, how they anchor or order the practices that unfold there, and how these investigations can reflect back on and enrich our understanding of the texts themselves. We contend that these crucial *how* questions can be productively pursued through concepts and methods derived from social sciences.

The Comics World collects essays that, each in their own way, seek to understand comics through concepts, theories, and methods derived from the social-scientific tradition. We seek to advance different ways of looking that reorient comics scholarship around the agents, institutions, and social fields that structure and are structured through their relationships with comics and graphic novels. Our intention with this volume is three-fold: (1) to help establish comics and graphic novels as an area of research within social-science disciplines, just as our colleagues have worked to make space in humanities disciplines; (2) to bring together examples of what this work might look like and present some findings from a range of case studies that can enrich our knowledge and understanding of contemporary and historical comics; and (3) to promote interdisciplinary dialog *across* the humanities/social sciences divide and thereby strengthen comics studies as a field. With Dale Jacobs (2019), we affirm that the path forward for comics studies lies in a reflective practice that "not only acknowledges . . . disparate disciplinary approaches but also attempts to capitalize on their various strengths."

We do not wish to limit "social-scientific inquiry" to particular disciplinary backgrounds or research methods, whether quantitative or qualitative. Contributors to this volume write as sociologists, political scientists, and social psychologists but also as historians, folklorists, business analysts, and rhetoric scholars, among other specialisms. Their work takes up a variety of theoretical and methodological approaches, but they all provide accounts of comics that are grounded in the social and cultural contexts where comics are made, circulated, and used. Rather than a collection of specific disciplines, we take "social science" to signify a certain quality of mind, a way of looking at the world that recognizes that the most intimate and personal aspects of our own experiences are the products of social, cultural, and historical forces that transcend the individual. This ability to link "personal troubles" and "public issues" is what C. Wright Mills famously called "the sociological imagination":

> The first fruit of this imagination—and the first lesson of the social science that embodies it—is the idea that the individual can understand his own experience and gauge his own fate only by locating himself within his period, that he can know his own chances in life only by becoming aware of those of all individuals in his circumstances. In many ways it is a terrible lesson; in many ways a magnificent one. (Mills 2000, 5)

That Mills speaks of helping people *understand* their own circumstances already points to the fact that meaning is constitutive of social life, and that's one important difference between social-scientific inquiry and other ways of knowing. The subjects of the social sciences are ultimately people, and people are meaning-making, agentic actors. Unlike rocks or atoms or books, they not only have their own ideas about the world, which may be radically different from the conceptual models researchers create, but they can also talk back to their would-be interpreters; they may even change their behavior on the basis of scholars' findings. At the same time, however, every actor plays a role, and social-scientific inquiry also recognizes that, while we may construct meaning in many ways, the institutions in which we live shape the possibilities and constraints for action. Social-scientific inquiry strives to understand and explain social action—that is, acts that are *both* subjectively meaningful *and* oriented to the behavior of others (Weber 1978, 4)—at the intersection of structure and agency.

This broadly social-scientific approach could be applied to comic books and graphic novels in many ways, and we note a recent turn in comics studies that seeks to supplement the close reading of texts with understandings of the contexts in which they are made meaningful. As part of her "call for a greater engagement with archives in comics studies," for instance, Margaret Galvan (2018) shows how an "overreliance on published and available texts skews the visible reality of what we analyze," as when scholars isolate the Alison Bechdel of *Fun Home* without noting how "grassroots" publications and their publics shaped and sustained her publishing career (409). Similarly, Leah Misemer has identified "correspondence zones" as discursive spaces that enable interchange between geographically distant creators (2018a) and among creators and their audiences over time (2018b), while others have shown how comics developed in dialog with other technologies (Smolderen 2014; Gardner 2012) or cultural forms and social movements, such as punk and riot grrl (Miller 2018). That is to say, key contexts tend to disappear from view when we take published books alone as objects of analysis, and they cannot be recovered simply by reading the texts "better." The social sciences certainly don't have a monopoly on interesting questions, and this volume is not intended as a template for how to do "social-scientific comics studies." We recognize the importance of allowing for gaps—whether they be the spaces between panels or spaces for new voices, methods, and approaches.

Yet, the call for a field that has traditionally thought of itself as a humanities (inter-)discipline to embrace the social sciences will nonetheless seem provocative (Woo 2019). Indeed, our provocation is intended to *problematize* comics and graphic novels, to encourage self-conscious reflection on how they appear as a problem to be investigated, on what we really want to know about them, and on the theories and methods that will enable us to answer those research questions (Sandberg and Alvesson 2011; see also Barnett 2015). We are, in other words, asking readers to think with and about comics differently. For the purposes of this collection, we have tried to be minimalists and employed a simple rule of thumb, soliciting contributions that try to understand comics in terms of some group of human beings that we might call, following Michael Warner (2002), a *public*. According to Warner, a public is both a kind of social space and a kind of relationship among persons that is created when people share an orientation to some object. While readers and audiences of texts are perhaps the most familiar publics, we want to extend Warner's idea that publics are constituted by "attention" (60–62) to think about the many publics created when people attend to comics. On this view, comics themselves are "boundary objects" that coordinate understandings and actions between these communities (Star and Griesemer 1989), enabling the constitution of what we may call a "comics world" from their interactions.

In *Comics versus Art*, Bart Beaty (2012) introduces the notion of the comics world to describe the field of cultural production oriented to comics and comic art. A comics world is a social system with distinctive ways of knowing, speaking, and doing comics. Beaty is drawing a parallel not only to lay conceptions of "the art world" but also to institutional approaches in the

sociology of art, such as those associated with Arthur Danto (1964), Howard
S. Becker (1982), and Richard Peterson (1985). According to Becker (1982), an
art world comprises everyone necessary for a work of art to be produced in
the way that it was in fact produced. These art worlds generally include—in
addition to the "artists" or "creatives" themselves—curators, agents, dealers,
critics, technical support staff, manufacturers of specialized equipment or
supplies, and the various real or imagined audiences who ultimately receive
the work. The comics world, by extension, can be understood as the social
actors who condition the production, mediation, and consumption of comics
in their myriad forms:

> Following Becker, we can define a comics world as one of many art
> worlds, and specifically as the collection of individuals necessary for
> the production of works that the world defines as comics. This divi-
> sion of labour would include, just on the level of production and cir-
> culation, writers, pencillers, inkers, colourists, letterers, editors, assis-
> tant editors, publishers, marketing and circulation personnel, printers,
> distributors, retailers, and retail employees. (Beaty 2012, 37)

There have been lively debates about the relative emphasis that ought to be
placed on comics produced in an "auteurist" mode versus the comic book
industry's more obviously commercially oriented works, which are typically
produced by collaborative teams (Chute 2008; Saunders and Chute 2009;
Beaty and Woo 2016; Hoberek 2019), but even the most Crusoe-like cartoonists must engage with a comics world at some point. As Roger Chartier
(1989, 161) reminds us, authors may create texts but it is publishers that make
(comic) books, and the transubstantiation of one into the other involves a
thousand mediations by many hands. We obviously find this conception of
the comics world extremely suggestive, yet it needs to be extended somewhat
if we are to encompass a broader range of social and cultural activity taking
place around comics than the specific art world Beaty describes.

First, we want to explicitly affirm that there is no single, unified comics
world. There are potentially as many worlds as there are kinds of comics—
and vice versa. For instance, while the term should not be taken as a straightforward substitute for "world comics" or transnational studies of comics (cf.
Berndt 2010), national and regional comics cultures are obvious candidates
for comics worlds, particularly when they seem to display characteristic
or distinctive aesthetic sensibilities and conventions, as in the case of the
Franco-Belgian bande dessinée or Japanese manga (see, e.g., Exner, this volume). Within these worlds, differences of genre, format, institutions, aesthetic

traditions, or readerships could be sufficient to distinguish another comics world if they are recognized as important by members. At the same time, these distinct comics worlds often overlap and interact with one another. Thus, "the comics world" does not name an object or closed system sitting out there in the world waiting to be discovered but a *problematic*, a way of posing questions about comics and the human activity that surrounds them.

Second, understanding comics through the concept of art worlds requires an expansion in the potential worlds involved. Beaty's definition explicates the comics world at "the level of production and circulation," and the recent turn to production and labor in comics studies (Brienza 2010; Brienza and Johnston 2016; Woo 2015) has certainly been one way of "sociologizing" comics studies (cf. Locke 2012). However, the meaning and uses to which comics are put are not necessarily determined by their producers. If we transpose the interactionist conception of an art world into a Bourdieusian key, we see that art worlds are *social fields* that encompass a wide variety of actors whose relations are structured by their position and symbolic capital (Bourdieu 1993, 1996; Bourdieu and Wacquant 1992). In this sense, the list of people involved in "producing" comics embraces anyone who participates in the field of comics and not just "industry" people.

Third, Beaty did not, in our view, fully articulate the implications of the perspectival shift he introduced. Comics scholars have frequently pointed to the multidisciplinary, interdisciplinary, or even *undisciplined* nature of the field (e.g., Hatfield 2010; Jacobs, 2019; Jenkins 2012; Steirer 2011). In actual practice, however, the bulk of comics scholarship resides comfortably within humanities disciplines. Early scholarship on comics mainly responded to a social problem framework and was taken up in fields like education, psychology, and mass communications, and scholars based in the social sciences or using social-scientific methods have made significant contributions to comics scholarship (see, e.g., Gordon 2017; Barker 1989; Pustz 1999; Brown 2001; Brienza 2010; Carpenter 2012), but the field today is unquestionably dominated by scholars trained and teaching in departments of literature. While not uncontested, the twin discourses of "comics as literature" and "the graphic novel" have nonetheless been decisive in comics studies' recent explosive growth, and, as Beaty and Woo (2016, 28) argue, "Comics studies, no less than the comics themselves, has been reshaped in order to find a place in literature departments." Looking to the comics world, rather than the comics themselves, as a locus of meaning and privileged site for explanation entails a very different way of doing comics studies, disrupting the taken-for-grantedness of criticism and interpretation as the field's raison d'etre.

The comics world, then, provides a flexible, pragmatic way of relating text to context—of drawing out the particular, contingent, and contested relationships that connect comics and society (Williams 1986). While the specific people, institutions, and practices that come into focus will depend upon the problems that we pursue, starting from this conception of the comics world prompts different questions, suggests different approaches, and requires different tools. It helps us to see comic books and graphic novels as part of a lived social reality that both shapes and is shaped by them. This kind of understanding is prerequisite—necessary, if not sufficient—to critical, reflexive engagement with the fields of social action oriented to comics. If we wish to confront controversies like #Comicsgate or working conditions in comics, if we want to ensure that marginalized audiences can see themselves represented in comics and marginalized creators have an opportunity to have their voices heard, if we want the field of comics studies to grow and thrive, then we will need to know something of how the comics world works.

Each chapter of this book engages with the social life of comic books and graphic novels, using specific texts, groups, or cultural practices to limn the contours of a comics world. Contributors demonstrate some of the ways people participate in comics worlds and how the relationships created in these spaces provide new perspectives on comics and comics studies. We've organized the chapters into three sections, reflecting three "moments" in the creation of meaning: production, circulation and re-mediation, and reception. This structure mimics classic models of communication (see Genosko 2012) while also loosely corresponding to overlapping "levels" in the comics industry (e.g., creators and publishers; distributors, retailers, and other intermediaries; fans and audiences). We recognize that this is a somewhat crude and merely analytic distinction; the people described in these chapters—and the social, cultural, and economic practices in which they are engaged—readily and regularly cross these boundaries. However, it also suggests how different points of entry can lead to similar lines of inquiry (compare, e.g., how Woo, Maynard, Sabeti, Galdieri, and Sinervo's chapters engage with questions of authorship and creativity or how gender plays out in contributions by Lent, Wieskamp, and Estrada Wilson), while the same object can take us to different places (see, e.g., Salkowitz's and Edmunds's different views on comic conventions). The range of sites for investigation and intervention showcased in the following pages is, of course, only the beginning, but they start to open up the complexity of how comics and graphic novels matter to different people at different times and for different reasons. Thus, we hope this volume directs our colleagues to the exciting, messy world *around* comic books and graphic novels. One of the virtues of the social-scientific model of inquiry we are advocating is that you never know what you're going to find until you look, so consider *The Comics World* an invitation to go exploring.

References

Appadurai, Arjun, ed. 1986. *The Social Life of Things: Commodities in Cultural Perspective.* Cambridge: Cambridge University Press.

Barker, Martin. 1989. *Comics, Ideology, Power and the Critics.* Manchester: Manchester University Press.

Barnett, Clive. 2015. "On Problematization: Elaborations on a Theme in 'Late Foucault.'" *nonsite .org.* 16, https://nonsite.org/article/on-problematization.

Beaty, Bart. 2012. *Comics versus Art: Comics in the Art World.* University of Toronto Press.

Beaty, Bart, and Benjamin Woo. 2016. *The Greatest Comic Book of All Time: Symbolic Capital and the Field of American Comic Books.* New York: Palgrave Macmillan.

Becker, Howard S. 1982. *Art Worlds.* Berkeley and Los Angeles: University of California Press.

Berndt, Jaqueline, ed. 2010. *Comics Worlds and the World of Comics: Towards Scholarship on a Global Scale.* Kyoto: Kyoto Seika University International Manga Research Center.

Bourdieu, Pierre. 1993. *The Field of Cultural Production: Essays on Art and Literature.* Edited by Randal Johnson. Cambridge, UK: Polity Press.

Bourdieu, Pierre. 1996. *The Rules of Art: Genesis and Structure of the Literary Field.* Cambridge, UK: Polity Press.

Bourdieu, Pierre, and Loïc J. D. Wacquant. 1992. *An Invitation to Reflexive Sociology.* Chicago: University of Chicago Press.

Brienza, Casey. 2010. "Producing Comics Culture: A Sociological Approach to the Study of Comics." *Journal of Graphic Novels and Comics* 1 (2): 105–19.

Brienza, Casey, and Paddy Johnston, eds. 2016. *Cultures of Comics Work.* New York: Palgrave Macmillan.

Brown, Jeffrey A. 2001. *Black Superheroes, Milestone Comics, and Their Fans.* Jackson: University Press of Mississippi.

Carpenter, Stanford W. 2012. "Ethnography of Production: Editor Axel Alonso and the Sale of Ideas." In *Critical Approaches to Comics: Theories and Methods,* edited by Matthew J. Smith and Randy Duncan. New York: Routledge.

Chartier, Roger. 1989. "Texts, Printing, Readings." In *The New Cultural History,* edited by Lynn Hunt, 154–75. Berkeley and Los Angeles: University of California Press.

Chute, Hillary. 2017. *Why Comics? From Underground to Everywhere.* New York: Harper.

Danto, Arthur. 1964. "The Artworld." *The Journal of Philosophy* 61 (19): 571–84. doi:10.2307/2022937.

Denney, Alex. 2018. "Cult Cartoonist Jesse Jacobs Selects His Favourite Frames." Dazed, April 23. https://www.dazeddigital.com/art-photography/article/39690/1/jesse-jacobs -comic-cartoonist-pick-his-favourites.

Galvan, Margaret. 2018. "'The Lesbian Norman Rockwell': Alison Bechdel and Queer Grassroots Networks." *American Literature* 90 (2): 407–38.

Gardner, Jared. 2012. *Projections: Comics and the History of Twenty-First-Century Storytelling*. Stanford: Stanford University Press.

Genosko, Gary. 2012. *Remodelling Communication: From WWII to the WWW*. Toronto: University of Toronto Press.

Gordon, Ian. 2017. "Ideological/Sociological." In *The Secret Origins of Comics Studies*, edited by Matthew J. Smith and Randy Duncan, 118–29. New York: Routledge.

Gordon, Ian. 2019. "Comics Studies in America: The Making of a Field of Scholarship?" In *The Oxford Handbook of Comic Book Studies*, edited by Frederick Luis Aldama. doi: 10.1093/oxfordhb/9780190917944.013.36.

Groensteen, Thierry. 2007. *The System of Comics*. Translated by Bart Beaty and Nick Nguyen. Jackson: University Press of Mississippi.

Hatfield, Charles. 2010. "Indiscipline, or, The Condition of Comics Studies." *Transatlantica* 1. http://transatlantica.revues.org/4933.

Hayman, Greg, and Henry John Pratt. 2005. "What Are Comics?" In *A Reader in Philosophy of the Arts*, edited by David Goldblatt and Lee Brown, pp. 419–24. Upper Saddle River, NJ: Pearson Education.

Hoberek, Andrew. 2019. "Building and Unbuilding a Comics Canon." *PMLA* 134 (3): 614–19.

Horrocks, Dylan. 2001. *Hicksville*. Montreal: Drawn & Quarterly.

Jacobs, Dale. 2019. "Comics Studies as Interdiscipline." *The Oxford Handbook of Comic Book Studies*, edited by Frederick Luis Aldama. doi:10.1093/oxfordhb/9780190917944.013.38.

Jacobs, Jesse. 2015. "Comics and Commerce in Canada." Originally published under the headline, "The Path to TCAF: Jesse Jacobs." *The National Post*, May 6. https://nationalpost.com/entertainment/books/the-path-to-tcaf-jesse-jacobs.

Jacobs, Jesse. 2017. "'So Many People Are Allergic to Ideas of Spirituality': An Interview with Jesse Jacobs." By Matthew James-Wilson. Hazlitt, November 7. https://hazlitt.net/feature/so-many-people-are-allergic-ideas-spirituality-interview-jesse-jacobs.

Jenkins, Henry. 2012. "Should We Discipline the Reading of Comics?" In *Critical Approaches to Comics: Theories and Methods*, edited by Randy Duncan and Matthew J. Smith, pp. 1–14. New York: Routledge.

Liew, Sonny. 2015. *The Art of Charlie Chan Hock Chye*. New York: Pantheon Books.

Locke, Simon. 2012. "Constructing a Sociology of Comics." Comics Forum (blog), January 13. https://comicsforum.org/2012/01/13/constructing-a-sociology-of-comics-by-simon-locke/.

Miller, Rachel. 2018. "From the Xeroxed Frontier: Mini-Comics, Anthologies, & Comics by Girls, Grrrls, & Wimmen in the 1990s." Paper presented at the first annual conference of the Comics Studies Society, Urbana-Champaign, IL, August.

Mills, C. Wright. 2000. *The Sociological Imagination*. Oxford: Oxford University Press.

Misemer, Leah. 2018a. "Hands across the Ocean: A 1970s Network of French and American Women Cartoonists." In *Comics Studies Here and Now*, edited by Frederick Luis Aldama, 191–210. New York: Routledge.

Misemer, Leah. 2018b. "Correspondence Zone." *Sequentials* 1 (2). https://www.sequentials journal.net/issues/issue2/misemer.html.

Misemer, Leah. 2019. "Taking Twitter Higher, Further, Faster: Leading the #Womenon-panels Event." TECHStyle (blog), March 8. http://techstyle.lmc.gatech.edu/taking-twitter-higher-further-faster-leading-the-womenonpanels-event/.

"On Hillary Chute's *Why Comics?*" 2019. Special section, *PMLA* 134 (3): 569–637.

Peterson, Richard A. 1985. "Six Constraints on the Production of Literary Works." *Poetics* 14 (1–2): 45–67.

Pustz, Matthew. 1999. *Comic Book Culture: Fanboys and True Believers*. Jackson: University Press of Mississippi.

Sandberg, Jörgen, and Mats Alvesson. 2011. "Ways of Constructing Research Questions: Gap-Spotting or Problematization?" *Organization* 18: 23–44. doi:10.1177/1350508410372151.

Seth. 2011. *The Great Northern Brotherhood of Canadian Cartoonists*. Montreal: Drawn & Quarterly.

Smith, Matthew J., and Randy Duncan, eds. 2017. *The Secret Origins of Comics Studies*. New York: Routledge.

Smolderen, Thierry. 2014. *The Origins of Comics: From William Hogarth to Winsor McCay*. Translated by Bart Beaty and Nick Nguyen. Jackson: University Press of Mississippi.

Star, Susan Leigh, and James R. Griesemer. 1989. "Institutional Ecology, 'Translations' and Boundary Objects: Amateurs and Professionals in Berkeley's Museum of Vertebrate Zoology, 1907–39." *Social Studies of Science* 19 (3): 387–420.

Steirer, Gregory. 2011. "The State of Comics Scholarship: Comics Studies and Disciplinarity." *International Journal of Comic Art* 13 (2): 263–87.

Warner, Michael. 2002. "Publics and Counterpublics." *Public Culture* 14 (1): 49–90. doi: 10.1215/08992363-14-1-49.

Weber, Max. 1978. *Economy and Society: An Outline of Interpretive Sociology*. Edited by Guenther Roth and Claus Wittich. 2 vols. University of California Press.

Williams, Raymond. 1986. "The Uses of Cultural Theory." *New Left Review* 1 (158): 19–31.

Woo, Benjamin. 2013. "How to Think about Comics as Social Objects: The 2013 Lent Award Lecture," *International Journal of Comic Art* 15 (2): 361–72.

Woo, Benjamin. 2015. "Erasing the Lines between Leisure and Labor: Creative Work in the Comics World." *Spectator* 35 (2): 57–64.

Woo, Benjamin. 2019. "What Kind of Studies Are Comics Studies?" In *The Oxford Handbook of Comic Book Studies*, edited by Frederick Luis Aldama, 3–15. New York: Oxford University Press. doi: 10.1093/oxfordhb/9780190917944.013.1.

The Comics World

Part 1. Production

Where do comics come from? How, by whom, and under what conditions are they brought into being? In this first section, we attend to the work of making and the people who do it. Long before a comic book or graphic novel appears on store shelves, is reviewed in the comics press or finds a readership, the people involved in its creation constitute its first publics. Although the productive labor of writers, artists, editors, publishers, printers, and intermediaries has been a long-standing interest of comic book fandom, it has only recently emerged as an area of significant interest among comics scholars. As Brienza and Johnston argue in the introduction to their collection *Cultures of Comics Work*, this focus on labor is radically inclusive: it "is agnostic toward many of the shibboleths of the study of comics while also having the ability to work around and within them." Comics work is "as applicable to Art Spiegelman's Pulitzer Prize–winning epic *Maus* as it is to a 12-page, photocopied, hand-stapled zine given out for free at a small-town comics convention attended by ten people, never to be seen again" (2016, 6, 7). It is also an obvious initial point of contact with other fields that have brought social-scientific approaches to bear on the products of human culture, such as sociology of art and literature, book history and publishing studies, and the political economy of communication and media industries.

We begin with three chapters on comics creators working in different global and industrial contexts. In "The Comics Workforce," Benjamin Woo offers a comprehensive picture of who makes English-language comics on the basis of a survey of 570 creative professionals conducted in 2014. Finding that respondents are roughly equally spread across publishing sectors and that relatively few make a stable living directly from comics, he argues that comics publishing "is not so much an industry as an ecology, a space where different kinds of comics making activities, many of them only semiprofessionalized, are taking place." An ecological approach complicates our understanding of production, disarticulating the monolithic "Industry" of much commentary and opening onto more complex accounts of how comics get made. Amy Louise Maynard follows with a qualitative picture of comics production in a single city, examining the opportunities and constraints available to creators given the particular mix of local institutions in Melbourne, Australia. Next, John A. Lent draws on decades of interviews with women cartoonists in Asia to refute claims that there are not or haven't been enough women making comics to represent them in historical retrospectives or awards programs. His analysis focuses on the genres and periodicals that have been coded as "feminine," as well as the differential career opportunities available to women who make comic art in Asia. Thus, the conventional wisdom that there just aren't very many women who make comics is not the unfortunate outcome of systemic forms of discrimination but an active contributor to these exclusions.

Once comics production is theorized as an ongoing social process, it becomes easier to see that this "system" is embedded in larger flows. Thus, Eike Exner and Ivan Lima Gomes ask how transnational forces and local politics together shape a comics world's development. In "Bringing Up Manga," Exner examines the influence of American newspaper strips on the development of Japanese cartooning in the prewar period, arguing that these strips in translation and their domestic imitators launched the Japanese comic strips that eventually became manga on a different formal and aesthetic trajectory. Where Exner is concerned with tracing influences, Gomes writes about an attempt to create an alternative comics world in the shadow of Dorfman and Mattelart's (2018) manifesto against cultural imperialism, *How to Read Donald Duck.* "Reshaping Comic Books in a Socialist Regime" recounts how Chile's state publisher used comics as tools for popular education and public communication during the socialist government of Salvador Allende (1970–73). In these chapters, the notion of "a comics world" productively crosses with that of "world comics," revealing that no art world is an island.

So, although our account of the comics world begins with worlds of production, where various actors must work together for a comic "to appear as it finally does" (Becker 1982, 2), it is not limited to a narrow productivism. Production is only one moment in the life of a comic, only one entry point into understanding how it acts and is acted upon in the social world. Instead, we see the publics that orient to making comics existing in dynamic relationships with intermediaries and audiences throughout their respective lifecycles.

References

Becker, Howard S. 1982. *Art Worlds*. Berkeley and Los Angeles: University of California Press.

Brienza, Casey, and Paddy Johnston, eds. 2016. *Cultures of Comics Work*. New York: Palgrave Macmillan.

Dorfman, Ariel, and Armand Mattelart. 2018. *How to Read Donald Duck: Imperialist Ideology in the Disney Comic*. New York: OR Books. Originally published in Spanish in 1971.

1.

The Comics Workforce

Benjamin Woo

Sometimes a photograph can say what no one will put into words. One day, for instance, Roland Barthes (1972) famously found a copy of *Paris Match* while waiting at the barbershop. The photograph on the cover of a uniformed, saluting Black youth said to him, "France is a great Empire, [and] all her sons, without any colour discrimination, faithfully serve under the flag" (116). At the mythic level of signification, this image symbolically incorporated French citizens of African descent in the national subject of the Republic, notwithstanding actual barriers to integration, and thereby assuaged white guilt over colonialism. But comics creators don't need Barthes to tell them that images can be very powerful indeed.

Some forty years later, Image Comics lined a group of writers and artists on stage at their annual expo to celebrate the new series that would soon appear in comic book stores. When pictures of this moment circulated online, people noticed that only two were women and most, if not all, were white (Clemente 2014; MacDonald 2014). The people on stage were not entirely representative of the titles announced at the expo (Hanley 2014), but, as Allison Baker (2014) suggested at the time, "The issue with the picture isn't that Image Comics is against diversity. The problem is the picture makes it look like they don't care about it." Absent clear, transparently produced, and publicly available data on who makes comics and graphic novels, these images perpetuated a myth that symbolically excludes women and visible minority creators from the comics world.

It has often been said that comic books are like our modern mythology. But mythology is presumptively unauthored; it is the gradual accretion of a culture's oral tradition. Comic books, by contrast, are generally produced by named people who are trying to make a living from their artistic labor. The "modern-mythology" rhetoric erases the labor performed by these people in the context of a complex, multifaceted cultural industry. Yet myths, in something like Barthes's (1972) sense, do indeed attend to their work. There is, for instance, no more enduring image of work in the comics industry than what Charles Hatfield (2012, 78) calls "the Myth of the Marvel Bullpen," which portrayed making comics as a job for whacky cut-ups with goofy nicknames. More recently, a short documentary produced for AT&T's U-verse Buzz tells a story about what it's like to be at the center of a "hot" industry like comics. The comic book artists of Toronto's RAID Studios are likened to rock stars; no less an authority than Alyssa Milano says, "They're just cool, they're fun to be around—and creative and inspiring" (Woo 2016). And we have the Image Expo photograph.

Comics readers don't necessarily have a very clear idea of how comics get made or—beyond familiarity with a handful of marquee names—by whom, and mythic discourses take root in this persistent gap between media producers and their audiences. This chapter reports some findings from a large-scale survey of creative workers in the field of English-language comics production. While the survey addressed a number of different issues related to work in comics, I will concentrate here on the makeup of the comics workforce and on some of the conditions under which they perform creative labor.

CONTEXT

This project responds not only to a pressing need among cartoonists for more systematic information about the industry in which they work but also to a significant turn towards work and production in media, communication, and cultural studies. Authors such as John Thornton Caldwell and Vicki Mayer have used the term "production studies," suggesting that it is time cultural production received the same thick description that cultural studies accorded to acts of reception and appropriation (Caldwell 2008; Mayer 2011; Mayer, Banks, and Caldwell 2009; Banks, Conor, and Mayer 2015). In the United Kingdom, the turn to work has been overdetermined by New Labour's creative industries agenda of the 1990s and 2000s. In particular, it has been fueled by the creative industries' failure to provide good work and social mobility to young people, especially after the 2008 financial crisis. For many of these writers, creative work has simultaneously served as *both* utopian model of unalienated labor *and* bellwether of actually existing trends towards casualization and precariousness in what Ulrich Beck (2000) has called "the brave new world of work" (Ashton and Noonan 2013; Banks 2007; Banks, Gill, and Taylor 2013; Hesmondhalgh and Baker 2011; McRobbie 2016;

Taylor and Littleton 2012). A third cluster of research focuses on the impacts of digital technologies (and the cultures of digital workplaces) on creative labor, including the digitally mediated immaterial labor of audiences and users (Deuze 2007; Fuchs 2014; Scholz 2013; Terranova 2000). The rise of the "produser" or "pro-am" not only impacts the nature of media-oriented leisure but also, in creating an army of people who do creative work for fun, may exert downward pressure on working conditions for creative professionals.

Determining who counts as a creative worker is an obvious conceptual problem. Most any job could be considered creative in some sense or another, yet, when one speaks of creative work in a cultural industry such as comics, one clearly has in mind some role that shapes content. However, in fields where much work is produced collaboratively, a notion of creativity is needed that can accommodate the contributions of both "above-the-line" and "below-the-line" workers, and high-status as well as low-status ones. It is also important that the definition of the population not screen out emerging or unsuccessful creators a priori. For the purposes of the study, I defined "creative workers in comics" as people who performed work, whether paid or not, that affected the content or aesthetic presentation of a comic book, graphic novel, minicomic, or webcomic that was made available to the public in English in 2010 or later. Because the contours of this population are unknown and an adequate sampling frame does not exist, probability sampling was abandoned in favor of generating the largest number of responses possible. A directory of active creators was constructed through two strategies: first, recent exhibitors listed on the websites of five major comic conventions (Comic-Con International in San Diego; the New York Comic Con; the Small Press Expo in Bethesda, Maryland; the Toronto Comic Art Festival; and the Thought Bubble festival in Leeds, United Kingdom) were recorded; second, three issues of the *Previews* catalogue, which comic shops use to order their inventory from Diamond, were randomly selected, and the credited creators of the five "premier" publishers (Dark Horse, DC, IDW, Image, and Marvel) were identified using the Grand Comics Database (GCD; www.comics.org). Publicly available contact information for both lists of creative workers was sought online.

The survey launched online in November 2013 and was accessible until February 2014. A total of 1,356 invitations to participate were sent by email. Additional creators were contacted through web-based contact forms on personal websites and DeviantArt accounts and through social media. Survey respondents were able to share a link to the survey through social media upon completion, and the survey launch was announced on a number of comics news websites. Finally, as a method of generating interest in the project, weekly updates based on preliminary data were posted on a project blog. A total of 570 completed surveys were collected, though respondents were able to skip questions they did not wish to answer, so some items have fewer responses.

FINDINGS

A relatively small field of cultural production, English-language comic and graphic-novel publishing nonetheless relies on the labor of a great deal of people. For instance, searching the GCD suggests that there were 5,531 comic books published in the United States in 2014, not including variants. Someone produced each of those comic books—usually several people working in a coordinated production process—and this is only a fraction of total output, as it does not include webcomics or minicomics/zines and may overlook other small-scale publishing activity. Scanning the exhibitors and guests of honor at a fan convention may give one an impression of who they are, but what do we really know about the people who make comics?

Of 519 valid responses to the question about current place of residence, nearly sixty percent live in the United States. Indeed, 13.7% live in New York or New Jersey alone. This is followed by Canada (10.6%), the United Kingdom and Ireland (7.1%), non-Anglophone Europe (5.8%), Asia (1.9%), Latin America (1.7%), Australia and New Zealand (1.2%), and other (0.2%). Given that the US publishing industry has made use of labor from Southeast Asia, Latin America, and eastern and southern Europe for some time now, the low numbers for these regions suggest that recruitment efforts did not adequately reach creators outside of the Anglophone world. However, table 1.1 does seem to validate the importance of major American publishers in these regions, as workers living in non-Anglophone countries are more concentrated in work-for-hire comics publishing than Anglophones residing outside the United States are.

In a 2014 article for the news and criticism website Comics Alliance, Andrew Wheeler introduced the "Harvey/Renee Index of Superhero Diversity." His intention was apparently to provide a punchy, Bechdel Test–like way of talking about the demographic diversity of comic books' casts as a ratio of "straight white non-Hispanic cisgender men" ("Harveys," after the DC Comics character Detective Harvey Bullock) to everyone else ("Renees," after Bullock's partner, Renee Montoya, a Latina lesbian). Somewhat ironically, this approach, which flattens all axes of difference into a single, binary dimension, helps us get beyond the perceptual biases that can lead us to see

TABLE 1.1. WHERE ARE COMICS CREATORS LOCATED?

Crosstab of place of residence by publishing sector. For each region, sector with most workers in bold.

		Publisher (work-for-hire)	Publisher (creator-owned)	Self-published (print)	Self-published (digital)	Other	Total
United States	n	**112**	62	110	82	5	371
	%	**30.2**	16.7	29.6	22.1	1.3	100
NY/NJ	n	21	14	16	19	1	71
	%	29.6	19.7	22.5	26.8	1.4	100
Canada	n	12	**15**	12	14	0	53
	%	22.6	**28.3**	22.6	26.4	0	100
UK & Ireland	n	9	**11**	9	6	0	35
	%	25.7	**31.4**	25.7	17.1	0	100
Europe	n	**19**	6	2	3	0	30
	%	**63.3**	20.0	6.7	10.0	0	100
Asia	n	**5**	0	3	1	0	9
	%	**55.6**	0	33.3	11.1	0	100
Latin America	n	**5**	0	1	3	0	9
	%	**55.6**	0	11.1	33.3	0	100
Australia & NZ	n	0	**2**	1	2	0	5
	%	0	**40.0**	20.0	20.0	0	100
Other	n	**1**	0	0	0	0	1
	%	**100**	0	0	0	0	100

a cast of white men with one or two women or visible minorities as "diverse." If the Harvey/Renee Index works for superhero teams, it can also help us understand the diversity (or lack thereof) in creative teams.

According to survey results (table 1.2), there are 1.2 Harveys for every Renee making comics. Virtual parity sounds quite good until we remember that the "Harveys" represent straight, white, cisgender men, while the "Renees" represent *everyone else*. Moreover, this is a conservative estimate due to problems inherent in coding race (here, "white" and "nonwhite") based on questions about ancestry, a similar but not quite identical construct. Respondents could select multiple ancestry groups and were coded as nonwhite if they reported descent from *any* non-European population group, alone or in combination, and this will likely produce an impression of greater diversity than a question on racial identity would. (For instance, according to the US

TABLE 1.2. HARVEY AND RENEE

Crosstab of gender identity, sexual orientation/identity, and race.

		Race		
		White	Non-white	Total
Male	Heterosexual	292	76	454
	Homosexual	11	2	13
	Bisexual	6	7	13
	Other sexual orientation	3	3	6
	Total	312	88	400
Female	Heterosexual	66	20	86
	Homosexual	4	1	5
	Bisexual	22	5	27
	Other sexual orientation	6	4	10
	Total	98	30	128
Other gender identity	Heterosexual	0	0	0
	Homosexual	1	1	2
	Bisexual	1	0	1
	Other sexual orientation	6	0	6
	Total	8	1	9
Total		418	119	537

Census Bureau, only 1.6% of the population are Native American or Alaskan Native alone *or in combination*,[1] yet, nearly 3.5% of survey respondents report Indigenous descent.) Nonetheless, 78% of comics creators report themselves to be of solely European ancestry (or, 428 of the 550 respondents who answered the questions on ancestry) in comparison to the 63.2% of Americans who identified in the "White alone, not Hispanic" category in the American Community Survey. It is worth noting that the comics workforce significantly underrepresents Black (2.7%) and Hispanic/Latinx (7.6%) creators relative to the US population as a whole (13.6% and 16.6%, respectively), while overrepresenting people of Asian descent (9.3% versus 5.7%) relative to the US population—though not, of course, to the world. Obviously, the gender profile of comics creators is completely disproportionate to the population at large, with 74.1% of respondents who answered the gender question identifying with a male gender identity, 24% with a female gender identity, and 1.8% with another gender identity. However, while a 2013 poll found that approximately 3.5% of American adults identify as lesbian, gay, bisexual, or

Figure 1.1. Harvey and Renee. Mosaic plot of race, gender identity, and sexual orientation. Harvey and Renee graphics adapted from Wheeler (2014) with original artwork by Michael Lark.

transgender (Gates and Newport 2015), 3.7% of respondents who answered the sexual orientation question identified as gay or lesbian, 7.5% as bisexual, and 4.2% as having another sexual orientation/identity. The whole picture is best represented by a mosaic plot (figure 1.1), where each combination of the three variables (race, gender identity, and sexual identity) is represented by a rectangle whose size is proportional to the number of matching respondents in the data set.

The median age of employed persons in the United States is 42.3 (Bureau of Labor Statistics 2015b). As Miranda Campbell (2013, 16–17) has suggested, official statistics often underrepresent young cultural workers since they are counted under the job where they spend most of their time, and this seems to be borne out in the case of comics and graphic novels, where the median age of survey respondents was thirty-six in 2014. Notably, the median age of respondents coded as Renees was slightly younger (34.64 years) than those coded as Harveys (38.3 years). Median career length was nine years, and the median age at career start was twenty-five. Comics creators appear to be a remarkably young workforce, although the online survey method may have underrepresented older creators. This youthfulness may also help explain why nearly eighty percent of creators claim no religious affiliation (almost the inverse of the US population; Pew Research Center 2015) as well as some of the respondents' household characteristics. For instance, fewer comics workers are divorced than average, and their households are slightly smaller. Most have no dependents. Roughly two-thirds of Americans own their homes, compared with forty-five percent of comics workers. Respondents' homes also tend to be smaller: more live in one-bedroom units and fewer in homes with four or more bedrooms. All these are characteristics one would expect of workers in an earlier stage of their life course.

Comics workers are also a well-educated group. About one-third of Americans twenty-five years and older have a bachelor's degree or higher. Nearly half of survey respondents have a bachelor's degree, and another twenty-two percent have credentials higher than a bachelor's (many of them MFAs). Although anecdotes abound of cartoonists encountering resistance from teachers in art school, about three-quarters report having received some training that is relevant to their work in comics, though only forty percent of those say that training was specific to comics. The professionalization of cartooning via correspondence courses, programs at the Columbus, Savannah, and Minneapolis Colleges of Art and Design, and institutions like the School of Visual Arts, Kubert School, and Center for Cartoon Studies is likely to change these numbers over time.

The survey defined four distinct publishing sectors or subfields, described to respondents as "ways that your work is made available to the public": via a publisher under a work-for-hire contract; via a publisher under a creator-ownership contract; self-published in print; and self-published digitally (this category would include webcomics). Most respondents appear to have some experience in multiple sectors, and the distribution was, broadly speaking, quite balanced between the four sectors. When asked which was the "main way" their work was disseminated during the previous three years, however, the most common response was work-for-hire publishing. A substantial plurality of respondents reported mainly working as a writer/artist in the previous three years, though most respondents had performed various roles within the production process over their careers.

As Hesmondhalgh and Baker (2015, 24–25) report, many cultural fields exhibit a gendered division of labor, where work is segregated by sex both vertically (in terms of status) and horizontally (in terms of particular occupational roles where men or women predominate). Examining the breakdown of sectors and roles in terms of diversity (tables 1.3 and 1.4), the least diverse roles (writer, inker, and letterer) are associated with the "industrial" mode of comics production typical in work-for-hire publishing (Rogers 2006), which is also the "Harviest" sector overall. That being said, a relatively high proportion of editors—also part of the industrial production model—are counted as Renees. It can, however, be a relatively low-status role, according with the broader tendency for women in many cultural industries to be disproportionately employed in production coordination roles, which are

TABLE 1.3. PRIMARY PUBLISHING SECTOR

Crosstab of main way work made available to public within previous three years by Harvey/Renee Index.

	Harvey		Renee		Total	
	n	%	n	%	n	%
Publisher (work-for-hire)	**115**	**68.0**	54	32.0	169	100
Publisher (creator-owned)	**64**	**62.7**	38	37.3	102	100
Self-published (print)	60	45.1	**73**	**54.9**	133	100
Self-published (digital)	47	38.5	**75**	**61.5**	122	100
Other	2	40.0	**3**	**60.0**	5	100

TABLE 1.4. PRIMARY OCCUPATIONAL ROLES

Crosstab of main role within previous three years by Harvey/Renee Index.

	Harvey		Renee		Total	
	n	%	n	%	n	%
Writer	**54**	**66.7**	27	33.3	81	100
Penciller	**15**	**53.6**	13	46.4	28	100
Inker	**12**	**70.6**	5	29.4	17	100
Letterer	**5**	**71.4**	2	28.6	7	100
Colorist	**23**	**63.9**	13	36.1	36	100
Editor	**16**	**59.3**	11	40.7	27	100
Writer/Artist	94	41.6	**132**	**58.4**	226	100
Multi-role artist	**51**	**63.7**	29	36.3	80	100
Other	**20**	**62.5**	12	37.5	32	100

discursively constructed as an extension of stereotypically feminized social reproductive labor (Hesmondhalgh and Baker 2015). By contrast, the role with the highest proportion of Renees—the only role where Renees are in the majority—is that of writer/artist. This is the role with the greatest amount of creative autonomy, but it is also in many cases (especially, when combined with a self-publishing model, also common for Renees) the most precarious. Asked to describe the nature of their employment in comics, most respondents identified as freelancers, with self-publishers coming in second (table 1.5). The casual, individualized nature of this work explains why nearly nine out of ten respondents do their creative work in a studio or office in their home. Most surveyed creators (83.7%) retain ownership rights to at least some of their published work, but less than half have ever received royalties.

TABLE 1.5. EMPLOYMENT STATUS

Crosstab of employment status by Harvey/Renee Index.

	Harvey		Renee		Total	
	n	%	n	%	n	%
Amateur	**20**	**58.8**	14	41.2	34	100
Freelancer	**151**	**62.7**	90	37.3	241	100
Freelancer (exclusive)	**13**	**52.0**	12	48.0	25	100
Self-publisher	81	45.5	**97**	**54.5**	178	100
Employee	**19**	**61.3**	12	38.7	31	100
Other	7	26.9	**19**	**73.1**	26	100

Although there were some irregularities in the data related to income, particularly at the extremes, respondents reported a median monthly personal net income of US $2,701.50 (or, $32,418 per year). Of that amount, how much comes from making comics? Respondents were also asked about the proportion of their income derived from different kinds of work, adapting Higgs and Cunningham's (2008) "creative trident" model with the addition of a fourth prong of completely non-cultural work (i.e., the proverbial "day job"): creative work in comics (on average, 32%), noncreative work related to comics (10.3%), creative work unrelated to comics (16.7%), and noncreative work unrelated to comics (35.5%). Whereas the US labor force as a whole works an average of 38.6 hours per week (Bureau of Labor Statistics 2015a), respondents worked a median of twenty-four hours and mean of twenty-nine hours a week on comics. Overall, this suggests most comics creators are unable to make their craft a full-time livelihood.

CONCLUSION

James Sturm's short comic "The Sponsor" (originally posted on the Nib and expanded for the Drawn & Quarterly twenty-fifth anniversary book) depicts a late-night meeting between a young cartoonist, Casey, and Alan, his older "sponsor" in an Alcoholics Anonymous–style support group for cartoonists. Casey has just been to another cartoonist's "packed" book launch, and he is gripped with jealousy and despair. She's younger than him, was profiled in the *New York Times*, raised $350,000 on Kickstarter, and has a contract with Drawn & Quarterly for her next book. Meanwhile, his own career is stalled. The comic he is serializing online hasn't found an audience after a year, and he's thinking of quitting—or, worse yet, going to grad school. This story is about the market for creative labor in comics and the anxieties it creates. It's about two cartoonists who are waiting for their "big break." They continue making comics—"Keep your eyes on your own drawing board. One panel at a time."—but, in the meantime, they are probably trying to make ends meet in other ways (Sturm 2015, 180–81).

Most people in the comics workforce resemble Casey and Alan more than the whacky cut-ups of the mythical Marvel Bullpen or the "rock stars" of RAID Studios.[2] If we look at the experiences of people making comics as a whole, rather than starting from notable comics and working backwards, we will develop a very different picture of what it means to make comics today. On average, creators derive relatively little of their income from making comics and do not work full-time at their vocation. Without diminishing the challenges that they have faced, we need to understand that even those artists legitimately complaining about their treatment by publishers are the successes in comics.

What I think this suggests is that comics production, as a field, is much broader and more complex than the Big Two of Marvel and DC—or even major minor publishers like Image and Dark Horse. Indeed, comics production cannot be reduced to comics publishing, at least as that word has traditionally been understood, without losing something important. What we're looking at is not so much an industry as an ecology, a space where different kinds of comics-making activities, many of them only semiprofessionalized, are taking place (Woo 2018). This may seem like nitpicking, but the change of perspective implied is significant because, as survey data show, writing off not-yet- and perhaps never-to-be-successful creators also whitewashes much of the diversity that does exist in the comics world. Future research would explore the determinants of "success" and "failure" in more detail.

Empirical data are not guaranteed to drive away myth. Barthes (1972) reminds us that myth is a mode of signification, a cascade of nested references that add up to more than the sum of its parts: "Every object in the world," including a table or graph, "can pass from a closed, silent existence to an oral state, open to appropriation by society" (109). Yet, they remain among the best tools we have for testing our hunches and systematizing anecdotal experience. A picture may be worth a thousand words, but numbers can be precious, too.

Acknowledgments

This research was conducted while the author held a postdoctoral fellowship at the University of Calgary with the financial support of the Social Sciences and Humanities Research Council of Canada.

Notes

1. Unless specified, population statistics are from the US Census Bureau's American Community Survey five-year estimates (2009–2013), available at http://factfinder.census.gov.

2. And, as some criticism of "The Sponsor" suggested, they are also more like Casey and Alan in that they are mostly straight white men.

References

Ashton, Daniel, and Caitriona Noonan, eds. 2013. *Cultural Work and Higher Education.* Basingstoke, UK: Palgrave Macmillan.

Baker, Allison. 2014. "Allison Types: Image Expo and the Public Perception Problem." Comic Book Resources. January 13, 2014. http://www.comicbookresources.com/?page=article&id =50252.

Banks, Mark. 2007. *The Politics of Cultural Work.* Basingstoke, UK: Palgrave Macmillan.

Banks, Mark, Rosalind Gill, and Stephanie Taylor, eds. 2013. *Theorizing Cultural Work: Labour, Continuity and Change in the Cultural and Creative Industries.* London: Routledge.

Banks, Miranda, Bridget Conor, and Vicki Mayer, eds. 2015. *Production Studies, The Sequel! Cultural Studies of Global Media Industries.* New York: Routledge.

Barthes, Roland. 1972. *Mythologies.* London: J. Cape.

Beck, Ulrich. 2000. *The Brave New World of Work.* Translated by Patrick Camiller. Cambridge, UK: Polity.

Bureau of Labor Statistics. 2015a. "Labor Force Statistics from the Current Population Survey: Employed Persons by Detailed Industry and Age." http://www.bls.gov /cps/cpsaat18b.htm.

Bureau of Labor Statistics. 2015b. "Labor Force Statistics from the Current Population Survey: Persons at Work in Agriculture and Nonagricultural Industries by Hours of Work." http:// www.bls.gov/cps/cpsaat19.htm.

Caldwell, John Thornton. 2008. *Production Culture: Industrial Reflexivity and Critical Practice in Film and Television.* Durham, NC: Duke University Press.

Campbell, Miranda. 2013. *Out of the Basement: Youth Cultural Production in Practice and in Policy.* Kingston and Montreal: McGill-Queen's University Press.

Clemente, Zachary. 2014. "D Is for Diversity: A Look at Image Expo." Multiversity (blog). January 17, 2014. http://www.multiversitycomics.com/columns/cross-canon-d-is-for -diversity-a-look-at-image-expo/.

Deuze, Mark. 2007. *Media Work.* Cambridge, UK: Polity.

Fuchs, Christian. 2014. *Digital Labour and Karl Marx.* New York: Routledge.

Gates, Gary J., and Frank Newport. n.d. "LGBT Percentage Highest in D.C., Lowest in North Dakota." Gallup. Accessed August 11, 2015. http://www.gallup.com/poll/160517/lgbt-percentage-highest-lowest-north-dakota.aspx.

Hanley, Tim. 2014. "Women in Comics Statistics: Image Expo 2014; or: Great Looking Books by a Lot of White Men." Straitened Circumstances (blog), January 9. https://thanley.wordpress.com/2014/01/09/women-in-comics-statistics-image-expo-2014-or-great-looking-books-by-a-lot-of-white-men/.

Hesmondhalgh, David, and Sarah Baker. 2011. Creative Labour: Media Work in Three Cultural Industries. London: Routledge.

Hesmondhalgh, David, and Sarah Baker. 2015. "Sex, Gender and Work Segregation in the Cultural Industries." In Gender and Creative Labour, edited by Bridget Conor, Rosalind Gill, and Stephanie Taylor, 23–36. Malden, MA: Wiley-Blackwell.

Higgs, Peter, and Stuart Cunningham. 2008. "Creative Industries Mapping: Where Have We Come from and Where Are We Going?" Creative Industries Journal 1 (1): 7–30. https://doi.org/10.1386/cij.1.1.7_1.

MacDonald, Heidi. 2014. "Is Image Just a Bunch of White Dudes? Yes and No. . . ." The Beat (blog), January 10, 2014. http://www.comicsbeat.com/is-image-just-a-bunch-of-white-dudes-yes-and-no/.

Mayer, Vicki. 2011. Below the Line: Producers and Production Studies in the New Television Economy. Durham, NC: Duke University Press.

Mayer, Vicki, Miranda J. Banks, and John Thornton Caldwell. 2009. Production Studies: Cultural Studies of Media Industries. New York: Routledge.

McRobbie, Angela. 2016. Be Creative: Making a Living in the New Culture Industries. Cambridge, UK: Polity Press.

Pew Research Center. 2015. "America's Changing Religious Landscape." http://www.pewforum.org/2015/05/12/americas-changing-religious-landscape/.

Rogers, Mark C. 2006. "Understanding Production: The Stylistic Impact of Artisan and Industrial Methods." International Journal of Comic Art 8 (1): 509–17.

Scholz, Trebor, ed. 2013. Digital Labor: The Internet as Playground and Factory. New York: Routledge.

Taylor, Stephanie, and Karen Littleton. 2012. Contemporary Identities of Creativity and Creative Work. Ashgate.

Terranova, Tiziana. 2000. "Free Labor: Producing Culture for the Digital Economy." Social Text 18 (2): 33–58.

Woo, Benjamin. 2016. "To the Studio! Comic Book Artists: The Next Generation and the Occupational Imaginary of Comics Work." In Cultures of Comics Work, edited by Casey Brienza and Paddy Johnston, 189–202. New York: Palgrave Macmillan.

Woo, Benjamin. 2018. "Is There a Comic Book Industry?" Media Industries 5 (1): 27–46. https://doi.org/10.3998/mij.15031809.0005.102.

2

The Melbourne Scene

COMICS PRODUCTION, CITY SPACES, AND THE CREATIVE INDUSTRIES

Amy Louise Maynard

The Melbourne comics scene began in the mid-1970s, and it has produced small-press comics, graphic novels, serial comics, and anthologies on a consistent basis since the 1980s. Today, Melbourne is one of the largest and most prolific centers of comics production in Australia. The city has a high ratio of publishers producing graphic novels, a prominent small-press scene, and an Eisner-winning comics store (All Star Comics). Mainstream media coverage of comics in Australia often focuses on the city's scene (Ridout 2012; Watts 2012; Russell 2014; Kartas 2015), and Australian comics academics frequently use Melbourne as a setting for their research (Patrick 2011; Bentley 2013). The scene is strong because the city's environment and culture are conducive to comics production and circulation.

Melbourne has branded itself as a city of culture and literature, and this increasingly includes comics. The city features retail stores, studios, galleries, and publishing houses that act as intermediaries, curating and circulating comics, brokering knowledge, and providing networking opportunities for both producers and audiences. In addition, literary and cultural centers, writers' festivals, and government arts agencies offer financial support for artists and events, consecrating comics by tying them into the broader art world.

After the decline of Australia's domestic mainstream comic book industry in the mid-twentieth century (Patrick 2012), comics production in Australia became focused on scene-based economies located in urban areas like Melbourne. The activity within these scenes is the result of stakeholders, cultural intermediaries, and institutions working together. They are both beneficiaries of and contributors to the creative economies of the cities where they are located. In this chapter, I will use Pierre Bourdieu's (1993) theories of the cultural field and contemporary creative industries studies approaches to examine the elements that encourage the production and circulation of comics in Melbourne. Based on interviews with Melbourne-based comics producers, I argue that the scene is defined by *innovation*, with comics-focused events and experiences constituting a new kind of cultural tourism; by *diversification*, as intermediaries seek to redress gender imbalances among both creators and audiences; and by *competition*, which produces more choice for consumers. As a result of these processes, Melbourne's comics scene has experienced high levels of sustainability and growth, contributing to its prominence as a center of comics culture in Australia.

METHODS OF ANALYSIS

Australian comics production, as a creative industry, relies on social networks, and these networks result in concentrated target markets that convert social into economic capital (McRobbie 1996; O'Connor, Cunningham, and Jaaniste 2011). Social networks, and clusters of production and consumption (scenes), are created through reciprocal social capital, knowledge, innovation, and individual and collective action (Hartley et al. 2013; O'Connor 2004).

Scenes are formed through movement and scale. By movement, I mean the human capital that is located in, moves to, or moves through geographical spaces where a culture has been built up, and scale refers to how many people are involved within the culture of the scene (Straw 2001; Williams 2011). But scenes are not static. They comprise a series of interlocking networks, which results in agglomeration economies (Straw 2001). An agglomeration economy contains a specialized labor market and sustained online/offline relationships between individuals and institutions (Berg and Hassink 2014). As a result, scenes have come to the attention of policy makers and creative industry theorists due to their contributions to local, state, and national economies (Hartley et al. 2013). They contribute to a city's reputation through cultural tourism and to "urban regeneration" by transforming city quarters and suburbs into distinct cultures (Hartley et al. 2013; O'Connor 2004; Evans 2009; Richards 2010).

To gather information about the Melbourne scene, I conducted seven interviews with comics producers who currently live and work in the city and have participated in the Melbourne scene. I recruited interviewees through email, with most being producers whom I had met previously; others were recruited through recommendation. The interviews were standard and conducted over email in May 2015. Four interviewees were men (Philip Bentley, Michael Fikaris, Bruce Mutard, and Jason Franks), two were women (Scarlette Baccini and Jo Waite), and one identified as nonbinary (Frank Candiloro). Throughout this chapter, I will refer to those who create comics as "producers." I have decided to use this term not only as a shorthand for editors, creators, artists, and writers but also because producers engage in other forms of labor besides making comics. They plan events, manage crowdfunding campaigns, write grant applications, and run businesses. They are "producing" something, even if it isn't necessarily creative (Heazlewood 2014; Hesmondhalgh and Baker 2011), and the Melbourne comics scene would not exist without all of these forms of labor.

Comics production, like other art worlds, is subject to its own internal logics (Bourdieu 1993; Becker 1976). Producers will define themselves by their peers and publics, forming strategies how best to enact their creative labor through the available methods of production and consumption (Bourdieu 1984, 1993). By defining cultural production as a field of positions, we shift from a view of comics as isolated pieces of work to seeing them as formed through social conditions of supply and demand (Bourdieu 1993).

INNOVATION

Comics production in Melbourne is driven by individuals and small-to-medium enterprises (SME). They act as entrepreneurs, making strategic decisions about how best to achieve more financial capital, cultural capital, or resources (Hesmondhalgh and Baker 2011; Potts 2009). Innovation in the Melbourne comics scene is fueled by collaboration and creativity, which facilitate the origination, adaptation, and retention of ideas and practices (Hartley et al. 2013). These two elements are embodied in the scene's intermediary institutions. In the comics industries, retailers and event organizers are likely to be cultural intermediaries, as they act as curators of content and circulate knowledge. These curation practices are defined by the tastes of cultural intermediaries and their knowledge of producers, products, and consumers (Woo 2012; Brown 1997). Indeed, the development of cultural intermediaries and institutions is one of the chief forms of innovation within the scene, enabling producers to adapt to changing conditions.

The Melbourne comics scene has its roots in comics fandom, which organized events such as swap meets and conventions. By bringing fans together and creating a culture of comics in the city, these events inspired fans to become producers. Melbourne-based producers created anthologies such as *Inkspots, Reverie,* and *Fox Comics* (Bentley 2013; Bentley, pers. comm). Anthologies were a preferred format because they allowed producers to collaborate together on production and circulation duties and could be made with few overhead costs (Bentley 2013). The producers of the *Inkspots* anthology (Greg Gates, Philip Bentley and Colin Paraskevas) also established Australia's first comics store, Minotaur Books in 1977.

Minotaur is still active and has been joined by All Star Comics. As retailers, they not only had a space where they could curate and circulate Australian comics but also hosted participatory events, such as book launches and signings, where producers and consumers could interact (Bentley 2013, 46–54). Similarly, Mitchell Davies, a proprietor of All Star Comics, said, "When we first opened the store [in 2011] there was already a strong comic-creating community in and around Melbourne, and we embraced that" (Russell 2014). All Star also hosts launches and signings and has established the All Star Women's Comics Club (Russell 2014; Kartas 2015). In addition to comic book stores, important local intermediaries include studio spaces, pubs, festivals, and publishers.

Local studios, such as Squishface Studio and Blender Studios, not only provide working space for producers but also organize innovative ancillary activities. These activities provide additional revenue streams and build goodwill for the comics scene. Squishface Studio is open to the public and sells comics, as well as hosts residencies, comics workshops for adults and children, and sketch nights. The inspiration to set up Squishface in 2012 came from Inherent Vice, an event where producers were watched by the public as they created their comics in the National Gallery of Victoria; billed as an "open residency," producers could also assist the public in making comics (Cuthbertson 2011; Rackleyft 2015, 14–15). The primary goals of the studio's owners are to become a recognizable cultural institution in the city and provide a "nice atmosphere" for people curious about cartooning and comics (Blumenstein 2013). Blender Studios hosts a comics collective (Silent Army) and is also open to the public for workshops, commissions, and consultations. It has developed into an important site of marketing and networking. Blender Studios has a shop and a gallery and holds an artist market every summer. According to Fikaris, the studio's relationship with the comics field has been a long and productive one since 2002, when the Silent Army collective first began working in the studio and selling its comics and zines in the shop.

The importance of studio spaces and artist-run centers is perhaps unsurprising, but, with the exception of their role as music venues, pubs are less commonly considered part of creative economies. In the comics scene, however, pubs function as important social spaces, hosting monthly "meets" where producers gather for personal and professional networking. There is evidence that meets grew out of the Australian versions of "comic jams," a practice adapted from the US industry where producers will either work together on their own material or pass a comic among themselves and collaborate together to make a story (Bentley 2013; Hatfield 2005). In interviews, Mutard and Franks both discussed the role meets have played in Melbourne comics culture since the 1990s; they are currently held at the Prince Alfred Hotel. Most importantly, meets are where producers will recommend each other for projects and partnerships. For instance, independent comics publisher James Andre was inspired to set up his imprint, Milk Shadow Books, after networking at the Melbourne meets. However, as will be discussed in more detail below, the reliance on pubs for networking and talent scouting has implications for who can pursue these opportunities.

Some Melbourne producers, such as Sarah Howell (Homecooked) and Luke Sinclair (Festival of the Photocopier), also work as festival organizers. Artistic events and festivals will often occur as an organic process, as producers within artistic subcultures and communities use collective action and temporary spaces to present their work to the public (Quinn 2010). The Festival of the Photocopier involves both small press comics and zines; comics and zines have historically had similar forms and practices, and these scenes began to integrate in Australia in the 1990s (Bentley 2013; Duncombe 1997). Like festivals in Europe and more recently Britain, Homecooked has successfully pursued grants from city and state funding bodies on the basis of their ability to draw tourists, locals, and international guests (Beaty 2007; O'Brien 2014). By becoming associated with a specific city (Melbourne) and even specific locations within the city, such as the Northcote Town Hall or Batman Park, the Homecooked Comics Festival joins the ranks of events like the Lakes International Comics Art Festival (Kendal, UK) and the Festival international de la bande dessinée d'Angoulême (Angoulême, France). These spaces contribute to the city's economy through a form of cultural tourism that is focused on experience, with consumers taking an active role in the artistic process. This form of tourism is designed to focus on small and/or consistent events that are embedded within local cultures (Richards 2010; Wynn 2016; Quinn 2010).

Intermediary work takes place by definition in between producers and consumers. Because of their role in financing and managing cultural production, publishers are typically counted among the ranks of cultural producers, not intermediaries. However, I argue that SME publishers that are grounded in local cultural scenes also take on important intermediary functions. Melbourne publishers such as Pikitia Press and Allen & Unwin take advantage of their strong connections in the scene, which have been fostered through anthologies and meets, to actively scout and develop talent, rather than accept unsolicited submissions. Furthermore, they collect information on which producers' work best represents their brand and the producers that have received recognition from critics and consumers (Rackleyft 2015; Bentley 2009). As a method of recruiting labor, talent scouting incorporates knowledge brokering, which refers to cases where a producer with high social capital will use their influence to connect other producers to projects and events (Putnam 2000; Boari and Riboldazzi 2014). Knowledge brokering produces innovation by integrating individual relationships with collective practices (Kühn 2015; Putnam 2000). It helps balance creativity with control and consolidation. There is always a risk when putting new products on the market, but this risk can be decreased if a cultural intermediary can "read the market" or, in other words, has an understanding of or reciprocal relationships with producers, competitors, and consumers (Hesmondhalgh and Baker 2011; Potts 2010).

The majority of my interviewees found the environment of Melbourne to be conducive to their comics work. For Mutard, the present and continual support of cultural intermediaries and institutions (e.g., galleries, bookstores, festivals), and producers taking initiative in approaching institutions, has helped to increase the cultural capital of Australian comics. The city is, in Candiloro's words, "a good environment for those who pursue arts": "it encourages artists to make something and put it in stores, or online, or organize launches, etc. So even if you don't get grants or government support, it is still an ideal place to make art." Through its economic and cultural support of the creative industries, Melbourne exemplifies "innovation through the creative consumption of global signs—a style, a look, a sound" (O'Connor 2004, 134). Melbourne's comics scene has become distinctive through its ability to integrate its practices into other creative industries.

In the Australian comics industry, institutions that act as gatekeepers to cultural capital include council, state, and federal funding bodies, as well as galleries, libraries, and festivals. In the comics field, many regard these institutions as consecrating bodies able to lend legitimacy and visibility to comics by hosting events (Patrick 2011; Roeder 2008). Local examples in Melbourne include Brunswick Arts Space (launches); the State Library of Victoria (exhibitions); the National Gallery of Victoria (the aforementioned Inherent Vice); the Wheeler Centre (panels, guest speakers and workshops); and the Melbourne Writers Festival (panels and workshops). Comics are receiving more respect within the Australian cultural sphere in general (Patrick 2011; Bentley 2011), and the willingness of Melbourne's institutions to support comics culture is also due to the city's commitment to arts and the creative industries in general. The city of Melbourne was made the UNESCO City of Literature in 2008, and the state government of Victoria pledged $7 billion to the arts and the creative-industries sector as of 2015. On this view, creative industries such as comics production promote the city's culture of artistic entrepreneurship, and encouraging creative labor promotes the city as a place of innovation to potential new residents as well as spurring development for those already residing within Melbourne's cultural quarters (McRobbie 1996, 2015; O'Connor, Cunningham, and Jaaniste 2011; Bennett 2010). While the chances of comics getting grants for their projects or events would have been slim in the 1980s, in the present, comics creators will often apply for—and receive—grants from councils and the state government (Mutard, Bentley; see also Bentley 2011; Rackleyft 2015). Comics are now considered to be a "valid medium" by mainstream cultural institutions (Fikaris). This cultural shift has made comics producers more assertive in applying for grants or inclusion on the program of writers' festivals (Mutard).

DIVERSIFICATION

This section considers efforts to diversify the Melbourne comics scene in two distinct senses. First, I'm interested in how producers and intermediaries use urban spaces. The Melbourne comics scene is not confined to a "quarter" but instead takes advantage of different inner-city areas and suburbs that furnish the spaces they need. Second, I'm interested in who is included in the scene.

Cities such as Melbourne that attract the so-called "creative class" have undergone significant gentrification, and the diversification of scene spaces is therefore borne of necessity as much as choice. The creative class not only encompasses artists such as comics producers but also white-collar professionals, and differences in culture and economic circumstances have caused some tensions, with spaces formerly occupied by artistic scenes being replaced by a commodified, middle-class culture (Bennett 2010, 24; Eltham 2011; Shaw 2013; Florida 2003). Many of the spaces utilized by stakeholders within the central business district (CBD) are institutions that rely on public patronage, such as libraries and public galleries, or retailers such as All Star and Minotaur. Blender Studios is one of the few comics production sites located within the CBD, but it also functions as a retail space. The ability of scene participants to occupy space in the CBD is dependent on whether they can afford to pay market rents—or convince institutions that can to sponsor events.

That being said, there is also reason to be skeptical of the thesis that gentrification effectively "ends" cultural scenes. Scenes have malleable boundaries, and this makes them resilient (McRobbie 2016; Straw 2001). In Australian comics scenes, creators will often utilize spaces such as warehouses for events. These spaces are small, low cost, and are easy to set up and even easier to dismantle. The suburbs give producers opportunities to gradually grow their enterprises and build up an agglomeration economy away from the constant activity downtown (Felton et al. 2010; Flew 2013). In the Melbourne comics scene, suburbs such as Brunswick (Squishface Studio and Brunswick Arts Space), Northcote (Northcote Town Hall, a space used by the Home-cooked Festival), and Fitzroy (Sentido Funf, a pub that been used for comics launches) benefit comics production by attracting artistic subcultures while still having areas where rent is cheap (Eltham 2011).

The theme of diversity also extends to demographics. In comics industries, and the creative industries more broadly, there have been concerns that men are favored over women for positions of power (MacDonald 2015; McRobbie 2011; Gill 2002). The Australian comics industry began as a white, male-dominated culture, and the Melbourne scene of the 1970s and '80s was a subculture that catered towards the interests of men. Comics stores were mostly populated with men—some of whom had questionable social skills—and early anthologies such as *Inkspots* and *Reverie* contained all-male production teams (Bentley 2013). Things began to change in the late 1980s and early 1990s, with women gaining increased autonomy and visibility through their own anthologies, such as "anarcho queer-punk zines" (Waite). Women also connected with each other through the website melbourne-comics.com. However, it is worth asking to what extent the informal social economy of the comics scene slowed progress on gender equity.

Women are also important on the cultural intermediaries side. For instance, Sarah Howell was the first director of Homecooked, and Erica Wagner was formerly the editor-in-chief of the graphic novels line at Allen & Unwin. Wagner now works at Twelve Panels Press, which also has Elizabeth MacFarlane as a publisher/talent scout. Katie Parrish, a comics creator and art editor at literary magazine the *Lifted Brow*, has spoken about her support for queer and female artists. According to Parrish, inclusivity is important, because there can still a "bro-y" vibe in certain scene spaces (Savage 2015).

Other businesses have also embraced diversity to reach additional consumer demographics. All Star Comics hosts the All Star Women's Comic Book Club, an all-women reading group. The idea for the club came from Cazz Jennings, a female employee at All Star. The club's purpose is to break down stereotypes of comics fans being men, but it is also a business initiative to draw more women into the store (Kartas 2015). Squishface Studio hosts women-only sketch nights every Thursday, giving women a social space to work and network away from pub meets.

Diversification increases resilience and reduces risk. On the one hand, by using different spaces across the city, the scene insulates itself from the vagaries of the rental market. On the other hand, the commitment to inclusivity is changing the composition of the scene at every level, with both cultural and financial benefits. "The support from family, peers and even strangers who might sympathize with what you are aiming at in your work will be more important [than commercial goals], but just as elusive as being paid for your work," says Waite. "Without encouragement, many will not continue to make art, especially women." These practices strengthen existing niches in the scene, with the goal of extending networks of culture and participation (Woo 2012).

COMPETITION

In the context of Australian comics production, competition takes place on both the "culture" and the "industry" sides. Within the cultural field, the logic of competition among producers is defined by the variety of comics produced and the values which are subsequently placed upon these comics, both inside and outside of the field (Bourdieu 1993). Within the creative industries, competition is something that can drive creativity; while the idea of "competition" calls to mind ruthless individualism, competition in a creative industry benefits from cooperation. Cooperation between producers prevents monopoly and stagnation (Hartley et al. 2013).

Producers within the scene were able to rationalize competition as existing within different forms rather than encompassing the scene as a whole. Competition—variety, cultural value, and cooperation—is visible in the "subscenes" within the Melbourne scene. According to David Blumenstein (2013), the Melbourne scene is divided into graphic novels, art or small-press comics, "genre" comics, and satirical/political cartoons. In an interview, Jason Franks similarly described a broad range of work being produced in Melbourne. Focusing on the quality of their own work was considered more productive than negatively judging others' differences (Fikaris; Candiloro). The cooperative nature of networks within the Melbourne scene was also seen as a strength by Franks, Baccini, and Mutard. As a writer, Franks finds it beneficial to be in a network with potential artistic collaborators and to "talk shop" with other producers. Candiloro often socializes with other producers via social media and saw the do-it-yourself ethic of scenes as key to producers having the freedom to set their own creative goals. Online connections are increasingly important to the Melbourne scene, being categorized as "essential" to event organization (Baccini; Bentley). These remarks support research that has been done on the benefits of social media in scenes, helping to foster a sense of community and collaboration (McRobbie 2016, 127).

The Melbourne comics scene is a participatory culture where consumers often become producers and producers are still enthusiastic audiences for their peers' comics (Baccini). According to Baccini, the scene's culture of sharing information and knowledge about grant opportunities, competitions, and festivals assists producers in networking with consumers. This knowledge is likely to be shared through spaces created by cultural intermediaries, who offer continual support to producers (Mutard), so there is a circular pattern between competition, diversity, and innovation.

CONCLUSION: CLUSTERS AND NETWORKS

This analysis of comics producers and intermediaries in Melbourne, Australia, is intended as a case study of how comics production could be considered a creative industry. While the term "creative industries" often conjures up images of transnational entertainment conglomerates, in Melbourne, the comics industry is organized in terms of a scene-based creative economy that brings individual producers, small and medium-sized enterprises, and public institutions together around the production and circulation of comics. While nationally prominent as a center of comics culture and producing works that garner international audiences, the Melbourne comics scene derives its vibrancy from its connections to a thriving urban community. I have argued that producers within this creative industry are directly influenced by their immediate local environment.

By studying the history and evolution of a scene in the context of a specific city, my research revealed that comics is not an isolated creative industry. Instead, producers integrate their practices with other creative industries and institutions. Producers seize innovative opportunities to extend their social networks, influence cultural policy, increase the medium's cultural consecration, and develop their target markets. While experiencing growth and sustainability through negotiation with cultural intermediaries and institutions, the Melbourne scene has also diversified its networks. This diversification has been in the form of producers, spaces, and forms that address specific issues. Lastly, competition between producers has led to a variety of comics forms being produced, which benefits a variety of consumers, even as it increases competition and invention among producers—enriching the overall community. Analyzing local, embedded networks, as I have in this chapter, demonstrates that context is essential to understanding how a creative industry grows and evolves. Its future remains in the hands of the many stakeholders that make and remake the scene as part of their social worlds.

References

Beaty, Bart. 2007. *Unpopular Culture: Transforming the European Comic Book in the 1990s.* Toronto: University of Toronto Press.

Becker, Howard S. 1976. "Art Worlds and Social Types." *American Behavioral Scientist* 19 (6): 703–18.

Bennett, Dawn. 2010. "Creative Migration: A Western Australian Case Study of Creative Artists." *Australian Geographer* 41 (1): 117–28.

Bentley, Philip. 2009. "Bernard Caleo Unmasked: Cartoonist, Tango Editor and Actor Interviewed" *Word Balloons* 9: 3–14.

Bentley, Philip. 2011. "Australian Comic Publishers Speak: Allen and Unwin, Black House and Gestalt Editors Interviewed." *Word Balloons* 12: 3–22.

Bentley, Philip. 2013. *A Life in Comics: A Personal History of Comics in Australia 1960–1990.* Sandringham: Second Shore.

Berg, Su-Hyun, and Robert Hassink. 2014. "Creative Industries from an Evolutionary Perspective: A Critical Literature Review." *Geography Compass* 8 (9): 653–64.

Blumenstein, David. 2013. "Stanleys 2013: The Australian Cartoonists Association Conference (Part 1)." Nakedfella Productions, October 28. http://nakedfella.com/blog/2013/10/ stanleys-2013-the-australian-cartoonists-association-conference-part-1/.

Boari, Cristina, and Frederico Riboldazzi. 2014. "How Knowledge Brokers Emerge and Evolve: The Role of Actors' Behaviour." *Research Policy* 1 (43): 683–95.

Bourdieu, Pierre. 1984. *Distinction: A Social Critique of the Judgement of Taste.* Cambridge: Harvard University Press.

Bourdieu, Pierre. 1993. *The Field of Cultural Production: Essays on Art and Literature.* Cambridge: Polity Press.

Brown, Jeffrey A. 1997. "Comic Book Fandom and Cultural Capital." *Journal of Popular Culture* 30 (4): 13–31.

Connell, R. W., and James Messerschmidt. 2005. "Hegemonic Masculinity: Rethinking the Concept." *Gender & Society* 19 (6): 829–59.

Cuthbertson, Ian. 2011. "Non-Stop Day in the Life of Comic Creators," *The Australian*, August 4th. http://www.theaustralian.com.au/arts/nonstop-day-in-the-life-of-comics-creators/ story-e6frg8n6-1226107678429

Duncombe, Stephen. 1997. *Notes from Underground: Zines and the Politics of Alternative Culture.* New York: Verso.

Eltham, Ben. 2011. "Hey Latte-Lovers, Art Works Just as Well on the Fringe," Crikey, June 3. http://www.crikey.com.au/2011/06/03/my-cup-of-tea-hey-latte-lovers-art-works-just-as-well-on-the-fringe/.

Evans, Graeme L. 2009. "From Cultural Quarters to Creative Clusters—Creative Spaces in the New City Economy." In *The Sustainability and Development of Cultural Quarters: International Perspectives*, edited by Mattias Legner, 32–59. Stockholm: Institute of Urban History.

Felton, Emma, Mark Nicholas Gibson, Terry Flew, Phil Graham, and Anna Daniel. 2010. "Resilient Creative Economies? Creative Industries on the Urban Fringe." *Continuum: Journal of Media and Cultural Studies* 24 (4): 619–30.

Flew, Terry. 2012. "Creative Suburbia: Rethinking Urban Cultural Policy—The Australian Case." *International Journal of Cultural Studies* 15 (3): 231–46.

Florida, Richard. 2003. "Cities and the Creative Class." *City and Community* 2 (1): 3–19.

Gill, Rosalind. 2002. "Cool, Creative and Egalitarian? Exploring Gender in Project-Based New Media Work in Europe." *Information, Communication & Society* 5 (1): 70–89.

Hartley John, Jason Potts, Stuart Cunningham, Terry Flew, Michael Keane, and John Banks. 2013. *Key Concepts in Creative Industries*. London: Sage Publishing.

Hatfield, Charles. 2005. *Alternative Comics: An Emerging Literature*. Jackson: University Press of Mississippi.

Heazlewood, Justin. 2014. *Funemployed: Life as an Artist in Australia*. South Melbourne: Affirm Press.

Hesmondhalgh, David, and Sarah Baker. 2011. *Creative Labour: Media Work in Three Cultural Industries*. London: Routledge.

Kartas, Georgia. 2015. "All Star Women's Comic Book Club." Red Magpie, June 25. http://www.red-magpie.com/?p=1638.

Kühn, Jan-Michael. 2015. "The Subcultural Scene Economy of the Berlin Techno Scene." In *Keep It Simple, Make It Fast! An Approach to Undergroudn Music Scenes*, edited by Paula Guerra and Tânia Moreira, 281–86. Porto: Faculty of Arts and Humanities, University of Porto.

MacDonald, Heidi. 2015. "How a Toxic History of Harassment Has Damaged the Comics Industry." The Beat (blog), October 1. http://www.comicsbeat.com/how-a-toxic-history-of-harassment-has-damaged-the-comics-industry/.

McRobbie, Angela. 1996. "All the World's a Stage, Screen or Magazine: When Culture is the Logic of Late Capitalism." *Media, Culture & Society* 18: 335–42.

McRobbie, Angela. 2011. "Reflections on Feminism, Immaterial Labour and the Post-Fordist Regime." *New Formations* 70 (1): 60–76.

McRobbie, Angela. 2016. *Be Creative: Making a Living in the New Culture Industries*. Cambridge: Polity.

O'Brien, Dave. 2014. "Comic Con Goes Country Life: On British Economy, Society and Culture." *The Comics Grid: Journal of Comics Scholarship* 4 (1).

O'Connor, Justin. 2004. "A Special Kind of City Knowledge: Innovative Clusters, Tacit Knowledge and the Creative City." *Media International Australia* 112 (1): 131–49.

O'Connor, Justin, Stuart Cunningham, and Luke Jaaniste. 2011. *Arts and Creative Industries: A Historical Overview; and an Australian Conversation*. Canberra: Australian Council of the Arts.

Patrick, Kevin. 2011. "In Search of the Great Australian (Graphic) Novel." *International Journal of Popular Culture* 1 (1): 51–66.

Patrick, Kevin. 2012. "The Cultural Economy of the Austrialian Comic Book Industry, 1950–1975." In *Sold by the Millions: Australia's Bestsellers*, edited by Toni Johnson-Woods and Amit Sarwal, 162–81. Newcastle upon Tyne: Cambridge Scholars Publishing.

Potts, Jason. 2009. "Creative Industries and Innovation Policy." *Innovation, Management, Policy and Practice* 11: 138–47.

Potts, Jason. 2010. "Can Behavioural Biases in Choice Under Novelty Explain Innovation Failures?" *Prometheus* 28 (2): 133–48.

Putnam, Robert D. 2000. *Bowling Alone: The Collapse and Revival of American Community.* New York: Simon & Schuster.

Quinn, Bernadette. 2010. "Arts Festivals, Urban Tourism and Cultural Policy." *Journal of Policy Research in Tourism, Leisure and Events* 2 (3): 264–79.

Rackleyft, Jessica. 2015. "Comic Book Artists." *Outline Magazine* 2 (1): 7–59.

Richards, Greg. 2010. "Tourism Development Trajectories—From Culture to Creativity?" *Tourism and Management Studies* 6 (1): 9–15.

Ridout, Cefn. 2009. "Picture This: The Future of Fiction." *The Australian*, April 1. Nexis Uni.

Roeder, Katherine. 2008. "Looking High and Low at Comic Art." *American Art* 22 (1): 135–47.

Russell, Stephen A. 2014. "Melbourne Comic Book Store Voted World's Best." *The Sydney Morning Herald*, July 28. http://www.smh.com.au/entertainment/books/melbourne -comic-book-store-voted-worlds-best-20140728-zxr56.html.

Savage, Ellena. 2015. "Meet Katie Parrish." *Spook Magazine*, January 27. http://www.spook magazine.com/meet-katie-parrish/.

Shaw, Kate. 2013. "Independent Creative Subcultures and Why They Matter." *International Journal of Cultural Policy* 19 (3): 333–52.

Straw, Will. 2001. "Scenes and Sensibilities." *Public* 22/23: 245–57.

Watts, Richard. 2012. "The Australian Comic Book Renaissance." Arts Hub, November 27. http://publishing.artshub.com.au/news-article/features/writing-and-publishing/ richard-watts/the-australian-comic-book-renaissance-192933.

Williams, J. Patrick. 2011. *Subcultural Theory: Traditions and Concepts.* Cambridge: Polity.

Woo, Benjamin. 2012. "Alpha Nerds: Cultural Intermediaries in a Subcultural Scene." *European Journal of Cultural Studies* 15 (5): 659–76.

Wynn, Jonathan. 2016. "Why Cities Should Stop Building Museums and Focus on Festivals." The Conversation, May 12. https://theconversation.com/why-cities-should-stop -building-museums-and-focus-on-festivals-57333.

3.

'Women and 'Asian Comic 'Art

GENDERED GENRES, FEMALE PORTRAYALS, AND WOMEN CARTOONISTS

John A. Lent

In January 2016, a brouhaha shook the Angoulême International Comics Festival when nine of the thirty cartoonists nominated for the prestigious Grand Prix removed their names from consideration because not one woman was among them. The uproar intensified when festival organizers defended their choices, saying it was difficult to find a woman with a significant body of work because of the lack of women in cartooning historically. In fact, only one woman had won the award in the festival's forty-three-year history.

This is a common refrain when discussing gender imbalances in the world of comic art. Yet, what Angoulême fest spokesmen and others overlook is that some women cartoonists have achieved greatness that has gone unrecognized, either because that accolade was reserved for men or because what women drew about has been systematically devalued. It is true that women do not make up a proportionate share of the global cartoonist community. Women (and some men) cartoonists have given reasons for this shortage: in some societies, women do not have much social or real-time mobility; they are expected to be demure and not funny or aggressive; and they are discouraged from entering what is considered male turf. In addition, most editors are men, and women are often overloaded with domestic duties that prevent them from continuing or starting cartooning careers. These factors came up in discussions I had with female cartoonists across Asia (see table 3.1 for a list of interviewees). This chapter attempts to grapple with the marginalization of women in comics, taking women cartoonists in Asia as its focus. Examining the gendering of periodicals and genres, stereotyped portrayals of women in cartoons and comics, and the careers and attitudes of

TABLE 3.1. LIST OF INTERVIEWEES			
Name	**Country**	**Place Interviewed**	**Date Interviewed**
Alam, Naima	Bangladesh	Dhaka, Bangladesh	Oct. 19, 2016
Au Yeung, Craig	Hong Kong	Hong Kong	March 24, 2012
Aventurado, Josie	Philippines	Tagaytay, Philippines	July 13, 2008
Bagalso, Terry	Philippines	Tagaytay, Philippines	July 13, 2008
Chang, Alice	Taiwan	Bethesda, Maryland	Sept. 14, 2000
Chatterjee, Rimi B.	India	Thrissur, India	March 22, 2009
Concepcion, Ofelia E.	Philippines	Tagaytay, Philippines	July 13, 2008
Fang Cheng	China	Beijing, China	June 10, 2001
Fong She Mei	Hong Kong	Hong Kong	March 20, 2012
Jaafar, Taib	Malaysia	Kuala Lumpur, Malaysia	July 21, 2000
Kaoru (Liew Yee Teng)	Malaysia	Kuala Lumpur, Malaysia	July 10, 2012
Laksami Wasitnitiwat	Thailand	Singapore	Feb. 23, 2011
Lam, Connie	Hong Kong	Hong Kong	March 22, 2012
Larasati, Dwinita	Indonesia	Bandung, Indonesia	July 13, 2013
Lau, Lily	Hong Kong	Bethesda, Maryland	Oct. 2, 2004
Lau, Lily	Hong Kong	Hong Kong	March 19, 21, 2012
Lee Wai-chun	Hong Kong	Hong Kong	March 22, 2012
Li Jianhua	China	Beijing, China	May 31, 2001
Li Qingai	China	Qiu Xian Cheng, China	May 28-30, 2009
Lucion-Rivera, Beth	Philippines	Tagaytay, Philippines	July 13, 2008
Ma, Ronnie Shuk-Chu	Hong Kong	Hong Kong	July 14, 1992
Mitu, Nasreen Sultana	Bangladesh	Dhaka, Bangladesh	Oct. 14, 2016
Nazar, Nigar	Pakistan	Singapore	Sept. 12, 2004
Pai, Anant	India	Mumbai, India	July 9, 1993
Pisey, Chan	Cambodia	Phnom Penh, Cambodia	June 22, 2010
Sarah Joan (Sarah Joan Mochtar)	Malaysia	Singapore	Feb. 21, 2011
Sekhar, Rukmini	India	New Delhi, India	July 14, 2009
Sudjai Bhromkoed	Thailand	Bangkok, Thailand	Dec. 4, 2006
Tan, Erlina	Indonesia	Bandung, Indonesia	July 12, 2013
Tanmoy, Syed Rashad Imam	Bangladesh	Dhaka, Bangladesh	Oct. 17, 19, 2016
Thirani, Jayshree	India	New Delhi, India	July 8, 2009
Wee Tian Beng	Singapore	Singapore	Dec. 1, 2016
Ye Liyun	Taiwan	Taipei, Taiwan	July 26, 2005
Yeo Hui Xuan	Singapore	Singapore	Dec. 1, 2016
Yonzon, Guia	Philippines	Guiyang, China	Sept. 10, 2007

female cartoonists, I am not only attempting to redress the false perception that no or few women have had significant careers as comic artists but also to explain how their careers have been rendered invisible.

GENDERED GENRES AND PERIODICALS

In North America, where most mainstream comics have been at least implicitly created for male fans and collectors for several decades, it is easy to forget that other audiences are possible. The history of magazine publishing has demonstrated the utility of targeting specific audience demographics in the design of a periodical, and gender is often a crucial axis of audience differentiation. Yet, cultural goods created for girls and women are typically viewed as less valuable or important than those created for men—or for the normatively male "general audience" (Huyssens 1986). And, to the extent that works created *by* women are often assumed to be necessarily *for* women, this has led to the ghettoization of many female cartoonists.

Gendered genre comic books are prevalent especially in Japan and South Korea. Other Asian countries/territories have histories of their own girls' comics to be discussed later; however, Japanese *shōjo* manga (girls' comics) and their Korean equivalents, *soonjung* manhwa, stand out because of their large pools of female creators, huge circulations, and impacts regionally, and to a certain degree, globally. Initially, shōjo stories were drawn by men, such as Shōsuke Kuragane in 1949 and Osamu Tezuka a few years later, and serialized in girls' magazines. Drawn in a "feminized" style, they concentrated on romance. By the late 1950s, a few women also drew these types of stories, and in the early 1960s, weekly shōjo manga magazines *Shōjo Furendo* ("Girls' Friend") and *Maagaretto* ("Margaret") came out. (Schodt 1983, 97) A group of women artists called *hana no 24 nen gumi* ("Magnificent 24s," because they were born about 1949, the twenty-fourth year of the Showa period) set the foundation for shōjo manga in the 1970s. These young women came to dominate staffs of shōjo manga, and increasingly, gender and sexuality figured in these female artists' stories. Fusami Ogi (2001, 151) said shōjo manga differed after the advent of the Magnificent 24s:

> instead of showing a *shoujo* dreaming of romance with a boy, they showed boys and focused on boys' love. In other words, not presenting texts for *shoujo* but showing the absence of *shoujo*, the texts have changed the position of women subjects and subjects of interest to women into the one which subverts the traditional concept of wom-

en. The women writers … displaced the theme of love as the principal concern of the text, taking on more social and political issues.

The male homosexuality theme in these books was a sharp contrast to traditional shōjo focusing on women's emotions and girl-boy love. In 1980, a subgenre of shōjo manga emphasized female sexuality, the first titles of which were Kodansha's *Be in Love* and Shogakukan's *Big Comic for Ladies*. Called *H-kei*, or ladies comics with soft pornography, they sold well in the 1980s, spurring many titles, particularly as depictions of sex became more explicit (Ito 2008, 189).

As with shōjo manga, soonjung manhwa were initiated in the 1950s by male artists who wrote/drew narratives that were either action, cheerful/ humorous, or family. Choo (2010) claims soonjung manhwa grew out of the family genre. In the 1960s, women entered the soonjung manhwa scene bringing to it their own stories or Western novels they dramatized, the drawing style of shōjo manga, and a feminine narrative sensibility that was very popular among female readers. Noh (2004, 282) credited the 1980s as the most important period in the history of girls' comics because it marked the emergence of a group of women with different themes and storytelling skills and the publication of *Renaissance*. Because of the influx of Japanese manga in the 1970s, these Korean female artists were unintentionally affected by Japanese creators' techniques and styles of creating characters, depicting human bodies, expressing moods, laying out pages, and transitioning scenes. The number of women cartoonists drawing soonjung manhwa continued to grow, so by 1997, when the number passed one hundred, the Korean Women Cartoonists Association (KWCA) was formed. Very few countries worldwide have an organization strictly for female cartoonists.

Cartoon periodicals specifically for women cartoonists and readers are rare in Asia, but they seldom exist elsewhere in the world. Perhaps this results from the exclusivity built into the definition of women's cartoon/comics periodicals—those originated by, staffed with, filled with content by, for, and read by women. Among the few magazines that have met this definition were *Renaissance* of South Korea and *Cabai* of Malaysia.

Renaissance started in November 1988 as an outgrowth of a group of women cartoonists who surfaced in the 1980s (e.g., Hwang Mina, Kim Hyerin, Kim Jin, Shin Eelsuk, and Kang Gyungok) and bypassed "stereotyped love stories of previous girls' comics" (Noh 2004, 282). They dealt with a broad span of serious topics (war, revolution, religion, etc.). *Renaissance* was sold in retail bookstores rather than borrowed from rental shops. By 2004, there were more comics magazines for women than for men; they had become specialized into biweekly/monthly and adults/teenagers/children. Adult comics magazines existed only briefly because, in Korea, "the time is not quite mature" for the taboo sexual topics found in some manga (293).

Cabai, first published April 1, 1997, was a Malaysian humor/cartoon magazine "exclusively for women," spearheaded by popular female cartoonist Cabai (Sabariah Jais). After high school, Cabai (a name taken from a type of spicy chili pepper) drew the female-related strips *Tiga Dara Pingitan* and *Joyah Sport* for the humor magazine *Gila-Gila*, which early on acknowledged the importance of the women's audience (Provencher 1999, 27–28). *Cabai* lasted only a couple of years, brought out by an appendage of Creative Enterprise, publishers of *Gila-Gila*. Creative Enterprise publisher Jaafar Taib explained to me that over the years, his company permitted its artists to start their own firms and then absorbed them (see Nik and Soom 1993).

What Dr. Dwinita Larasati initiated in Indonesia in 2008 qualifies (at least in its beginnings) as comics generated by a woman artist/publisher with stories written, drawn, and read by women. While pursuing postgraduate studies in Europe, Larasati regularly sent borderless story diaries to her mother in Bandung, keeping her abreast of Larasati's activities. When she returned home, an acquaintance suggested that the two of them start a company, Curhat Anak Bangsa ("Outpouring of a Nation"), to publish Larasati and other women cartoonists. Larasati readily agreed, knowing her types of drawing would lack mainstream market value in Indonesia. The first seven books and series were all female authored (Larasati 2011, 141). Larasati and her company have not shied from experimenting with comics as she explained in our interview. In 2009, CAB paired four female artists with four HIV/AIDS-affected children to tell the kids' stories in a graphic diary, *Berbagi Hidup* ("Sharing Life"), and the same year invited nine artists to create seven pages of graphic diary within a week, which became an annual anthology, *Seven*. Definitely, Larasati and CAB went a different direction from manga-inspired publishers in Indonesia, giving females adequate chances to create in their "own styles, stories, and characteristics" (Larasati 2011, 137).

PORTRAYALS OF WOMEN

For much of their history, comic books portrayed women and girls as supportive, passive, and dependent, as dimwitted, house-bound servants to their husband masters, as damsels in distress, waiting for a prince charming to come to their rescue, or as sexy, hourglass-shaped superheroines, attractive to the male gaze. These stereotypes remain in Asian comics, but with the entry of more women into the ranks of cartoonists, metamorphoses have occurred.

Aruna Rao contends that female comics characters closely reflect the status of women in a society, and for India, she categorizes women comics figures as goddess, warrior, demon, victim, lover, vamp, capricious woman, and companion (Rao 1999). Anant Pai, creator of the very popular *Amar Chitra Katha* comic book series in India, told me something similar while defending himself against accusations that he depicted women negatively. Negative portrayals were necessary, he said, to preserve historical accuracy (see Lent 2004). B. S. Jamuna, in her analysis of *Amar Chitra Katha*, reports that women are bestowed an image which becomes "metaphorically a dispossession of identity," are "transformed to a spectacle for men's pleasure and of women's helplessness," are "relegated to a peripheral position," and are treated harshly and afflicted with the "women in refrigerator syndrome" (Jamuna 2010, 511–14, 522). Rukmini Sekhar, with her *Vivalok Comics*, attempted to blot out the common Indian comics stereotype of "long-suffering women who obey and revere their husbands, no matter how poorly they are treated in return" (quoted in McLain 2009, 31).

Representations of women also depend on the intended gender audience of a comic book. This is especially important in Japan and South Korea where genres are divided into male (shōnen) and female (shōjo), shōnen presenting stories about experiences, often with much action, and shōjo expressing the feelings and personalities of characters with a concern for the inner being of the characters. *Kawaii*, or cuteness, is often associated with girls' comics, one writer explaining that such cuteness fights against the type of beauty that is perfection and maturing and suggesting even a plain girl can make herself cute (Shiokawa 1999, 107). Read by teenaged and adolescent women, today's shōjo portray same-sex relationships about as often as they do romance between heterosexual couples. Female readers are huge consumers of *yaoi* (boy to boy romance and sex) because these comics are a safe haven for them to fantasize about full sexual freedom, which traditionally was solely the prerogative of males. The early shōjo manga generally, and those mainstream today, have presented stories as fairy tales of princesses with magical powers, romances deeply rooted in a Cinderella complex. Weekly Japanese male comics tend to show women as helpless and powerless, victims of exploitation in traditional pink-collar occupations. Many stories insult women's intelligence and integrity and stereotype them as sex objects. Shōnen have featured many close-ups of women's body parts—crotches, hips, breasts, and vulvae (the latter symbolized as clams)—as well as portrayals of rape, gang rape, and sexual harassment, and images of women masturbating, urinating, and defecating. In these comics, the power hierarchy was very obvious. (Ito 1994) In contemporary Japan, female essay comics, which differ from and sell better that shōjo and ladies manga, have allowed their authors to express personal experiences and daily activities. Autobiographical and appearing in general interest or women's magazine, the essay comics concern domesticity, marital life, pregnancy, childbirth and care, and single women's lives (Nakagaki 2012, 236; see Sugama-Shimada 2011).

Korean girls' comics are consumed primarily by women and for years have had tastes cultivated by manga. Boy-meets-girl love stories and dreamy romances have been favorites, and when there were heroines, they were portrayed as paragons of beauty—a Western standard of beauty. As with shōjo, Korean girls' comics are expanding into every type of human relationship—romance, friendships, homosexuality, and lesbianism—and are being subdivided into increasingly diverse groups. No matter the type of story, soonjung manhwa aim to capture feelings and complexities of relationships. Some critics think Korean girls' comics reinforce gender stereotypes and roles, while others regard them as revolutionary, even subversive against patriarchy; among the latter are those with boy-to-boy love and science-fiction themes. Noh (2004, 290) contends that making men objects of sexuality, as yaoi do, provides women the excitement of subverting tradition, and displaying women with supernatural powers can subvert patriarchal dualism by showing femininity as superior to masculinity (Noh 2008, 230).

A third determinant of women's portrayals in comic books is the gender of their creators. As already stated, in Japan and South Korea, female depictions in girls' comics changed significantly after women joined or replaced men as the storytellers. As a result, in Japan, females gained a "subject" position (Ogi 2008b, 148), and stories were told from a female point of view, expressing girls' fantasies, dreams, and hopes (Ito 2008a, 202). Whereas traditionally, shōjo manga presented girls in a Cinderella dream world, where they had to have magical powers to be a princess, in more contemporary works, the girl character is strong without the need for magic (Ogi 2008a, 178).

Throughout other parts of Asia since the last third of the twentieth century, isolated instances existed of the imaging of women differently from the traditional, hackneyed way. In India, Manjula Padmanabhan created the newspaper strip *Suki* in 1982, featuring a character described as the "quintessential free spirited urban Indian woman struggling to make her choices in a seriously unfriendly world" (Mandira Moddie, quoted in Stoll 2013a, 370). In Hong Kong, Lee Wai-chun drew *13-Dot Cartoon* (1966–1980), which, she told me, was about a modern girl who "can do what she likes, make her own decisions, have her own ideas"; and in Malaysia, starting in the 1980s, the very popular humor/cartoon magazines dealt with gender and marital issues because of economic and social changes affecting female and male roles (Provencher 1999).

Cartoons, comics, and graphic novels drawn by Asian women today are often autobiographical, sometimes following the frustration and turmoil in the authors' lives, and issue-related, usually dealing with problems encountered by women in everyday life. Such are Ayesha Tariq's 2016 graphic novel, *Sarah: The Suppressed Anger of the Pakistani Obedient Daughter*, a semi-autobiographical account of the frustrations of a teenage girl in a conservative, boy-favored Pakistani family (Sokan 2016), and Kripa Joshi's *Miss Moti* comic book series in Nepal, which deals with the author's own struggles with her body image and serves as a role model for heavy women (Lent 2015, 296).

FEMALE CARTOONISTS' CAREERS AND ATTITUDES

Canvassing fifteen Asian countries in 1992 and 1993, I often asked male cartoonists, "Where are the female cartoonists?" Invariably, the answer was that they did not exist, or a name or two would be given with no further knowledge of their careers. Japan was an exception, having many long-serving, female manga artists, some well-known and wealthy. In the rest of the continent there were few others, and, for the most part, they were not in the limelight. Today, the situation is considerably better because of changing professional and public attitudes towards women in cartooning. So, where *are* the female cartoonists? In this discussion, women are categorized as entrepreneurs, members of collectives, corporate-affiliated cartoonists, freelance artists/writers, and women engaged in cartooning auxiliary activities.

Entrepreneurs

Taking into account the minimal role women were permitted to have in a number of Asian cultures, and their delayed entry in the comics/cartoons realm, few of them have attained the status of owner or head of cartooning enterprises. Those who have did so by starting their own studios/companies. They include Rukmini Sekhar of India, Laksami Wasitnitiwat of Thailand, Guia Yonzon of the Philippines, Fong She Mei of Hong Kong, the already discussed Dwinita Larasati of Indonesia, and Sabariah Jais (Cabai) of Malaysia.

Noncartoonist Rukmini Sekhar took an entirely different route to developing a series of Indian comic books called *Vivalok Comics* in 2001. In my interview with her, Sekhar said *Vivalok* aimed to resist the "homogeneity of kinship, clothing, customs, and rituals" in India; use an "intellectual approach"; link "today's reality with regional legends—the classics interpreted at the grassroots level," and deal with gender and other social issues. As the cofounder (at the mere age of twenty-five) of Thailand's EQ Plus Publishing in 2004, Laksami Wasitnitiwat told me that she sought to promote Thai cartoonists' works and to integrate Thai culture into comics. An offshoot of Dim Sum Studio, EQ Plus publishes cartoon biographies, Thai fables, folktales, classic novels, myths, and science, following Thai children's "interests and their school curriculum."

For many years, Guia Yonzon has partnered with her cartoonist husband, Hugo Yonzon III, in attempting to rejuvenate the Philippines' rich *komiks* tradition. To accomplish this, the couple set up a publishing house, Mango Comics, in 2001, where they published comic books for an upscale audience and magazines such as the bimonthly shōjo-manga-style *Mango Jam* for, about, and by girls, and the political humor magazine, *Mwahaha*, and reprinted classic komiks such as *Darna* and *Lastikman* (Lent 2009, 136). Like the Yonzons, Fong She Mei is in partnership with her husband cartoonist Ma Long as owners/operators of Century Culture Ltd., a children's comics publisher in Hong Kong. In a 2012 interview, Fong She Mei told me that she conceptualizes, researches, and writes the stories that Ma Long draws.

Collective Participants

Women have actively participated in collaborative working groups in parts of Asia, which give them opportunities to talk and receive feedback about their work, participate in live drawing, and seek outlets for their cartoons in collective anthologies and other venues. These collectives often approach cartooning outside the industrial framework, treating comics in alternative, independent terms, with community replacing corporation.

Comic art collectives that sprouted in parts of India in recent years included a few women, such as Vidyun Sabhaney, cofounder of Captain Bijli Comics in Delhi, Tina Thomas, co-operator of Studio Kokaachi in Cochin, and Parismita Singh of Pao Collective in Delhi. Typical of Indian comics collectives, the Pao Collective was organized in 2008 to publish anthologies of the organizers' works and to help them earn their daily bread (*pao*) from their art (see Stoll 2013a, 2013b, 2015). Jeremy Stoll (2013a, 378) describes how Singh and her four male Pao collaborators support Indian comics culture by creating excellent visual narratives, to collaborating creativity, holding comics events, developing anthologies of creators' works for publication, and generally publicizing the creative potential of the medium as a powerful one. Separately, each of these five creators has contributed an individual voice and style to Delhi's comics community.

Another group of Indian women who met in a 2014, week-long workshop, sponsored by Zubaan Books, came out with an anthology, *Drawing the Line: Indian Women Fight Back*, meant to "encourage more women to step into the realm of sequential art and graphic storytelling," and draw about issues pertinent to women (Kuriyan 2014).

Similar types of collectives, each involving only one or two women cartoonists, have existed in Hong Kong, Bangladesh, and Indonesia. Cartoonist Craig Au Yeung told me that in 1997, he pulled together a small informal group of Hong Kong alternative comics creators, called Cockroach, with the aims to encourage, exhibit, and publish members' comics in the organization's oversized periodical of the same name (see Lent 2015, 66–67). The sole woman among them was Lily Lau, who created five comic books that she described to me as exposures of gender inequality and hypocrisy, touching upon people's "deepest fears, loneliness, desire for love." The Bangladeshi Cartoon People community was started as a platform where budding cartoonists and other artists can interact, meet and learn from local cartoonists, watch self-made tutorials on the group's YouTube channel, and join a "sketch walk" around Dhaka every Saturday, founder Syed Imam Tanmoy explained to me. Female member Naima Alam said the group is meaningful to women because they normally are insecure in cartooning. In Indonesia, the rebirth of comics production in the early 1990s, and, in some cases continuing until today, can be attributed to organized campus and professional communities. Two women, Dr. Rahayu Hidayat and Edi Sedyawati, separately, had much to do with this revival, Hidayat as organizer of the community, Lembaga Pengkajian Komik Indonesia ("Indonesian Comics Studies Committee"), and Sedyawati as a guiding spirit of the first Pekan Komik dan Animasi ("Comics and Animation Week"), out of which the campus comics community Masyarakat Komik Indonesia emerged. Scores of similar groups have appeared throughout Indonesia, often made up of art institute and other students, hobbyists, and professional cartoonists (Lent 2015, 139–40); they initiate art community events, stimulate discourse and evaluations among cartoonists, sponsor competitions, and publish independent and occasionally mainstream comics. The many groups allow artists, women among them, to work independently while forming collectives with friends who support their individuality (Berman 2005). In July 2013, I was the guest of active comics communities in Jakarta (Akademi Samali) and Bandung (Komikara), at both of which there were only a few female participants, though the afore-mentioned Dwinita Larasati was the main organizer of Komikara. These examples suffice to give the range of activities females can participate in as members of these collectives.

Corporate-Affiliated Cartoonists

Women have been affiliated with Asian corporate cartooning for decades, seldom as full-time staff, but more likely as regular adjunct or occasional freelance cartoonists. Full-time staff positions as cartoonists on major news-papers and magazines are rare for women and men alike in large sectors of Asia. In cases where there is a full-time newspaper slot(s) for an artist, invariably, the person hired to fill it is expected to draw illustrations, but seldom cartoons.

An exception to this practice has been China where, since at least 1949, women occupied full-time art and cartoonist positions at daily newspapers or magazines. The country's first female cartoonists, Yu Feng and Liang Baibo, published cartoons as early as 1929 and the early 1930s, but probably not as staff members, although Yu Feng worked as a "cartoon journalist" for *Jiuwang Ribao* in 1937, and Liang Baibo drew a front-page strip called *Miss Bee* in *Li Bao* for twenty-five days in 1935 (Wei 1998, 3). More likely, the first female, full-time staff artist on a newspaper was Chen Jinyan, who served as art editor of *Beijing Ribao* from the early 1950s to the 1960s. Her famous car-toonist husband, Fang Cheng, told me Chen's duties were to supervise other cartoonists and draw paintings and headings; she drew her own cartoons for *Beijing Ribao* and other dailies in her spare time. In the early 1950s, cartoonist Mao Yunzhi also served as art editor of the dailies *Dazhong Ribao* and *Jinan Ribao*, while drawing cartoons, and more recently (1980–2000s), Li Jianhua held a full-time position in the Art Editorial Department of the English-language *China Daily*. Until retirement, Li was a full-time political cartoonist at *China Daily*, a rarity among women worldwide (see Lent and Xu 2003). Taiwan's first woman cartoonist, Ye Liyun also was a full-time staff member, drawing for comics publisher Wen Chang Publishing House in the 1960s. In my interview with Ye, she related that she started at Wen Chang when she was fourteen years old, and by sixteen, "I drew a lot of comics already and my wages were more than my teachers." After high school graduation, Ye's comics career ceased because of the shutdown of Wen Chang and pressure from her husband to quit.

Though it is difficult to determine their exact employment status, women cartoonists have been affiliated with mainstream periodicals and publishing houses elsewhere throughout Asia. Those not salaried employees often are regular contributors of comic strips, political or gag cartoons to a newspaper or magazine, serving in what might be termed an adjunct capacity, usually without medical or other benefits. A common payment arrangement for comic book creators is through royalties on individual stories or entire books or series conceptualized by the writer/artist. Those who are fortunate to have their own continuing books and series are more apt to be aligned with one publisher. Of course, there are freelance cartoonists who feel no loyalty to one medium or publisher; they submit works to multiple outlets based on the possibility of acceptance and rate of payment. Any or all of these arrangements can exist in a country's comic art industry.

Examples of women cartoonists working in different planes of Indian political cartooning have been Samita Rathor, who drew a regular newspaper pocket cartoon, *Mrs. and Mr.*, and a one-panel gag cartoon, *Chill Pill*; Maya Kamath, a political cartoonist with three dailies and creator of a family strip, *Gita*, and a syndicated current affairs series, *The World of Maya*; and Manjula Padmanabhan, who had a popular strip, *Suki* (Lent 2009b, 22). In the comic book realm, Anant Pai told me that nearly one-fourth of the total 436 stories that made up the classic *Amar Chitra Katha* comic book series were written by the firm's female associate editor, Kamala Chandrakant.

There are a few Asian women cartoonists who have experienced the whole range of working arrangements. Pakistan's first female cartoonist, Nigar Nazar, is one such person. While finishing art school, Nigar Nazar created a girl character called Gogi, who exuded light, down-to-earth humor on everyday life. In 1971 and 1972, Nazar drew *Gogi Giggles* daily for Karachi's the *Sun*. On the move with her diplomat husband, in Turkey, Nazar drew freelance for two monthly magazines and three daily newspapers; then in Libya, she contributed *Gogi Giggles* to two newspapers, drew cartoons for a children's monthly magazine, produced children's shows for Libya TV, hosted a weekly women's radio program, and published the first Gogi cartoon book. Back in Pakistan in 1979, Nazar worked as a cartoonist and woman's editor of the Islamabad daily, the *Muslim*, where *Gogi Giggles* appeared for years. Nazar told me that for humanitarian and social consciousness-raising purposes, she and her Gogi Studios have painted murals on the walls of hospitals and sides and backs of buses promoting care for children with psychological ailments and other public awareness messages (Rehman 2014; see Lent 2006).

Over the years, women have maintained working relationships with mainstream comic book publishers on an ad hoc level, doing a story or part of a story for a specific title, which might be a one-time opportunity, and on a quasi-staff basis, handling all aspects of a book or series of books under their own names. Examples of creators working in an ad hoc capacity are many female komiks writers in the Philippines; as one of them, Ofelia E. Concepcion, told me, "We don't have regular jobs; we take jobs when they come." She added that these can come from NGOs, religious groups, government institutes, novel and magazine publishers, film, radio, and television studios, as well as komiks companies. In a sense, they are freelance writers except that they have some inkling where they can be published—where publishers know of them. Among seven women komiks writers I interviewed in 2008, Josie Aventurado said she was under contract for ten years to write one pocket book monthly, though she said she was a freelance writer. At another level, Terry C. Bagalso was an editor at Atlas in charge of assigning komiks stories to writers who also did "outside writing." Beth Lucion-Rivera said that discrimination did not exist concerning payment rates, in that writers were paid according to seniority, skills, and saleability, not gender. What they are responsible for when given a job varies; for example, idea conceptualization can be their own, or that of the client or readers. These women carry on a line of female komiks writers in the Philippines dating to Flor Afable Olazo in the 1950s, followed by Elena Patron, Nerissa Cabral, Gilda Olvidado, and Pat V. Reyes, all of whom were extremely prolific (Gimena 2009, 126–30; see Casis 2009).

There are women comics creators who work for one company in a quasi-staff arrangement; they abound in Japan and South Korea but also exist elsewhere. In Singapore, Yeo Hui Xuan has her own series (ten volumes) of the title *A Dream Walker* with TCZ Studio. She has a work space in the studio and receives a forty percent royalty on sales of her books, which she told me is the same rate given to any artist (including students) published by TCZ. In neighboring Malaysia, Liew Yee Teng (Kaoru) is *Gempak* cartoon magazine's leading shōjo artist; in her first twelve years at parent company Art Square, she created four one-volume compilations of her stories, the eight-volume *Helios Eclipse*, and an ongoing series *Maid Maiden*. Kaoru has her own tiny cubicle at Art Square, where, she explained to me, she does all aspects of her stories (see Gan 2011).

Popular girls' cartoonist Lee Wai-Chun preferred to create her *13-Dot Cartoon* and its paraphernalia from her crowded Hong Kong apartment. From 1966 to 1980, she wrote and drew 178 issues of *13-Dot Cartoon*, which were printed by Hong Kong's largest publisher. The comic book featured an attractive young woman engaged in "unrealistic scenarios, luxurious life, charity work, and fantastic adventure" (Wong and Cuklanz 2000, 38) and wearing a vast array of fashionable clothing that Lee designed. Lee, in our interview, said of Miss 13-Dot's wardrobe: "She would go into the toilet with one dress on and come out in another"; the first twenty-eight issues had 1,728 different pieces of clothing. Female readers, according to Lee, took *13-Dot Cartoon* to their tailors to have them copy the patterns. The books have often been reprinted and are still popular today (see also Wong 2014).

Freelance Cartoonists

That most Asian women cartoonists are working as freelancers is not a startling revelation; that is the reality of large sectors of cartoonists (of all genders) nearly everywhere. They do not normally live off their cartooning efforts, and they do keep their day jobs. In interviews worldwide, I have met female cartoonists with a wide diversity of day jobs: Turkey's leading soprano, housewives, teachers, a proprietor of real estate and taxi firms, an advertising agency employee, painters and sculptors, a commune council worker, novelists, and illustrators of children's books.

In Asia, the situation is about the same. Taiwan's Alice Chang, for example, rattled off to me a list of things she did for a living—designed albums, wrote an internet column and a love advice column, and even served as creative director for Taiwan's ruling president at one time. She also wrote love novels under the penname "Aquarius Whale." The pioneer female cartoonist in Cambodia, Sin Yang Pirom, in the late 1980s, worked her day job at a commune council and in the evenings wrote illustrated novels that were turned into comics. Nasreen Sultana Mitu of Bangladesh told me that she makes her living as a teacher and submits political cartoons to the daily *New Age* and to *Unmad* humor magazine. Indian graphic novelist Rimi B. Chatterjee is employed as a corporate consultant. To publish her three-book series, *Kalpa Shadowfalls*, Chatterjee told me she hired artists from a small studio and used up all three advances given by her publisher to produce the first book. She expected proceeds from this initial book to finance the second and those from the second to produce the third. Freelance cartoonists who work as housewives have taxing schedules trying to squeeze in idea formation and drawing. Chan Pisey, one of the three women cartoonists in Cambodia's history, told me that she usually draws when her three small children are asleep. Similarly, Nigar Nazar of Pakistan explained that she juggled home duties and cartooning by beginning to draw at 4 a.m. and stopping at 7 a.m. when her three children awoke.

Cartooning Auxiliary Personnel

In some instances, Asian women have been heavily involved in elevating the cartooning profession through organization, promotion, and education. Like Dr. Rahayu Hidayat and Edi Sedyawati of Indonesia, they have not always been cartoonists themselves. Three Asian women who have spent long periods promoting comic art are Li Qingai of China, Connie Lam of Hong Kong, and Sudjai Bhromkoed of Thailand. Of the three, only Li is a cartoonist. With her cartoonist husband, Chen Yuli, Li started a training and semiprofessional facility, Frog Cartoon Group, in the most unlikely of places, among the vegetable and cotton farmers of Qui County, Hebei Province, China. Started in 1983, the Frog Cartoon Group, as Li proudly told me, mentored more than 2,000 farmers and other workers, many starting at early ages in the so-called Tadpole Cartoon Class. Li and Chen provide most of the training and professional guidance, occasionally assisted by China's top-notch cartoonists who visit for short periods. Since 2004, Connie Lam has been executive director of the Hong Kong Arts Centre, where she has given considerable energy to building a strong professional infrastructure for both alternative and mainstream comics. Significantly, she and the Hong Kong Arts Centre have sponsored comics-awareness activities; set up an academic degree program in comics; organized exhibitions of Hong Kong comics and a series of workshops, screenings, and seminars locally and in about a half-dozen countries; compiled and published books on the history of Hong Kong comics; assisted in publishing alternative artists' comic books; and acquired a four-story building to be converted into a comics facility. In Thailand, Sudjai Bhromkoed cofounded Cartoonthai Institute in 2003, the aim of which, she told me, is "to combat bad comics here, those with violent and sexually explicit content" and to support "good" cartoonists. The institute, supported by the Foundation for Children, enhances cartooning with missions in the academic, networking, and production realms.

Other noncartoonists have been associated with the production and distribution of comics, including Jayshree Thirani, who managed Campfire Comics for her husband, Keshav Thirani, in India; Ronnie Ma Shuk-Chu, who was general manager of Tin Ha comics in Hong Kong, which belonged to her brother, Ma Wing-Shing; and Erlina Tan, who was owner-operator of the oldest and largest reprinter/distributor of Indonesian classic comics. Tan inherited Maranatha Books in Bandung upon the death of her husband, Marcus Haddy. In our interview, she described her dismay at taking over the business: "At first, I did not understand the business. I was used to taking care of the kids, taking them to school, working in the kitchen. I knew nothing about the comics business. After my husband died, I had to love the business."

CONCLUSION

A mere generation ago, a conclusion like this on women and Asian comic art would have been rather dismal. Few women cartoonists outside of Japan and Korea existed or were acknowledged to exist, and a negative attitude prevailed among male editors and cartoonists that women did not have the commitment, sense of humor, or toughness needed to succeed in the profession. Traditionally, when women were portrayed in comic art, often they appeared as ladies in distress waiting for a male rescuer, sex objects designed for male pleasure, or servile, sometimes battered, housewives. In the span of about twenty years, significant change has occurred.

Today, Asian women are engaged in cartooning at nearly all levels—in administration, staff and corporate-affiliated positions, as members of comics collectives, and as freelance artists. In many instances, they work alongside male cocreators under equitable conditions. Sometimes this happened because men opened doors for female creators; sometimes, because brave women took down the doors. The situation is not yet ideal. The imbalance in numbers of male and female cartoonists is still huge, for many reasons: religions and cultures that hold women to be inferior to men, the predominance of male editors who control publishing gates, and the women themselves, reluctant to enter cartooning for various reasons, including heavy workloads inside and outside the home. Portrayals of women in Asian comic art have changed partly because of increasing numbers of female creators, content that is of more interest to women, and female-friendlier reading venues such as bookstores and online sales agencies replacing shabby rental shops and stalls. Though old stereotypes of women in cartoons and comics persist, they are less frequent and in some instances are offset by stories of independent, self-assured, and outspoken women.

The roles and portrayals of Asian women in comic art are improving at an ever-accelerating rate. One can expect a marked increase in the number of women in the comic art community over the next generation, which will, in turn, continue to improve their portrayals in cartoons and comics. However, we should always remember that these new cohorts will not be starting from nothing. When people argue, as the Angoulême festival's spokespeople did, that they don't know any significant women cartoonists, it often turns out that they simply haven't been looking. As my interview research demonstrates, there is in fact a rich history of women creating and promoting comics in many Asian countries. They have rarely had the same opportunities as their male peers, but this should not be seen as an excuse for neglecting their contributions. Rather, we should understand the constraints on women cartoonists' careers and celebrate the achievements that have been made in spite of them.

References

Berman, Laine. 2005. "Comic Hey-Day! Indonesia's Comic Scene Is in a Golden Age but the Industry Remains Marginal and Plagued by Self-doubt." *Inside Indonesia*, July-September. http://www.insideindonesia.org/edition-83/comic-heyday.

Casis, Aileen P. 2009. "Women Cartooning: An Art That Demands Courage." In *The First One Hundred Years of Philippine Komiks and Cartoons*, by John A. Lent, 56–57. Manila: Yonzon Associates.

Choo, Kukhee. 2010. "Consuming Japan: Early Korean Girls Comic Book Artists' Resistance and Empowerment." In *Complicated Currents: Media Flows, Soft Power and East Asia*, edited by Daniel Black, Stephen Epstein, and Alison Tokita, chap 6. Melbourne: Monash University ePress.

Gan, Sheuo Hui. 2011. "Manga in Malaysia: An Approach to Its Current Hybridity through the Career of the Shojo Mangaka Kaoru." *International Journal of Comic Art* 13 (2): 164–78.

Gimena, Glady E. 2009. "Women in Komiks, in a World of Men." In *The First One Hundred Years of Philippine Komiks and Cartoons*, by John A. Lent, 126–29. Manila: Yonzon Associates.

Ito, Kinko. 1994. "Images of Women in Weekly Male Comic Magazines in Japan." *Journal of Popular Culture* 27 (4): 81–95.

Ito, Kinko. 2008a. "Masako Watanabe: 50 Years of Making Girls' and Ladies' Comics in Japan." *International Journal of Comic Art* 10 (2): 199–208.

Ito, Kinko. 2008b. "The Touching and the Sensual in Japanese Ladies' Comics: An Interview with Asako Shiomi." *International Journal of Comic Art* 10 (2): 186–98.

Jamuna, B. S. 2010. "Strategic Positioning and Re-presentations of Women in Indian Comics." *International Journal of Comic Art* 12 (2–3): 509–24.

Kuriyan, Priya, Larrisa Bertonasco, and Ludmilla Bartscht, eds. 2014. *Drawing the Line: Indian Women Fight Back*. New Delhi: Zubaan Books.

Larasati, Dwinita. 2011. "So, How Was Your Day? The Emergence of Graphic Diary and Female Artists in Indonesia." *International Journal of Comic Art* 13 (2): 134–42.

Lent, John A. 2004. "India's *Amar Chitra Katha*: Fictionalized History or the Real Story?" *International Journal of Comic Art* 6 (1): 56–76.

Lent, John A. 2006. "Nigar Nazar: Pakistani-Cartoonist-Woman." *The Comics Journal*, November: 191–92.

Lent, John A. 2009a. *The First One Hundred Years of Philippine Komiks and Cartoons*. Manila: Yonzon Associates.

Lent, John A. 2009b. "An Illustrated History of Indian Political Cartooning." *International Journal of Comic Art* 11 (2): 3–25.

Lent, John A. 2015. *Asian Comics*. Jackson: University Press of Mississippi.

Lent, John A., and Xu Ying. 2003 "Chinese Women Cartoonists: Historical and Contemporary Perspectives." *International Journal of Comic Art* 5 (2): 351–66.

McLain, Karline. 2009. "*Vivalok Comics*: Celebrating All That Is Small in India." *International Journal of Comic Art* 11 (2): 26–43.

Nakagaki, Kotaro. 2012. "Expanding Female Manga Market: Shungiku Uchida and the Emergence of the Autobiographical Essay." *International Journal of Comic Art* 14 (1): 236–50.

Nik Naizi Husin, and M. Hafez M. Soom. 1993. "Cabai Kartunis Wanita Yang Gigih." *Sasaran* July: 111–13.

Noh, Sueen. 2004. "The Gendered Comics Market in Korea: An Overview of Korean Girls' Comics." *International Journal of Comic Art* 6 (1): 281–98.

Noh, Sueen. 2008. "Science, Technology, and Women Represented in Korean Sci-Fi Girls' Comics." *International Journal of Comic Art* 10 (2): 209–34.

Ogi, Fusami. 2001. "Beyond Shoujo, Blending Gender: Subverting the Homogenized World in *Shoujo Manga* (Japanese Comics for Girls)." *International Journal of Comic Art* 3 (2): 151–61.

Ogi, Fusami. 2008a. "*Hana yori dango* (*Boys over Flowers*) as a Trans-National Comics for Girls beyond Japan." *International Journal of Comic Art* 10 (2): 170–85.

Ogi, Fusami. 2008b. "Shojo Manga (Japanese Comics for Girls) in the 1970s' Japan as a Message to Women's Bodies: Interviewing Keiko Takemiya—A Leading Artist of the Year 24 Flower Group." *International Journal of Comic Art* 10 (2): 148–69.

Provencher, Ronald. 1999. "An Overview of Malay Humor Magazines: Significance, Origins, Contexts, Texts, and Audiences." In *Themes and Issues in Asian Cartooning: Cute, Cheap, Mad and Sexy*, edited by John A. Lent, 11–36. Bowling Green, OH: Popular Press.

Rao, Aruna. 1999. "Goddess/Demon, Warrior/Victim: Representations of Women in Indian Comics." In *Themes and Issues in Asian Cartooning: Cute, Cheap, Mad and Sexy*, edited by John A. Lent, 165–82. Bowling Green, OH: Popular Press.

Rehman, Sonya. 2014. "Interview: Pakistan's First Woman Cartoonist Shapes Young Minds and Society," Asia Society, November 7. https://asiasociety.org/blog/asia/interview-pakistans -first-woman-cartoonist-shapes-young-minds-and-society. Accessed October 28, 2015.

Schodt, Frederik L. 1983. *Manga! Manga! The World of Japanese Comics*. Tokyo: Kodansha.

Shiokawa, Kanako. 1999. "Cute but Deadly: Women and Violence in Japanese Comics." In *Themes and Issues in Asian Cartooning: Cute, Cheap, Mad and Sexy*, edited by John A. Lent, 93–126. Bowling Green, OH: Popular Press.

Sokan, Kenny. 2016. "An Obedient Daughter? Pakistani Author Acts Out Frustrations in Graphic Novel." *The World*, March 3. http://www.pri.org/stories/2016-03-03/obedien tdaughter. Accessed March 7, 2016.

Stoll, Jeremy. 2013a. "A Creator's History of the Comics Medium in India." *International Journal of Comic Art* 15 (1): 363–82.

Stoll, Jeremy. 2013b. "Bread and Comics: A History of the Pao Collective." *International Journal of Comic Art* 15 (2): 117–44.

Stoll, Jeremy. 2015. "From Corporate to Collaborative Comics in India." *International Journal of Comic Art* 17 (1): 483–99.

Sugawa-Shimada, Akiko. 2011. "Functions and Possibilities of Female 'Essay Manga': Resistance, Negotiation, and Pleasure." *International Journal of Comic Art* 13 (2): 103–15.

Wei, Shaochang, ed. 1998. *Miss Bee*. Jinan: Shandong Pictorial Press.

Wong, Wendy Siuyi. 2014. "Fifty Years of Popularity of Theresa Lee Wai-chun and *Miss 13-Dot*: Changing Identities of Women in Hong Kong." *International Journal of Comic Art* 16 (2): 582–96.

Wong, Wendy Siuyi, and Lisa M. Cuklanz. 2000. "The Emerging Image of the Modern Woman in Hong Kong Comics of the 1960s & 1970s." *International Journal of Comic Art* 2 (2): 33–53.

Yong, Fei, ed. 1997. *Chinese Modern Cartoonists Dictionary*. Hangzhou: Zhejiang People's Press.

4.

Bringing Up Manga

HOW EDITORS IN THE 1920s AND 1930s HELPED CREATE CONTEMPORARY JAPANESE COMICS

Eike Exner

Although expansive definitions of comics, such as Scott McCloud's (1994, 9) or David Kunzle's (1973, 1–4), consider most or all forms of graphic narrative throughout history "comics," there are significant differences between the currently dominant form of comics, which first appears in strips by Rudolph Dirks and Frederick Burr Opper in the *New York Journal*, and other, pre-1900 forms. As Thierry Smolderen (2009, 7) argues in *The Origins of Comics*, the comic strip—and with it modern comics—came into existence around the turn of the century, when artists in the United States, in competition with (still silent) cinema, strove to make graphic narrative more mimetic by abandoning external narration and instead representing sound, motion, and other, more abstract elements visually through devices like speech balloons and speed lines.

More than two decades after the creation of this new, mimetic form of comics, editors at magazines and newspapers in Japan, through the importation and translation of such comic strips from abroad, drastically changed the trajectory of graphic narrative there. Their efforts between 1923 and 1940 led to the adoption of the American comic strip as the primary model for Japanese graphic narrative, and modern manga, including the influential works of Tezuka Osamu,[1] should be considered the offspring of these translated comic strips.

PREVAILING PERSPECTIVES ON THE ORIGINS OF MODERN MANGA

The significance of the importation of American comic strips in prewar Japan has not yet been widely acknowledged. Broadly speaking, there are two prevailing narratives on the development of contemporary Japanese comics, though these should be taken as historiographical tendencies rather than absolutes.

The first holds that these comics, which since the 1980s have come to be widely known abroad as manga, are the product of a centuries-old Japanese tradition of graphic narrative with admitted occasional—but tangential—foreign influence.[2] This view is promulgated, for example, by Brigitte Koyama-Richard's (2007) *One Thousand Years of Manga*, the permanent exhibition at the Kyoto International Manga Museum, and the work of Shimizu Isao (1987; 1991; 2007; 2009), Japan's most prolific manga historian. It is, perhaps unsurprisingly, even endorsed by the Japanese government. Paul Gravett (2004, 18) writes that, with the introduction of a new national art curriculum for junior high schools in 2000, teachers were provided with material "to help them convey the uninterrupted continuity between historic picture scrolls and prints and [contemporary] manga." Gravett himself rejects this view, as does Kure Tomofusa, who likens proclaiming Hokusai's manga or the *chōjūgiga* picture scrolls ancestors to present-day manga to arguing that the abacus is an early computer—they might both be used for similar purposes, but one didn't lead directly to the other (Kure 2007, 118).

According to the second view, and in the words of Matsushima Masato, curator of Japanese painting at the Tokyo National Museum, "The [contemporary] manga found in Japan are a medium that developed after being introduced from the West and widely permeating Japanese society from the Meiji Period [1868–1912] onwards" (Matsushima 2015, 269, translated from the Japanese). Matsushima is referring to a development that actually began in 1862, a few years before the Meiji Restoration, when foreign resident of Yokohama and staff artist for the *London Illustrated News* Charles Wirgman founded the *Japan Punch*, Japan's first graphic humor magazine. Though originally targeted at other Anglophone expatriates, the magazine attracted a native readership as well. The influence of the *Japan Punch* was so immense that cartoons became known in Japan as *ponchi-e* ("Punch pictures"). Because of their popularity, Japanese, too, began to publish graphic humor magazines, such as the *E-Shinbun Nipponchi* in 1874 and the *Maru Maru Chinbun* in 1877. The *Japan Punch* ceased publication in 1887, but the influx of European cartooning continued. By the same year, a translation of Wilhelm Busch's *Max und Moritz* had appeared and introduced Busch's picture story to Japanese readers (Sasaki 2012, 74). The earliest reported use of the word "manga" in its contemporary meaning (in this case denoting a four-panel cartoon copied from a foreign magazine) occurred on April 27, 1891, in the newspaper *Jiji Shinpō* and likely originated with Imaizumi Ippyō (Miyamoto 2003, 109).[3] Imaizumi had traveled to the United States to study caricature a few years prior and upon his return in 1890 joined his uncle Fukuzawa Yukichi's *Jiji Shinpō* as its illustrator. Imaizumi was succeeded in this position by Japanese painter Kitazawa Rakuten (also spelled "Racten" by Kitazawa, whose legal given name was Yasuji). Rakuten had studied cartooning in Yokohama under the Australian Frank Arthur Nankivell and in 1902 created Japan's first newspaper cartoon page for the *Jiji Shinpō*. He christened said page *Jiji Manga*, a decision that led to "manga" eventually replacing the term "ponchi-e."[4] In 1905 Kitazawa founded the influential magazine *Tokyo Puck* and became the most important manga artist of the early 20th century. His prominence a decade later was rivaled only by Okamoto Ippei, who worked as a cartoonist for the newspaper *Asahi Shinbun* from 1909 onwards and wrote illustrated stories that he referred to as *manga manbun*. With the success of Kitazawa and Okamoto's works contemporary Japanese comics were born and, the story goes, ready to be picked up and popularized further by Tezuka Osamu after the end of World War II. However, like the continuity narrative advocated by Shimizu, this account does not sufficiently explain significant changes that occurred in manga between the (pre-1923) works of Kitazawa and Okamoto and those drawn by Tezuka.

The vast majority of multipanel narrative manga before 1923 look markedly different from today's *story manga*. Okamoto's manga, consisting of separate pictures and text, resemble the picture story model of Wilhelm Busch more than they do Tezuka's comics, for example. This is unsurprising given Okamoto's admiration of Busch's work (Okamoto 1930, 255; 1936) and multiple adaptations of his stories (Takeuchi 1995, 32–33), including one of *Max und Moritz* for the magazine *Ryōyū* in 1923 (Sasaki 2014, 74). In both *Max und Moritz* and manga manbun, sound is generally not expressed through visual devices such as speech balloons, as is the case in most comics (Japanese and other) today. Instead of presenting the reader with an "audiovisual stage" (Smolderen 2009, 137) upon which the story is acted out mimetically, external narrative text is usually necessary to relay what is going on.

FROM PICTURE STORIES TO COMIC STRIPS

The current, globally dominant form of expression in comics is essentially that of the American comic strip created and popularized by Rudolph Dirks and Frederick Burr Opper at the close of the nineteenth century.[5] The distinctive features of the comic strip compared to earlier forms of graphic narrative are (a) the abandoning of the outside narrator, who mediates between images and reader through extradiegetic text adorning the panels, and (b) a marked increase in transdiegetic content in the images. Transdiegetic signs make visible that which otherwise would be difficult or impossible to express visually in still images. In Saussurean terms, transdiegetic signs consist of an *extra*diegetic signifier and an *intra*diegetic signified:[6] speech balloons signifying intradiegetic dialog, stars expressing pain, or dust clouds that *symbolize* movement rather than *depicting* actual dust (a device referred to as "briffits" by Mort Walker [2000, 30]). In all of the above, a phenomenon within the story world (i.e., an intradiegetic signified) that is nonvisual within a still image, such as movement or sound, is made legible to the reader via a visual device that exists outside the story world (i.e., an extradiegetic signifier). Whether or not the difference between Busch's *Max und Moritz* or Okamoto's *manbun manga* on the one hand and Dirks's *Katzenjammer Kids* or Tezuka's story manga on the other is significant enough to mark the creation of a new medium—that is to say, whether the latter are "comics" while the former are not—is arguable, but differences of form between the two are undeniable. What the historical narratives outlined above fail to explain is how Japanese comics came to so closely resemble the American comic strip rather than the Buschian picture story.

Kitazawa and Okamoto were both familiar with the newer form of graphic narrative that had come to dominate American print media by the 1920s, but neither was quick to adopt it. Kitazawa was enamored with Outcault's *Buster Brown*, which served as an inspiration for his characters Chame and Dekobō and from which he appears to have copied ideas (see Jo 2013, 34). He also published a translation of Jimmy Swinnerton's *Mr. Jack* in the November 10, 1908, issue of the *Tokyo Puck* (likely the first printing of an American newspaper comic strip in Japan), and there are occasional instances in which he experimented with the form. Okamoto, on the other hand, visited the comics department of Pulitzer's *New York World* in 1922 and wrote an article for the *Asahi Shinbun* about American comics in general and George McManus's *Bringing Up Father* and Bud Fisher's *Mutt and Jeff* in particular, but neither artist embraced strip conventions such as transdiegetic sound until *after* they had become dominant in Japan as well.

1923: SUZUKI BUNSHIRŌ'S *ASAHI GRAPH, SHŌ-CHAN NO BŌKEN,* AND *BRINGING UP FATHER*

As pointed out by Sasaki Minoru (2014), 1923 brought about significant changes in manga, which can be traced back to two decisions by Suzuki Bunshirō, editor in chief of Japan's first tabloid newspaper, the *Asahi Graph.* For the *Graph's* first issue on January 25, 1923, Suzuki devised a manga strip inspired by the London *Daily Mirror's Pip, Squeak and Wilfred* (Suzuki 1952, 190). Although others have disputed his account (Takeuchi 1995, 70–72), Suzuki claimed to have written the first scripts himself, having them illustrated by artist Kabashima Katsuichi, with Oda Nobutsune later taking over as writer. The new strip, *Shō-chan no bōken*, chronicled the adventures of a boy called Sho and his squirrel companion. It was an immediate success and, after the protagonist's original school uniform cap was replaced by a knit hat with a pompom, Sho's style of headwear even rose to national fame as a *Shō-chan bo* ("Shō-chan/Little Sho hat") and generated a corresponding fashion trend among Japan's children (Suzuki 1938; Ōtsuka 2013, 89–90).[7]

Whereas Kitazawa had previously experimented with the convention, *Shō-chan no bōken* was Japan's first serialized four-panel graphic narrative regularly using speech balloons. However, it used few other transdiegetic devices and, like most narrative manga at the time, *Shō-chan no bōken* still relied heavily on extradiegetic narration printed next to or underneath the panels to convey events to the reader. George McManus's *Bringing Up Father*, which began appearing in the *Asahi Graph* on April 1, 1923, did not, and it became the first true "audiovisual" comic strip serialized in Japan. Suzuki (1938, 44) writes that he had been following the strip in an American newspaper for many years before deciding to license it from International Features' (the syndicate holding the distribution rights and today's King Features) representative in Tokyo. Under its Japanese title, *Oyaji kyōiku*, the strip's weekday edition ran in the *Asahi Graph* until the Great Kantō Earthquake on September 1, 1923. After the quake, the *Asahi Graph* appeared only intermittently and without comics until November 14, when it again appeared regularly, now on a weekly basis. The new, weekly version of the *Asahi Graph* published the Sunday edition of *Oyaji kyōiku* until July 31, 1940.[8] This made *Bringing Up Father* by far the longest-running serialized manga in Japan, surpassed by others only after the end of World War II. The daily edition of *Bringing Up Father* was also published in the *Tokyo Asahi Shinbun* from October 25, 1923, to November 21, 1925, the *Osaka Asahi Shinbun* from February 15, 1924, to April 22, 1925, and the women's periodical *Zen-Kansai Fujin Rengōkai* from December 1925 to March 1928.

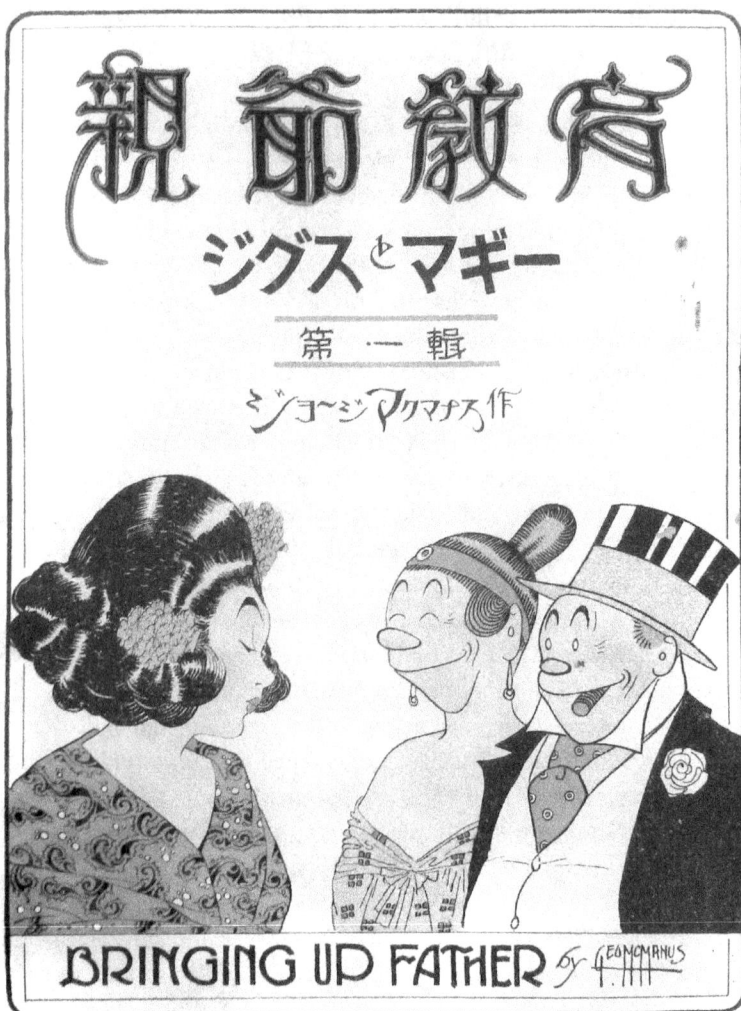

Figure 4.1. Greyscale photograph of *Bringing Up Father* anthology cover.

In 1924 and 1925, two volumes collecting *Bringing Up Father* strips in Japanese translation were published as well. The first of these book volumes featured exclusive cover art and a letter "To Japanese Readers" by McManus himself (see figure 4.1 for a greyscale photograph of the cover). In it, McManus expresses that he is "extremely proud that any work of mine has found favor in a land so far from the United States as the land of the Rising Sun

[sic]." According to Suzuki's article in the October 19, 1938, *Asahi Graph*, Mc-Manus was so pleased to see his strip's protagonists Jiggs and Maggie speak Japanese that he published an article or cartoon about this development in the magazine *Editor and Publisher* (44). In its November 16, 1938, issue, the *Asahi Graph* featured a telegram by McManus commemorating his strip's fifteen-year anniversary in the publication: "I am honored and pleased to learn that jiggs and his family and friends have been entertaining the readers of asahigraph for fifteen years stop My heartiest congratulations and best wishes for a continuance of our relationship banzai [sic]" (44). McManus may have considered his work's enormous success in Japan particularly amusing in light of a joke in the foreword to a collected volume of *Bringing Up Father* strips published in the United States in 1919, four years before Jiggs and Maggie spoke Japanese for the first time: "The greatest rooter for this series is the Mikado of Japan who, in his annual message to the Japanese parliament, made the flat-footed statement: '[made-up Japanese] BRINGING UP FATHER [made-up Japanese].' The italics are all his own" (McManus 1919, i).

Whether the Japanese emperor later actually became a fan is unknown, but *Bringing Up Father*'s immense popularity is beyond doubt. Evidence for it can be found in the appearances made by Jiggs and/or Maggie in a variety of advertisements in Japanese newspapers and magazines, where they endorsed products such as insurance, bicycle parts, stoves, and alcoholic beverages in more than two dozen different ads between 1923 and 1932, most of which appeared multiple times and in multiple publications. Advertisements featuring Jiggs and/or Maggie far exceed in number those featuring Shō-chan, Nontō, or Mutt and Jeff, although they appear to have been overtaken in popularity by Tagawa Suihō's Norakuro, Popeye, Betty Boop, and Mickey Mouse in the 1930s. A play based on the strip even was staged in Tokyo in August 1924, with articles covering it in the *Tokyo Asahi Shinbun* on August 16 and 23. *Bringing Up Father*'s success induced other editors to follow Suzuki's lead, sparking a comics translation boom. Between the first and last Japanese appearance of Jiggs and Maggie in the *Asahi Graph*, dozens of other American comic strips (and some non-American foreign ones, such as the British *Bonzo* or the Swedish *Adamson*) were featured in Japanese newspapers, magazines, and books. Among these, one finds a large share of what today is considered the canon of prewar American comics, including Jimmy Swinnerton's *Little Jimmy* (daily strip in the *Kokumin Shinbun* from April 16, 1923, to June 8, 1926; Sunday edition in the monthly magazine *King* from January 1925 to March 1926), Bud Fisher's *Mutt and Jeff* (*Osaka Asahi Shinbun* from November 14, 1923 to July 17, 1925; *Zen-Kansai Fujin Rengōkai* January 1925 to March 1928),[9] Cliff Sterett's *Polly and Her Pals* (*Tokyo Nichi Nichi Shinbun*, July 1 to August

19, 1923),[10] and Fred Opper's *Happy Hooligan* (January 11, 1925, to January
26, 1930), *Mr. Dough and Mr. Dubb* (as an intermittent replacement), *Our
Antediluvian Ancestors*, and *And Her Name Was Maud* (as topper strips)
in the *Jiji Shinpō*. Kitazawa Rakuten's inclusion of Jimmy Swinnerton's *Mr.
Jack* in a single issue of the *Tokyo Puck* had been an anomaly in his work as
an editor until 1925, but as the editor of the *Jiji Manga* Sunday supplement,
he was likely responsible for introducing Fred Opper's strips to Japan. On
February 2, 1930, these strips were replaced by Pat Sullivan/Otto Mesmer's
Laura and *Felix the Cat*, the latter of which continued until December 31, 1932.
Kitazawa left the *Jiji Shinpō* in 1932, and the overlap between his tenure and
the above-mentioned strips suggests he was instrumental in bringing them
to the *Jiji Shinpō*. What led Kitazawa to regularly print American comic strips
remains unknown, but the sustained success of *Bringing Up Father* appears
the most plausible explanation.

Despite the multitude of other foreign strips published in prewar Japan,
few rivaled *Bringing Up Father*'s longevity. Suzuki (1952, 190–91) claims that
a successful comic strip requires a discerning editor, because it is often the
case that newspaper staff will tire of a comic strip before the readership does,
become overly critical of it and end up canceling it. According to the article
accompanying McManus's 1938 telegram, the *Asahi Graph*, too, considered
dropping *Bringing Up Father* at some point, but decided against it because
of readers' overwhelming support for its continuation, a point corrobo-
rated by Suzuki (1938, 44). This support may have been the result of Suzuki
Bunshirō's personal interest and involvement in the strip's translation and
publication. Although Suzuki (1938, 44) declares that the other American
comics published in Japan were simply "not funny," it is more probable that
Jiggs and Maggie's outstanding popularity was rather due to Suzuki dis-
carding episodes whose jokes did not translate well into Japanese and only
publishing those that he personally deemed able to preserve their humor in
translation—a practice that almost led to occasional shortages of material.[11]

THE FIRST JAPANESE COMIC STRIPS

The popularity of the new American strips was not lost on editors at newspapers without translated comics, and it soon led to the appearance of
Japanese strips that adopted the format. The first and most significant of
these early strips was *Nonki na tōsan* (often colloquially shortened to *Nontō*
and rendered in English as "Easy-Going Daddy"), which became the most

successful domestically produced strip of the 1920s besides *Shō-chan no bōken*. According to Suzuki, *Nontō* was spawned by *Hōchi Shinbun* editor-in-chief Takada Tomoichirō's request that manga artist Asō Yutaka produce a strip in the same vein as *Bringing Up Father* in order to compete with McManus's creation (1952, 189; 1938, 44). Asō's strip began serialization in the *Hōchi Shinbun* on April 29, 1923, and became the first regular strip by a Japanese author to fully embrace the American format. Unlike *Shō-chan no bōken*, *Nontō* did not feature extradiegetic narration and instead made extensive use of transdiegetic content beyond speech balloons, such as sight and motion lines, music notes, pain stars, and briffits.

That Asō and other Japanese cartoonists were closely following *Bringing Up Father* is particularly evident from the comics' reading order. The *Asahi Graph's Bringing Up Father* had originally preserved the American reading order for panels and speech balloons (left to right, top to bottom), but used the Japanese order for dialog (top to bottom, right to left). Conflicting reading directions are obviously confusing to the reader, and *Bringing Up Father* switched to rendering Japanese dialog in the original English reading direction on May 16, 1923.[12] On June 3, *Nonki na tōsan*, too, suddenly featured dialog written from left to right. Two weeks later, Asō changed the order of panels to match that of McManus's strip as well. The success of the left-to-right strips destabilized the established Japanese reading order in manga—in fact, the dominance of strips like *Bringing Up Father* and *Nonki na tōsan* may have even been a factor in making left-to-right writing of horizontal Japanese text acceptable. Horizontal text used to be virtually always written right-to-left, and it is only during the mid-1920s that regular examples of left-to-right Japanese text appear (e.g., in advertisements); today, left-to-right has become the norm for horizontal Japanese. In December 1923, an anonymous Japanese strip called *Chikame no Shō-chan* appeared in the *Hōchi Shimbun* and used the American order for panels and text. In 1924, Shimokawa Hekoten, one of Kitazawa's disciples, published a comic strip called *Shinsetai* in the *Chuō Shinbun*, in which he combined a Japanese reading order for panels with an American reading order for text, and fellow Kitazawa pupil Nagasaki Batten's *Pī-bō monogatari*, switched between American and Japanese reading orders in alternate issues of the *Jiji Shinpō* between November 1923 and June 1924. *Shō-chan no bōken* also began to experiment with left-to-right reading for dialog or titles and subtitles, and for a period in 1925 even appeared written entirely (dialog, titles, *and* external narration) in the American reading direction. At least fifteen of the earliest Japanese-drawn comic strips used left-to-right reading at some point. Eventually, Japanese artists stopped using the same reading direction as American comics, but they retained the abolition of extradiegetic narration and the reliance on transdiegetic elements that such strips had introduced.

The Buschian picture story model did not disappear from Japanese publications overnight. Okamoto Ippei's most prolific student, Miyao Shigeo, wrote a series of successful graphic narratives during the 1920s, such as *Dango kushisuke man'yūki* (Takeuchi 1995, 11–13), and Shimada Keizō's *Bōken dankichi* was popular in the 1930s. However, this previously dominant form of graphic narrative kept steadily losing ground to the American comic strip model. The percentage of manga in eight Tokyo newspapers up to 1945 that used extradiegetic narration (*setsumeibun*) continually declined from 1923 onwards, with this model of graphic narrative becoming entirely absent from the newspapers surveyed by 1937 (Jo 2013, 291–92, 299). Although examples of pictures stories in the tradition of Busch and Miyao persisted in other publications (notably, *Bōken dankichi* in the monthly *Shōnen Kurabu*), the ascent of the comic strip manga and decline of the picture-story manga statistically documented by Jo can be observed across Japanese print media of the 1920s and 1930s.

KUBO AKIRA AND MATSUI KOMAZŌ'S *MANGA MAN*

This shift towards the American comic strip model was reinforced in August 1929 with the appearance of the monthly magazine *Manga Man*, published by Tokyo Manga Shinbun-sha ("Tokyo Manga Newspaper Company"). Tokyo Manga Shinbun-sha was founded specifically to publish *Manga Man*, an effort led by Kubo Akira, *Manga Man*'s publisher, and Matsui Komazō, who wrote the first issue's editorial. Inspired by Matsui's collection of approximately thirty years' worth of the *American Weekly* (the *San Francisco Examiner*'s Sunday supplement), *Manga Man* aimed to introduce the visual splendor of large-format, color American newspaper comics to Japan, as stated in the first issue (30).[13] Thus, *Manga Man* at first appeared in quadruple *shi-roku-han* format (approximately 38 cm by 26 cm), featuring over a dozen pages printed entirely in color. *Manga Man*'s visual content consisted of a combination of foreign "nonsense" cartoons ("nonsense" as opposed to political cartoons or those depicting scenes from everyday life) and comic strips. The magazine's most iconic feature was Harold Knerr's *The Katzenjammer Kids*, which ran on a color-printed full double-page spread during *Manga Man*'s color period and remained a feature in black and white until May 1930. *Manga Man* featured foreign strips like Knerr's *Dinglehoofer und His*

Dog, Russ Westover's *Tillie the Toiler, Bonzo,* and *Adamson*; cartoons by artists such as Otto Soglow and William Ridgewell; and domestic comic strips by Asō Yutaka, Miyao Shigeo (a rare example of Miyao employing the new format), and Shishido Sakō.

Manga Man's aspirations soon clashed with economic reality. Although its second issue optimistically proclaimed that the first one sold out and that a circulation of ten to fifteen thousand copies should be achievable in the future, the magazine's fourth issue in November 1929 featured an apology for a twenty percent price increase from 25 to 30 sen, justifying it as the only option to keep the magazine afloat due to the high costs of color printing.[14] In February 1930, the magazine changed strategy and lowered its price to 20 sen while shrinking its format and abandoning color printing. Although this decision led to significant sustained growth in circulation for a while (based on circulation numbers printed in the back of the magazine, which may have to be taken with a grain of salt), the magazine's size was reduced further in December 1930, and *Manga Man* disappeared from newsstands five to six months later.[15]

Despite the magazine's brief lifespan and its American (and American-style Japanese) comics' failure to reach the popularity of *Bringing Up Father,* it nonetheless had a significant impact on the development of Japanese comics. In 1929, an aspiring *mangaka* by the name of Yokoyama Ryūichi purchased one of the first *Manga Man* issues from a newsstand in Katase outside of Tokyo (Yokoyama 1997, 44). Yokoyama, who had become a "manga fan" because of "foreign manga" (i.e., cartoons and/or comic strips) he had seen in magazines, began to submit his own work to *Manga Man* and soon became a regularly featured contributor. At the magazine, he met and befriended other manga artists, most notably Kondō Hidezō, Yazaki Shigeshi, Yoshida Kanzaburō, and Sugiura Yukio. In his autobiography, Yokoyama (1997) makes a strong claim for the influence of foreign comics and cartoons on him and his peers:

Japanese magazines at the time weren't aware that foreign manga were copyrighted and reprinted them freely. This meant that we were able to see a lot of great foreign manga, but eventually syndicates complained and [magazines] started paying for translation rights from then on. Because of this we weren't able to enjoy good manga in magazines anymore. So depending on your perspective it seems like you could say that we were able to learn a lot thanks to the editors who prepared pirated copies. (Yokoyama 1997, 189–90; from the Japanese)

When Yokoyama speaks of learning from foreign manga, he may not only mean reading them. One of the tasks given to the permanent *Manga Man* artists was to trace, copy, and edit the foreign cartoons and strips for publication in translation (Minejima 1984, 86). It is possible that some of the foreign manga in *Manga Man* were traced and edited by Yokoyama and that through this process he acquired hands-on experience drawing in this new format.[16] *Manga Man* had been important not only because it acquainted emerging artists like Yokoyama with foreign comics and cartoons, but also because it was one of the few magazines that would print work by authors who were yet unknown to the public (Kōmori 2009, 65–6). When *Manga Man* ceased to exist in 1931, these artists' most important venue for publication disappeared. In order to better market their work to publications reluctant to feature less established artists, Yokoyama and the mangaka he had befriended at *Manga Man* founded the *Shin Manga-Ha Shūdan* (usually rendered in English as "New Manga Group") the following year, electing Yokoyama as their leader. Although the New Manga Group turned out a success, Yokoyama himself had already become a rising star on his own.

INUI SHIN'ICHIRŌ AND *SHINSEINEN*

In January 1931 Inui Shin'ichirō, an editor for the monthly magazine *Shinseinen*, saw the current *Manga Man* issue at a newsstand at Ōtsuka station, much like Yokoyama had over a year earlier in Katase (Inui 1991, 57–59). Inui purchased a copy of the magazine and liked Yokoyama's contribution so much that he decided to pay the *Manga Man* offices a visit to ask for his address. As luck would have it, the *Manga Man* address was within walking distance from the station, and unbeknownst to Inui was actually Yokoyama's personal address, which in January 1931 *Manga Man* had begun to use for official purposes (for unknown reasons). Yokoyama's work was featured in the February issue of *Shinseinen*, and he as well as other members of the New Manga Group became frequent contributors. Five years later, Yokoyama created the popular character Fuku-chan, whose comic strip became a long-running success both before and after the war, eventually even surpassing *Bringing Up Father*'s longevity in Japan.[17]

It was no accident that Inui had taken a liking to Yokoyama's work inspired by foreign comics. Inui had been hired by *Shinseinen* editor Mizutani Jun about a year earlier (Inui 1987, 21), and one of his main responsibilities in the new job was the copying and translation of foreign manga for the magazine. The reason for *Shinseinen*'s embrace of (predominantly) American comics and cartoons was that they were an easy way of giving the magazine the "modern" appearance it was striving for (Mizutani 1936, 56). The Japanese cartoonist establishment around Kitazawa and Okamoto was seen as too old fashioned (Mizutani 1936, 56; Inui 1991, 54–55). Mizutani considered American comics and cartoons more advanced than others primarily because they had sought to "drive out" explanatory text as much as possible and instead relied mostly on visual means of conveying information (Mizutani 1936, 56).[18] It would have been hard to find someone more qualified for his job than Inui Shin'ichirō. Inui had been born outside of Seattle, Washington, in 1906 and lived in the United States until, at seven years of age, he was sent to Japan to attend school there against his will. Due to his foreign upbringing, he was treated as an outsider and missed the land of his birth, eagerly consuming American books and magazines sent by his mother (Inui 1991, 8–12). Although Inui wanted desperately to return to his native Seattle, this was made impossible by the anti-Japanese Immigration Act of 1924. Forced to stay in Japan, he hoped to study English literature at Aoyama Gakuin University but, because of his caretaker uncle's fierce opposition, had to enroll in its economics department instead. As a university student, Inui discovered and became a fervent reader of *Shinseinen*, which was publishing translations of foreign detective and humoristic novels. He enjoyed the translations and decided to try his hand at literary translation himself. Although Inui did not expect his work to be received particularly well, he submitted it to *Shinseinen*, which published his translations of P. G. Wodehouse's *The Romance of a Bulb-Squeezer* and a story by Ellis Parker Butler in May of 1928 (13–18).

Two years later, Inui found himself cutting comic strips and cartoons out of foreign magazines for reproduction in *Shinseinen*. Unlike other publications at the time, the magazine did not publish any translated comics in narrative continuity over successive months, but it provided by far the greatest overall diversity in foreign manga material found in prewar Japan. *Shinseinen* featured cartoons by artists like Gluyas Williams, William Ridgewell, Dr. Seuss, and Otto Soglow (and Soglow's strip *The Little King*), as well as comic strips like George Herriman's *Krazy Kat* (June 1930, April and May 1931, and December 1934) and E. C. Segar's *Thimble Theatre*, home of Popeye (several pages in April 1934). As a student, Inui had wondered why such "new style manga" were not appearing in Japan and had searched bookstores for copies of English and American magazines "to still my thirst for manga" (Inui 1991, 55). It is questionable whether classics such as *Krazy Kat* and *Thimble Theatre*, both of which make extensive use of non-standard English, would have appeared in prewar Japan had it not been for someone like Inui, who had grown up speaking English and had already been intimately acquainted

Figure 4.2. Greyscale scan of a Mickey Mouse page from the April 1931 issue of *Shinseinen*.

with Anglophone cartoons and comics. *Shinseinen* is furthermore the only Japanese publication to print Floyd Gottfredson's *Mickey Mouse* comic strip (April 1931, May and September 1932; see figure 4.2 for a greyscale scan of one of the *Mickey Mouse* pages from the April 1931 issue),[19] and a full forty-eight pages of Alex Raymond's *Secret Agent X-9*, likely the only example of the new American genre of adult adventure strips emerging in the 1930s to reach Japan.[20] *Shinseinen* also partly published Milt Gross's silent graphic novel *He Done Her Wrong* as *Tokkan koji* in July 1937.

Since the *Shinseinen* translations were produced and published without regard for the originals' copyrights and there was no need to be consistent due to the absence of narrative continuity over multiple issues, Inui was free to experiment with various translation strategies. Different strategies in the translation of comics between Japanese and European languages have received academic attention only since the 1980s when Japanese manga first appeared in Europe and North America on a commercial scale, but the translation of foreign cartoons and comics in prewar Japan demonstrates that the same issues faced by Western translators had already been explored in Japan fifty to sixty years prior. The *Shinseinen* translations feature different combinations of reading orders, explanatory notes on said reading orders, both replacement and preservation of intradiegetic and transdiegetic writing, and even instances of left-right inverted panels (in addition to merely rearranging the panels), a translation strategy that has been widely discussed in contemporary studies of Japanese comics (e.g., Sell 2011; de la Iglesia 2016; Brienza 2016). Any analysis of comics translation between Japanese and European languages should take into account the prewar translation of foreign works into Japanese, and Inui's translations in particular.

TAGAWA SUIHŌ AND TEZUKA OSAMU

Publications like the *Asahi Graph*, *Manga Man*, and *Shinseinen* changed the dominant form of graphic narrative in Japan by popularizing it through translations of mostly American comic strips and inspiring a new generation of artists, such as the New Manga Group, Shishido Sakō, and Tagawa Suihō to make use of the form.[21] Tagawa Suihō, in particular, contributed to the establishment of the "American comic strip format" with his popular *Norakuro* (Takeuchi 1995, 49, 61, 112). Tagawa started out as a *rakugo* writer and modernist painter but became a manga artist after being encouraged to do so by *Omoshiro Kurabu* editor Nakashima (90). Shimizu Isao (1991, 136) claims that the idea for *Norakuro* came most likely from *Shōnen Kurabu* editor in chief Katō Ken'ichi, who, inspired by *Felix the Cat* in Kitazawa's *Jiji Manga*, proposed a comic strip about a dog playing soldier. Anthropomorphic animals had been virtually nonexistent in Japan prior to *Felix the Cat* but began to proliferate soon after its publication in translation (Takeuchi 1995, 144). Takeuchi Osamu and Komatsu Sakyō, too, suspect that Tagawa was likely inspired by American comics (Takeuchi 1995, 92; Ōshiro et al 1982, 185).

By the time Tezuka Osamu began publishing manga in the 1940s, the American strip format had already become well established. However, Tezuka did not merely follow this new domestic tradition but was himself influenced directly by previously published translations. Tezuka was born in 1928, five years after the influx of translated American comics began, but his father kept a well-stocked comics library in his study, where Osamu would later discover and read them (Ban 1994, 31). Among the magazines and newspapers were issues of *Shinseinen*, the *Asahi Graph*, and the *Asahi Shinbun*, in which Tezuka read *Bringing Up Father* (Tezuka 1997c, 63).[22] Tezuka's thorough familiarity with the foreign comic strip characters that had appeared in Japanese translation is evident from a scene in his 1948 work *Lost World* (Tezuka 2009, 238–39). This mass scene of various comics characters features Jiggs and Maggie, Blondie and Dagwood, Mickey Mouse and Donald Duck, Popeye and Betty Boop, the Little King, Henry, and Adamson (as well as Oswald the Rabbit, whom Tezuka likely knew only as an animated character). All of these characters had appeared in translated comic strips during Tezuka's childhood. *Lost World* furthermore also features characters that are obvious copies of Mickey Mouse and Popeye.[23] Furthermore, the recurring Tezuka character Ham Egg is based on the villain from Milt Gross's *He Done Her Wrong*, which Tezuka had seen in *Shinseinen* (Ban 1994, 252; Tezuka 1997b, 90), and besides copying characters from foreign comics Tezuka also recalls drawing skyscrapers based on those in *Bringing Up Father* (Tezuka 1997a, 125–26). One of Tezuka's first (at the time unpublished) comics, *Shōri no hi made*, even features a four-page scene with Jiggs and Maggie.

One reason why Tezuka is sometimes treated as the originator of modern manga may be that his active period coincided with the diverging of Japanese and American comics. Between the end of World War II and the late 1980s there was little exchange between US and Japanese comics artists. Although some American comics, most notably *Blondie*, which appeared in *Shūkan Asahi* until 1956, were still popular in the early postwar years, the number of such strips paled in comparison to the amount of foreign material made available by prewar newspaper and magazine editors. Thus, the big eyes that are now seen as a hallmark of manga aesthetics descend from prewar American comic strips and animation conventions that fell out of favor in the United States but survived in Japan, likely due to Tezuka's popularity. Rather than creating or reinventing modern manga, Tezuka Osamu continued and refined a form of graphic narrative that had been introduced from abroad in 1923 by Suzuki Bunshirō and other editors, and domesticated by the likes of Asō Yutaka, Yokoyama Ryūichi, and Tagawa Suihō since. There are significant differences between Tezuka's oeuvre and the pre-1923 works of Kitazawa Rakuten and Okamoto Ippei, and in terms of narrative and stylistic conventions Tezuka's comics are instead remarkably similar to the comic strip model represented by McManus's *Bringing Up Father* (Tezuka himself writes about being influenced by McManus in Tezuka 1997c, 63).

CONCLUSION

None of this is to say that Japanese comics are merely an offshoot of American works. Similar to what happened in the case of the *ritsuryō* administrative system, the tea ceremony, modern warfare, animated film, car manufacturing, and video games, (mostly) men in positions of power and influence imported an idea or technology that had been created abroad, but which was thoroughly domesticated and developed further at home. The myriad Japanese innovations in style and content are one major reason why Japanese comics appear irreconcilably foreign to so many in "the West" and why claims of an entirely separate tradition are still taken at face value, even though the lineage of today's manga is more closely connected to the work of George McManus than to that of Hokusai or the creators of the chōjūgiga scrolls.

When examining the history of an art form, it is tempting to focus on the contributions of artists, but the editors who imported comic strips or encouraged Japanese artists to imitate them played a pivotal role in the establishment of the "audiovisual" stage model in Japan. Though their contributions tend to be overlooked, editors like Kubo Akira, Matsui Komazō, Inui Shin'ichirō, Takada Tomoichirō, Katō Ken'ichi, and—first and foremost—Suzuki Bunshirō were responsible for the genesis of contemporary Japanese comics no less than artists were. Without them, modern manga might have developed very differently.

Notes

1. I am keeping Japanese names in their original order, with the family name followed by the given name.

2. Although it in English generally denotes contemporary Japanese comics, in Japanese, the term "manga" has a much broader meaning, or rather several meanings. In addition to longer *story manga*, it originally referred to sketches by Hokusai and other artists, came to encompass all forms of humorous drawings (such as single-panel cartoons), and even used to refer to what we now call "anime." Nowadays, some scholars write the word in the katakana or hiragana scripts to distinguish its meaning of contemporary comics from other, older meanings, for which it is written in kanji (Chinese characters).

3. Shimizu (2009, 25) cites an even earlier appearance of the word "manga" in an announcement in the *Jiji Shinpō* on February 6, 1890, but said announcement refers to a sketch of a boat in the February 11 issue which does not exhibit any of the traits associated with caricature or cartooning.

4. Miyamoto Hirohito argues that the change from "ponchi-e" to "manga" was more than a simple linguistic shift. For a summary of this debate, see Stewart (2014).

5. See Exner (2018) for a detailed explanation of this process.

6. Randy Duncan's (2011, 45) "non-sensory diegetic images" can be considered a subcategory of the transdiegetic.

7. The January 7, 1925, issue of the *Osaka Asahi Shinbun* on page 2 even featured an article about a Shō-chan-themed new year's gathering, with reportedly 237 children attending. An accompanying photograph shows most of them wearing Sho-chan hats.

8. The Asahi database Kikuzo II lists *Bringing Up Father* for the subsequent issue as well, but this appears to be a mistake.

9. *Mutt and Jeff*'s first appearance was actually on September 1, 1923, in the *Asahi Graph*, the day of the Great Kantō Earthquake, with an announcement that the strip would appear regularly. Apparently, that plan was abandoned because of the earthquake, but the strip was eventually taken up by other Asahi publications.

10. The translation of *Polly and Her Pals* appears to have been the first Japanese comic strip without extradiegetic narrative text to use typeset lettering for dialog, now the norm in Japan.

11. The hypothesis that translatability was a determining factor in the longevity of a foreign strip is supported by the fact that the second-longest running strip, Oscar Jacobson's *Adamson*, featured almost no dialog (it has even been translated into English under the title *Silent Sam*) and thus was less hampered by lackluster translations or untranslatable humor than other strips.

12. Although the majority of translated American comics after *Bringing Up Father* followed this example and preserved their original reading order, the *Tokyo Puck*'s 1908 translation of *Mr. Jack* rearranged panels to accommodate the Japanese top-bottom, right-left reading order.

13. It is unclear what exact position Matsui had at the magazine. The first issue's mission statement was written by him, and in a new year's greeting in the January 1931 issue, his name is the only one listed before Kubo's. Later editor's notes are usually signed "K," implying that they were written by either Matsui (Komazō) or Kubo. Kubo is the only *Manga Man* staff referred to in accounts by artists working for the magazine.

14. See also Inui (1991, 171) on the cost of color printing then. Suyama (1968, 141) speculates that *Manga Man*'s short lifespan was also due to competition from other manga magazines founded around the same time. Indeed, the *Shuppan nenkan* publication directory for 1930 lists all of *Manga Man*'s competitors at a unit price of 20 sen (501; data from February 1930).

15. Suyama (1968, 142), Ozaki (1987, 179), and Shimizu (1987, 212) claim that *Manga Man* ended in June 1931, but no public records of a June 1931 issue survive.

16. Later, around the year 1933, Yokoyama also lettered Nakazato Tomijirō's translations of *Bringing Up Father* for the *Asahi Graph*, work that he writes paid better than drawing original works for most magazines (Yokoyama 1997, 190).

17. One of the strip's characters bears a striking resemblance to the Captain from Knerr's *Katzenjammer Kids*, which Yokoyama must have been intimately familiar with through *Manga Man*.

18. This of course being precisely the trend that had been introduced in Japan with Suzuki Bunshirō's publication of *Bringing Up Father*. Mizutani speculates that this shift was inspired by the cinema. From his examples, it is apparent that Mizutani is mostly talking about single-panel cartoons when he says "manga" (calling comic strips [*tsuzuki manga*] and animation a different topic), but his comments apply to both.

19. The *Tokyo Nichi Nichi Shinbun* and the women's magazine *Shufu no Tomo* published *Mickey Mouse* in comic strip form (December 6, 1936, to January 17, 1937, and May to October 1934, respectively), but both appear to have been adapted from animated Mickey Mouse cartoons, rather than being translations of the original *Mickey Mouse* strip. The same pattern can be found in the magazine *Hi no de* with comic strips adapted from Max Fleischer animated films, most notably *Betty Boop* and *Popeye* (December 1932 to February 1938). The original *Betty Boop* comic strip by Bud Counihan was published in *Shinseinen* in December 1934.

20. This work appeared so different from the other cartoons and comics that *Shinseinen* labeled it an "adventure novel/illustrated talkie" instead of "manga."

21. Shishido's familiarity with American comics can be gleaned from his discussion of them and mention of specific Japanese translations in Shishido 1929, 3–7.

22. Tezuka claims that the *Asahi Shinbun* copies were from 1927 or 1928, but *Bringing Up Father* ceased to be printed in the *Asahi Shinbun* in 1925, so perhaps he is misremembering the dates or confusing the *Asahi Shinbun* and the *Asahi Graph*.

23. When criticizing Disney for plagiarizing from Tezuka's *Kimba the White Lion*, one should remember that Tezuka copied Mickey long before Disney copied Kimba.

References

Ban Toshio and Tezuka Production. 1994. *Tezuka osamu monogatari—osamushi tōjō 1928–1959*. Tokyo: Asahi Shinbunsha.

Brienza, Casey. 2016. *Manga in America: Transnational Book Publishing and the Domestication of Japanese Comics*. London: Bloomsbury Academic.

de la Iglesia, Martin. 2016. "The Task of Manga Translation: 'Akira' in the West." *The Comics Grid: Journal of Comics Scholarship* 6. http://doi.org/10.16995/cg.59.

Duncan, Randy. 2011. "Image Functions: Shape and Color as Hermeneutic Images in *Asterios Polyp*." In *Critical Approaches to Comics: Theories and Methods*, edited by Matthew J. Smith and Randy Duncan, 43–54. New York: Routledge.

Exner, Eike. 2018. "The Creation of the Comic Strip as an Audiovisual Stage in the *New York Journal* 1896–1900." *ImageTexT* 10 (1). http://www.english.ufl.edu/imagetext/archives/v10_1/exner/

Gravett, Paul. 2004. *Manga: Sixty Years of Japanese Comics*. London: Laurence King.

Inui Shin'ichirō. 1991. *Shinseinen no koro*. Tokyo: Hayakawa Shobō.

Jo En. 2013. *Nihon ni okeru shinbun rensai kodomo manga no senzenshi*. Tokyo: Nihonkyohosha.

Komatsu Sakyō. 1982. "Taiken toshite no mangashi." In *OH! Manga*, edited by Ōshiro Noboru, Tezuka Osamu, and Matsumoto Reiji, 179–92. Tokyo: Shōbunsha.

Kōmori Ikuya. 2009. "Manga purodakushon-ron (1)." *Senshū Kokubun* 85: 63–82.

Koyama-Richards, Brigitte. 2007. *One Thousand Years of Manga*. Paris: Flammarion.

Kunzle, David. 1973. *The Early Comic Strip: Picture Stories and Narrative Strips in the European Broadsheet from c. 1450 to 1825*. Vol. 1 of *The History of the Comic Strip*. Berkeley: University of California Press, 1973–90.

Kure Tomofusa. 2007. *Gendai manga no zentaizō*. Tokyo: Futabasha.

Kyoto International Manga Museum. Permanent exhibition. Kinbuki cho 452, Nagakyo-ku, Kyoto. Visited 2015, February 8.

Matsushima Masato. 2015. "Chōjūgiga ha manga wo unda no ka." In *Masterpieces of Kosan-ji Temple: The Complete Scrolls of Choju Giga, Frolicking Animals*, 269–74. Tokyo: Asahi Shinbunsha.

McCloud, Scott. 1994. *Understanding Comics: The Invisible Art*. New York: HarperPerennial.

McManus, George. 1919. *Bringing Up Father—Third Series*. New York: Cupples & Leon Company.

Minejima Masayuki. 1984. *Kondō Hidezō no sekai*. Tokyo: Seiabō.

Miyamoto Hirohito. 2003. "Ponchi to manga, sono shinbun to no kakawari." In *Shinbun manga no me—hito seiji shakai*, 106–9. Yokohama: Newspark.

Mizutani Jun. 1936. "Amerika manga ni tsuite." *Tōyō* 1 (6): 56–7.

Okamoto Ippei, ed. 1927. *Shōgakusei zenshū—jidōmangashū*. Tokyo: Kōbunsha.

Okamoto Ippei. 1930. "R-shi ni fukai wo kanjitsutsu mangaka shokun ni kukan su." In *Ippei Zenshū*, 244–58. Tokyo: Senshinsha.

Okamoto Ippei. 1936. "Manga zadankai." *Tōyō* 1 (6): 29–51.

Ōtsuka Eiji. 2013. *Mikkī no shoshiki*. Tokyo: Kadokawa Sensho.

Ozaki Hideki. 1987. *Sashie no 50 nen*. Tokyo: Heibonsha.

Sasaki Minoru. 2012. *Manga-shi no kisomondai*. Tokyo: Office Heliar.

Sasaki Minoru. 2014. "Sutōrī manga no hajimari." Presentation at Hibiya Library & Museum, Sept. 6, Tokyo, Japan.

Sell, Cathy. 2011. "Manga Translation and Interculture." *Mechademia* 6: 93–108.

Shimizu Isao, ed. 1987. *Manga zasshi hakubutsukan 10—mangaman*. Tokyo: Kokushokankōkai.

Shimizu Isao. 1991. *Manga no rekishi*. Tokyo: Iwanami Shoten.

Shimizu Isao. 2007. *Nihon manga-shi*. Kyoto: Rinsen Shoten.

Shimizu Isao. 2009. *Yonkoma manga*. Tokyo: Iwanami Shoten.

Shishido Sakō. 1929. *Amerika no yokoppara*. Tokyo: Heibonsha.

Shuppan nenkan shōwa 5 nen. 1977. Tokyo: Bunsendō.

Smolderen, Thierry. 2009. *Naissances de la bande dessinée*. Brussels: Les Impressions Nouvelles.

Stewart, Ronald. 2014. "Manga Studies #2: Manga history: Shimizu Isao and Miyamoto Hirohito on Japan's first modern 'manga' artist Kitazawa Rakuten." Comics Forum, June 14. http://com icsforum.org/2014/06/14/manga-studies-2-manga-history-shimizu-isao-and-miyamoto -hirohito-on-japans-first-modern-manga-artist-kitazawa-rakuten-by-ronald-stewart/.

Suyama Keiichi. 1968. *Nihon manga 100 nen—seiyō ponchi kara SF manga made*. Tokyo: Haga Shoten.

Suzuki Bunshirō. 1938. "Sono koro no omoide." *Asahi Graph*, October 19: 44–45.

Suzuki Bunshirō. 1952. *Bunshirō bunshū*. Tokyo: Dai Nihon Yūbenkai Kōdansha.

Takeuchi Osamu. 1995. *Kodomo manga no kyojintachi*. Tokyo: San'ichi Shobō.

Tezuka Osamu. 1997a. *Tezuka Osamu taidanshū 2*. Tokyo: Kodansha.

Tezuka Osamu. 1997b. *Tezuka Osamu taidanshū 3*. Tokyo: Kodansha.

Tezuka Osamu. 1997c. *Tezuka Osamu manga no ōgi*. Tokyo: Kodansha.

Tezuka Osamu. 2009. *Tezuka Osamu bunko zenshū: Rosuto wārudo, metoroporisu*. Tokyo: Kodansha.

Walker, Mort. 2000. *The Lexicon of Comicana*. Lincoln, NE: iUniverse.com.

Yokoyama Ryūichi. 1997. *Waga yūgiteki jinsei*. Tokyo: Nihon Tosho Center.

5.

Reshaping Comic Books in a Socialist Regime

QUIMANTÚ, *PARA LEER AL PATO DONALD* AND THE CHILEAN COMICS WORLD DURING UNIDAD POPULAR (1971–1973)

Ivan Lima Gomes

The nearly one thousand days of Salvador Allende's socialist government in Chile (1970–1973) are remembered, along with the Cuban Revolution (1959), as one of the twentieth century's most significant experiences of left-wing national rule in Latin America. The Chilean experience of socialism drew the attention of much of the international left in those Cold War years because it promised that the transformation of the capitalist system into a socialist one was not only possible but also could be initiated democratically (Moulián 2005, 35–56). The Unidad Popular (UP) became a reference for those who wanted to transform the political reality of their countries towards socialism and social reforms. But right-wing parties and politicians were also paying close attention to the UP. In Chile, the political climate was highly polarized, culminating in a coup: the presidential palace of La Moneda was bombed, and President Allende was killed. A seventeen-year period of military rule—marked by violence, repression, and the dismantling of the national economy—followed the episode (Zárate 2001).

The fall of Allende and the limited popular reaction to it took most of Chile's left by surprise. Maybe the Chilean left wing believed the population had already become aware and educated enough to realize the social improvements Allende's socialist rule promoted. After all, education and media were two very important fronts to the popular government, as is made clear in the UP program:

These media (radio, publishing, television, press, and cinema) are fundamental to help in the formation of a new culture and a new man. So they should receive an educational orientation and they also should be released from their commercial nature. Measures should be adopted to ensure that social organizations dispose of these means of communication and that the ominous presence of monopolies be eliminated from them. (*Programa de la Unidad Popular* 1969)[1]

One of the UP's most important initiatives in this area was to acquire a share of a publisher called Zig-Zag, then considered one of the largest Latin American companies in the publishing area. Under state control, the publishing house was inaugurated on February 12, 1971, and assumed the name Quimantú. It undertook the printing of an impressive amount of publications—including comic books.

This chapter examines Quimantú's theory of comics and its impact on Chile's comics world. An analysis of what were seen as the "meanings" behind comics—with an emphasis on the influence of intellectuals associated with Quimantú, like Armand Mattelart, Ariel Dorfman, and Manuel Jofré—is followed by a description of how Quimantú and its editorial line were created. This is followed by a brief case study of how Quimantú adapted the superhero genre to its mandate. From these, we are able to better understand historical peculiarities present in UP's cultural policy, which were important in establishing and consolidating the "Chilean road to socialism" among children and youth and its efforts to reshape the Chilean comics world.

DEBATING CULTURE AND COMICS

Creating a state-controlled publisher was a goal of various social actors involved with UP (Subercaseaux 2010, 174–76). Only one month into Allende's presidential term, a group of writers and intellectuals, including poet Enrique Lihn and writer Ariel Dorfman, published a manifesto in the magazine *Cormorán* arguing that it was now necessary for intellectuals and writers to assume the position of "vanguard of thought." In this spirit, they conducted a series of reflections on overcoming "underdevelopment" and "dependency." They also proposed the creation of a Corporation for the Promotion of Culture (Corporación de la Cultura de Fomento) and, as one of its branches, an Institute of Books and Publications (Instituto del Libro y Publicaciones). Among other responsibilities, the latter would advise a state publisher in order to keep criticism of bourgeois culture a priority in its publications (*Cormorán*, 8 December, 1970, 7–9).

This proposal was part of a broader concern with the role of culture in the lives of ordinary Chileans. For example, in a series of lectures on "media's social responsibility," Armand Mattelart, a Belgian scholar then based in Chile (Zarowsky 2009), proposed a direct link between the quality of mass media and the quality of political institutions. The daily newspaper *La Nación* covered the event and quoted some of Mattelart's main ideas. According to Mattelart, any attempt to transform media without first transforming society would be fruitless. In a bourgeois society, "the messages which spread through media tend to have the purpose of impacting the receiver (the individual) in order to convince him of the 'goodness' inherent to a bourgeois rule (freedom, democracy, equality, etc.)." Instead, social organizations should become "more than receptors, they should transmit messages as well." Making this possible would allow an authentic and emancipatory mass communication ("Se iniciaron jornadas sobre la responsabilidad social de los medios de comunicación" 1970, 17; "Jornada del colegio de periodistas" 1970, 6). Critiques of this sort were also specifically targeted at comic books.

Until relatively recently, Dorfman and Mattelart's (1971) *Para leer al Pato Donald* (*How to Read Donald Duck*) was arguably the best-known work of comics studies in the world. It was, moreover, the locus of much of the debate around comics in Chile when published by Ediciones Universitarias de Valparaiso in 1971. Even if *Para leer al Pato Donald* was not published by Quimantú, the right-wing newspaper *El Mercurio* suggested a common ideological orientation between the book and the Unidad Popular government. According to *El Mercurio*, left-wing writers close to the UP project chose Donald Duck as a high-profile enemy in order to distract from more serious problems—one which was, they ironically argued, a shortage of birds that allegedly threatened Chile at the time ("El Pato Sedicioso" 1972, 01–11, 3).

Mattelart has said their focus on Disney comics was based on a symbolic criterion: the United States' comics world was "a culture we did not want and was opposed to what we were trying to start building" (Gomes and Mattelart 2013, 202). A similar thread runs through *Superman y sus amigos del alma* ("Superman and His Soul Mates"), which provides valuable insight into contemporary debates about the social meanings of comics in socialist Chile. Written by Dorfman and the sociologist Manuel Jofré as a result of research carried out within Quimantú between 1971 and 1972, it was published in Argentina two years later. (When the coup happened, the book was ready for printing.) It had the initial title of "Secret Documents about the Inner

Life of Superman and His Soul Mates," most likely a reference to a very successful Quimantú book at that time, *Documentos Secretos de la ITT* ("ITT's Secret Documents"; Dorfman 1978, 16). Written in a language that sometimes resembles an essay and a political pamphlet, the book uses Umberto Eco and Roland Barthes as theoretical references—plus Dorfman and Mattelart, of course—to define comics in the capitalist world.

In the original prologue—supposedly written in comic book format and lost during the seizure of the book by the military—Dorfman said he sought to "link the ideology behind superheroes with the insurgent efforts of Chile's dominant class, which was for the moment out of national executive power" (Dorfman 1978, 15–16). Jofré's analysis in the book's second part followed this tune. Jofré points out that the comic book initially developed as a supposedly innocent entertainment for children, leading to the infantilization of the form. He argued comic book stories had very simple plots; they were fast reads with an "eminently pragmatic structure," through which the "values of bourgeois ideology" carried by the characters are absorbed by readers. Fragmentation and naturalization of reality, individualism, vertical relations of power, emphasis on adventure compared to the daily life, legalism, irrationalism and prejudice of race and class were some of the elements listed as defining "traditional bourgeois comics," from Superman to Dick Tracy (Jofré 1978, 101–13). According to Jofré, the comic book

denies or distorts the historical fact that there are developed and underdeveloped countries (the scenarios are often no man's lands—e.g. the West, the jungle or the gothic city of Batman). . . , it also denies the possibility of social transformations driven by the people (superheroes always triumph, be it Batman, Tarzan or Zorro) . . . , it denies the insurmountable contradictions of capitalism (superheroes always save the day no matter how big the injustice was before he solved it) . . . , it denies the social sphere of life (the hero is always alone), it denies humanity (superheroes are painted as Messiahs who impose justice and order, and are endowed with eternal powers), it denies the justice of classes (superheroes solve problems that justice cannot) . . . , it denies freedom (superheroes punish those who rebel, recapturing them in the name of the system) . . . , it denies the necessity to work (characters are always stranded), it denies creativity (resulting in a repetitive world) and of course, in addition to denying many more things, the ideology of comics denies itself (no character ever reads comics). (95–96)[2]

It is worth noting that Jofré did not distinguish between different narrative genres in his critique; jungle comics and westerns were equated with super-heroes like Batman, which were popular enough to inspire Enríque Lihn to write a book about the tensions of Chilean culture at the time (Pachas 2015). To be fair, Jofré did point out a small distinction between comic book genres when he said superheroes are "one of the most widespread trends in the history of comic book." However, the statement was just a generalization: Superman and his "soul mates"—the "superheroes" of other popular comic book genres, such as Zorro, Roy Rogers, the Phantom, Tarzan, Dick Tracy, Flash Gordon, Prince Valiant and, of course, Super Mouse—were usurping the role of the transformers of reality, a mission intrinsic to the proletarian class: "in a world protected by Superman, Marx and Che Guevara are un-necessary" (Jofré 1978, 101–2, 98).

Thus, comics and the ideologies they expressed needed to be understood in light of the social relations of production, where they served as a form of ideological compensation for the alienation produced by capitalism. Work-ers must recognize the need for revolutionary emancipation before it can be realized, or, as Jofré declares, "Men must observe themselves to find out they are economically and humanly poor: comics keep them from doing so" (1978, 91). The strategy that followed from this was to use this medium with a revolutionary purpose and thereby assist in building a new society endowed with new values:

> Comics are weapons. The media are weapons. But the use we make of them is not to destroy. It is to defend, because our weapons are different. Truth, freedom, human fulfillment. All in all, our weapon is the unity of human beings. Under socialism there will be no weapons. Under socialism there will be no murders. Under socialism there will be no men who kill other men, neither by means of labor exploitation nor by guns. Because there will be no bullets, no weapons, no comics, no Capital. (93)

Yet, thanks to Quimantú, there *were* comics in socialist Chile. It was up to the publisher's writers, artists, and editors to determine what a comics world founded on the "unity of human beings" might look like.

DEFINING SOCIALIST COMICS

On November 6, 1970, three days after Salvador Allende took office as president of Chile, all ninety employees—including designers, writers, and workers in the printing plant—of Zig-Zag voted to go on strike—possibly because they were excited about the newly elected government (Albornoz 2005, 154). The decision to split Zig-Zag into two publishing houses—and one of them to become a state publisher—came soon after. After a series of strikes and public accusations of indebtedness and monopoly against the publishing house, the government decided to buy all Zig-Zag assets, which basically consisted in its physical space, machinery, staff, and some of the magazines whose circulations were weak at the moment. The state also assumed all of the publishing firm's debts. Some of the comic books that became part of the state publisher were *Far West*, *Jinete Fantasma* ("Jinete the Ghost"), *Espía 13* ("Spy 13"), *El Siniestro Doctor Mortis* ("The Sinister Doctor Mortis"), *Intocable* ("Untouchable"), *Jungla* ("Jungle"), *Agente Silencio* ("Agent Silence"), *Guerra . . . !* ("War . . . !") and *5 por Infinito* ("Five times Infinity"). Zig-Zag, in turn, would be entitled to continue with more successful titles (Bergot 2004, 06) like the comic book *Condorito* ("Little Condor"), the magazine *Ercilla*,[3] and the newspaper *Vea* ("See") in addition to titles from Disney universe such as *Disneylandia* ("Disneyland"), *Tío Rico* ("Rich Uncle," i.e., Uncle Scrooge) and *Tribilín* (i.e., Goofy). Zig-Zag also received the promise that the state would ensure the printing of these publications.

Quimantú had a profound impact on Chilean society: it is estimated that the press published more than eleven million books before the coup of September 11, 1973. Quimantú's nine collections of books were launched on the market under three thematic blocks that emphasized their "didactic and pedagogical aspects" and a "clear political and secular commitment": the goal of collections such as *Quimantú para todos* ("Quimantú for Everyone"), *Minilibros* ("Little Books"), *Cordillera* ("Mountain Range") and *Cuncuna* ("Caterpillar") was to make national and foreign literature available to both children and adults in Chile; collections like *Camino Abierto* ("Open Way"), *Cuadernos de Educación Popular* ("Journal for Popular Education") and *Clásicos del Pensamiento Social* ("Classics of Social Thought") were more concerned with disseminating themes and values directly linked to the left-wing political debate; the third thematic block of collections, among which were *Nosotros los Chilenos* ("We, the Chilean People"), discussed issues related to daily life and national culture in general (Bergot 2004, 16). However, it not only printed books and magazines aligned with UP's political perspectives but also many comic books, usually fortnightly (Bergot 2004, 19–23).

The first months following the agreement with Zig-Zag were a time of evaluation and reorganization at Quimantú. From February to June 1971, discussions were held about which titles should remain or be canceled and about the political and editorial policies that would guide the publisher's comic books. At first, the plan was to maintain all publications remaining after the November 1970 negotiations, with a few exceptions, and then decide which ones should be canceled. Some titles did not survive this first evaluation, such as *El Siniestro Dr. Mortis* and the women's magazine *Confidencias*. When I interviewed the sociologist Arturo Navarro in Santiago de Chile in January 2013, he told me he was responsible for reviewing many thematic magazines: sports, television, gastronomy, and so on. This illustrates how the Quimantú team organized their publishing program and how new ideas were proposed. He talked a lot about *Confidencias*. He stated he had a "structuralist point of view" back then, and that was why he proposed replacing the translations of American love stories with *fotonovelas*:

> A fotonovela is a love story narrated with pictures. My boss ended up finding it very interesting. She told me, "Well, who can do it?" "I can!" I answered. And that was it. I was part of an arts group at the University. It was called *Sexta Experiencia*. We were students of sociology, psychology, along with several photographers. So I called my friends and colleagues of *Sexta Experiencia* to create the fotonovela.

When asked about the commercial result of this move, Navarro readily stated that it resulted in the end of *Confidencias*. It was, in his own words, a "disaster." They were aware of how daring the proposition was—after all, it was a new format, and the audience was very specific: "very romantic older people, mainly women." The fotonovela format was not the only change proposed by Navarro's group. At some point, they also began experimenting with the plots. For example, in one story, a beautiful middle-class young woman falls in love with two young men, one rich, and the other poor. Typical of the genre, the whole story revolves around the woman's dilemma, and finally, on the last page, she wonders, "Well, who will I stay with?" At this point, a photographer appears in the fotonovela and says, "I do not know who you will be with! You have to decide for yourself!" Navarro reported the plot of this fotonovela in a humorous tone. He highlighted what a "complete delight it was to have a major publishing house … at your disposal to publish the follies you wanted." Magazine editors at Quimantú were free to produce "follies" that ran directly counter to the known expectations of the community of readers. However, Navarro also acknowledged that this autonomy was because comic books and fotonovelas were not Quimantú's priority. In general, magazines were considered of lesser importance than, for example, works of literature and of political education. So, if such changes in style turned fotonovelas and comic books into successful publications, even better for a book publishing house like Quimantú; if not, as they could be cancelled at any time—which effectively happened to several publications.

In our interview, Navarro pointed out that Quimantú employed many artists and writers in a department aimed at producing comic books, but this section was regarded as less important than the other departments at the publisher, such as those dedicated to publishing books for political education or new authors of Latin American literature. Considered "less politically relevant," the artists were classified by sociologists like Navarro as "pateros"—that is, as people who drew "ducks"—a clear reference to the character Donald Duck, prime target of the cultural theorists aligned to the Chilean left wing. One of these theorists was the aforementioned Mattelart, who was responsible for establishing evaluation policies for the editorial production of comic books in Quimantú. Asked about his involvement with the publishing house during an interview I conducted in October 2013, he said the reason he opted for discussing plots and creative solutions for the comics with designers rather than a more explicit intervention in their production was because comics were secondary at Quimantú (Gomes and Mattelart 2013).[4] Nonetheless, Quimantú attempted to develop a comics magazine that could work as reference for a new comics world, one aligned with the Chilean democratic way to socialism rather than the capitalist comics world.

CASE STUDY: "*CABROCHICO*, A MAGAZINE FOR TODAY'S BOY"

Cabrochico ran comics that were notably different from those that spread "ideological values of the bourgeoisie." It was the first Quimantú comic book developed exclusively for children, published after an initial reorganization of the publisher, and can be understood as an attempt to put into practice several of the theses discussed above. Through an analysis of the early issues of *Cabrochico*, we can infer some of Quimantú's editorial policies for comic books. Generally speaking, *Cabrochico* criticized all juvenile stories, including fairy tales and many other genres present in comics. However, superheroes were again a notable absence; *Cabrochico* and Quimantú as a whole simply preferred to not talk about them—with a few exceptions.[5]

Simple lines, parody and criticism of the superhero genre, and contrasts between fantasy and reality were employed in *Año 2.200* ("Year 2200"), a science-fiction series illustrated by Guidú and written by Saúl Schkolnik that presented the Cold War imagery around the space race, and, at the same time, comment on Chilean reality. An *Año 2.200* story published in the third issue of *Cabrochico* discussed the relevance of a superhero in the lives of children from a distant planet (9–16). After a distress call, the characters Gagarito,[6] Proton, and others land their ship on a distant planet and find kids throwing themselves from a cliff toward a tree in the hope of flying and saving their mascot, Miu, which is stuck at the top. Their actions are inspired by a character called Super-Super, as indicated by the capes they are all wearing. Repeated attempts to rescue Miu fail, and they all display minor injuries. Nonetheless, the boys remain faithful to their comics icon—to the point of attacking Gagarito and his friends with stones when the protagonists say Super-Super was just a story. The protagonists soon learn the power of Super-Super. They see his influence everywhere: not only in comic books but also on TV shows, commercials, and public monuments (figure 5.1). Superheroes were a problematic "*lieu de mémoire*" (Nora 1997, 14) of capitalism within the socialist project. Just like in *Año 2.200*, Dorfman and Jofré "sensed" Superman "was in all corners of Chile" and had become "the most dangerous" adversary to be fought (Dorfman 1978, 15–16). Against the extraordinary individualization of action inspired by the superhero, the *Cabrochico* characters defend teamwork. The cat owners' behavior changes when one of them injures his head trying to fly. He needs the medical aid of the Chilean characters, who promptly propose collective cooperation as a strategy to save the mascot. After this, the boys finally realize they no longer need Super-Super to solve their problems. They thank the protagonists, who go back into space.

This satire of superheroes and their readers was unusual within Quimantú's editorial project and must have pleased *Cabrochico*'s editors. It inspired a special supplement for parents to explain why they criticized superhero culture and, thereby, to explain *Cabrochico*'s educational policy. During the first four issues, they had worked hard to deconstruct several narratives and characters who inhabited the Chilean comics world until then. In response to critical letters they received, the editors found themselves compelled to attach a supplement for parents to issue five arguing in defense of its editorial line and against fairy tales and conventional children's genres. *Cabrochico*'s editors criticized the ethnocentrism of Disney comics, which they described as full of "stupid natives" depicted in a derogatory manner, and the morally degrading violence of horror comics.[7] But, most importantly, the supplement questioned whether parents should really believe that one man was capable of solving all the problems of "our country and world," or if these problems should not be resolved through unity and cooperation.

Figure 5.1. Superheroes everywhere in *Año 2.200*. Detail from *Cabrochico* #3 (1971, 13).

Instead of supporting individualism, as acclaimed by superhero narratives, parents should support narratives about the "union of all Chileans to the country's progress." The text called on them to "show [kids] that it is better to help each other as adults do," instead of waiting for Superman (33). To replace them, the supplement suggests comics that showcase the importance of working and practicing sports, not only for the healthy development of children but also for the development of cooperation and unity among the Chilean people. [8]

Figure 5.2. Supplement for parents. *Cabrochico* #5 (1971, 30).

Even some advertisements featured in *Cabrochico* seem to take part. Figure 5.3 portrays the strength a child will obtain by drinking milk. However, in the young boy's mind, the strong body he gains will not turn him into a superhero but "a first-class worker" like his father. Health and physical education were important elements of the visual culture of socialist regimes like the USSR (O'Mahony 2006). Their importance for the Chilean socialist project can be seen in *Cabrochico* through creative low-cost food recipes, health recommendations, and guidelines about vitamins and medicines,

Figure 5.3. Advertisement in *Cabrochico* #4 (1971, 43).

among others, in issues three and four. In order to build a body politic strong enough to fight off cultural domination and US policies, it was necessary to deconstruct the superheroes' reputation for physical strength. "Super-Supers" were thought to be invulnerable and free of marks, above any historical determination, and treated like celebrities (Bukatman 2013, 179). They should be overcome by other national heroes; to this end, local history and the everyday were locations to find new (super)heroes to forge the canon of a Chilean comics world.

CONCLUSION

After September 11, 1973, Quimantú was attacked and closed by military forces. Its books and magazines were publicly burned, as reported by Ariel Dorfman in his memoir (1974, 10). A "transformation of visual memory" followed (Errázuriz and Quijada 2012). Not only were political and social projects related to UP dismantled, but images and symbols referring to the years of social transformation advocated by Unidad Popular also disappeared. Resuming activities months later, Quimantú was renamed after poet Gabriela Mistral by the military dictartorship. The new government maintained some series but edited the content in order to compliment militarism and delete the credits of the authors (Erráruriz and Quijada 2012, 45–65). As for the comic books, in general, they returned to pre-Quimantú style plots for a few years, although it was common to see small messages such as "the country rose in September," "the armed forces safeguard our sovereignty," and "for today, tomorrow will be a great day for Chile" at the bottom of pages in comic books like *El Manque* (these examples are from issue 282). They were finally canceled, and Editora Nacional Gabriela Mistral went bankrupt in 1984.

Looking back at Quimantú's publishing activities under the Unidad Popular, three main changes were made to the comic book line. First, some magazines had their content radically altered. Second, new titles were created in keeping with Quimantú's editorial line, the best-known example of which is *Cabrochico*. Third, Quimantú canceled some series that, because of their content or their poor commercial performance, could not be seriously modified in their content by the publisher. Such was the case of *El Siniestro Doctor Mortis*, which was a horror magazine and therefore unsuited to Quimantú's editorial vision for comics. While these changes should remind comics scholars of the need to account for publishers and their political orientations, the presence of comics theoretically oriented to reshape the comics world in Chile, the gradual departure of others, and *Cabrochico*'s cancellation in December 1972 all suggest that the UP's project of ideological demystification did not achieve the expected results in a market already consolidated through publications as *Mampato* (Flores 2010, 563). In fact, Quimantú's writers and artists cannot be understood outside of that tense and polarized context. If the political project was mainly taken up by intellectuals who joined the publishing house after its nationalization, several workers did not notice major differences between their activities at Zig-Zag and the nationalized Quimantú because premises, machinery, and workers remained the same (Hurtado 2005, 54). Many of them, however, felt uncomfortable with the presence of intellectuals who sought to interfere in the content of the publications. When asked about experiences of censorship at Quimantú, Juan Marino said, "there were conflicts due to minds that should not be in places of management":

> However, despite all the efforts of these people, they were not able to eliminate all of my three comics because these comics were the ones which economically sustained Quimantú . . . They wanted to censor *Jungla*, for example. And for that they sent a sociologist—a great man of culture, currently in the United States doing a very good job—who soon understood that *Jungla* was a research work supported by the Embassy of India. The sociologist then gave up meddling with our editorial choices and left. (*Juan Marino: el siniestro Dr. Mortis* 2014)

Another worker commented that "sociologists" were responsible for putting clothes on Mizomba, an act that changed the Tarzan-like lead of *Intocable* beyond recognition. Following the state takeover and Quimantú's new editorial guidelines, the character became an agitator of the masses in Africa, leaving behind his wild past as a jungle man (Navarro 2007). Chile's community of comic book readers landed in the middle of a dispute between pateros and sociologists.

Given the above, it appears that there was also no consensus about these ideas at *Cabrochico*. On the one hand, the editorial line was clearly affiliated with the conclusions reached by Dorfman and Mattelart (1971) in *Para to leer al Pato Donald*. On the other hand, not all comics in the magazine made explicit criticisms of imperialism or attempted to show readers their own alienation at the hands of foreign culture. The controversy around Quimantú's editorial project remains alive today, but as Arturo Navarro (2007) has written, "in a society like Chile, the fact of spreading culture is itself 'revolutionary'": "It is not necessary to quibble about content. If there is any text that does not share the collection line, just don't publish it, but one should never change a text that is widely known by previous generations."[9]

Notes

1. Translated from Spanish by the author.
2. Translated from Spanish by the author.
3. Ercilla is a Spanish given name.
4. It is worth mentioning that *Para leer al Pato Donald* was not published by Quimantú, but by a university press in Valparaiso. Disagreements inside Quimantú concerning the thesis behind Dorfman and Mattelart's book were fundamental to ensure it would never be published there:

We presented the book to the people in Quimantú we knew the most—a section director was a guy who belonged to the Socialist Party. He tried to ask their colleagues to
see if it was possible to publicate our book by Quimantú . . . So the only solution for
us was to release it from the Catholic University of Valparaiso, which could publish
it quickly . . . But, you know, all this was treated with the utmost discretion. This
kind of thing was not advertised to the public. To do otherwise would be to confess
tensions within Quimantú. And that would be very bad . . . We presented the book
to Quimantú also as a matter of courtesy, because we had little doubt about its very
low chances to be accepted there. (Gomes and Mattelart 2013, 207–8)

5. *Supercauro* was one such exception. The protagonist was a very thin and poor boy. He
acquired special powers and became Supercauro after ingesting "protein," possibly through
milk, referencing the UP government's daily distribution of half liter of milk to Chilean
children (Zárate 2013, 184). However, Supercauro did not solve the problems using physical
strength. Instead, he defeated his enemies—the black market, illiteracy, currency leakage,
a copper strike, and opposition to state-owned enterprises—with reasoning and collective
organization, demonstrating that superheroes were not necessary (Flores 2010, 586–87).
Supercauro was published in *La Firme* ("The Firm"; Kunzle 1978), a series that attempted
to make political education more palatable. Armand Matellart called *La Firme* the only
Quimantú production that achieved its purpose; it was distinct from the publisher's other
comics in being neither "Manichean" nor full of "shallow defenders of the people" (Gomes
and Mattelart 2013, 208).

6. Spanish for "Little Gagarin."

7. Here, they echoed the well-known attacks on horror and crime comic books in several
other places (Lent 1999).

8. Similarly, Quimantú's sports magazine *Estadio* replaced its coverage of football teams,
turf, and international sports with reports on community sports activities and health tips.

9. Translated from Spanish by the author.

References

Albornoz, Cesar. 2005. "La cultura en la Unidad Popular: porque esta vez no se trata de
    cambiar un presidente." In *Cuando hicimos historia. La experiencia de la Unidad Popular*,
    edited by Julio Pinto, 147–76. Santiago de Chile: LOM Ediciones.
Allende, Salvador. 1973. "Última alocución de Salvador Allende en 'Radio Magallanes.'"
    Salvador Allende (Website). Accessed February 5, 2012. http://www.salvador-allende.cl/
    Discursos/1973/despedida.pdf. (site discontinued).
Bergot, Solène. 2004. "Quimantú: editorial del Estado durante la Unidad Popular chilena
    (1970–1973)." *Pensamiento crítico* 4.
Bergot, Solène. 2005. "Quimantú: une maison d'édition d'État au Chili." *Le bulletin de l'Institut
    Pierre Renouvin* 21: 91–112.
Borges, Elisa. 2011. "¡Con la UP ahora somos gobierno! A experiência dos Cordones Industriales
    no Chile de Allende." PhD diss., Universidade Federal Fluminense.

Bukatman, Scott. 2013. "A Song for the Urban Superhero." In *The Superhero Reader*, edited by Charles Hatfield, Jeet Heer, and Kent Worcester, 170–98. Jackson: University Press of Mississipi.

Dorfman, Ariel. 1974. *Ensayos quemados en Chile*. Buenos Aires: Ediciones de la Flor.

Dorfman, Ariel. 1978. "Prólogo no qual se mostram super-homens de verdade em ação." In *Super-homem e seus amigos do peito*, edited by Ariel Dorfman and Manuel Jofré. Rio de Janeiro: Paz e Terra.

Dorfman, Ariel, and Armand Mattelart. 1971. *Para leer al pato Donald*. Valparaíso: Ediciones Universitarias de Valparaíso.

"El Pato Sedicioso." 1972. *El Mercurio*, Santiago de Chile, January 11, 3.

Erráruriz, Luis Hernán, and Gonzalo Leiva Quijada. 2012. *El golpe estético: ditadura militar en Chile, 1973–1989*. Santiago de Chile: Ocho Libros.

Flores, Jorge Rojas. 2010. Historia de la infancia en el Chile republicano, 1810–2010. Santiago de Chile: JNJI.

Gascón y Martín, Felip. 2002. "Transformaciones sociales, redes y políticas de comunicación en Chile (1967–2001). Elementos para una ecología política de las comunicaciones." PhD diss., Universidad Autónoma de Barcelona.

Gomes, Ivan Lima, and Armand Mattelart. 2013. "Entrevista Armand Mattelart." *Revista História e Cultura* 2 (2): 197–212.

Hatfield, Charles, Jeet Heer, and Kent Worcester, eds. 2013. *The Superhero Reader*. Jackson: University Press of Mississippi.

Hurtado, Marcela Angelica Neira. 2005. "*Zig-Zag*: un gigante de papel." Bachalerate's diss, Universidad de Chile.

"Instituto Nacional del Libro: iniciativa de UC porteña." 1970. *La Nación*, Santiago de Chile, August 29, 6.

Jofré, Manuel. 1978. "As histórias em quadrinhos e suas transformações." In *Super-homem e seus amigos do peito*, edited by Ariel Dorfman and Manuel Jofré. Rio de Janeiro: Paz e Terra.

"Jornada del colegio de periodistas: proceso a los medios de comunicación de masas." 1970. *La Nación*, Santiago de Chile, November 26, 6.

Juan Marino: el siniestro Dr. Mortis (website). Accessed January 1, 2014. http://cancionero delapatagonia.cl/cancionero/mortis.html.

Kunzle, David. 1978. "Chile's *La Firme* versus ITT". *Latin American Perspectives* 1 (5).

Lent, John, ed. 1999. *Pulp Demons: International Dimensions of the Postwar Anti-Comics Campaign*. Madison, WI: Fairleigh Dickinson.

Moulián, Tomás. 2005. "La vía chilena al socialismo: itinerario de la crisis de los discursos estratégicos de la Unidad Popular." In *Cuando hicimos historia: la experiencia de la Unidad Popular*, edited by Julio Pinto Vallejos, 35–56. Santiago de Chile: LOM Ediciones.

Navarro, Arturo. 2007. "Quimantú o la propagación de los niños." Arturo Navarro (blog). http://arturo-navarro.blogspot.com/2007/11/quimant-o-la-propagacin-de-los-nios.html.

Nora, Pierre, 1997. *The Realms of Memory: Rethinking the French Past*. New York: Columbia University Press.

O'Mahony, Mike. 2006. *Sport in the USSR: Physical Culture—Visual Culture*. London: Reaktion Books.

Pachas, Daniel Rojas. 2015. "Batman en Chile o la deformación histriónica de un mito."
    Aisthesis 57, 43–57.

"Programa de la Unidad Popular." 1969. Salvador Allende (website). Accessed February 1,
    2012. http://www.salvador-allende.cl/Unidad_Popular/Programa%20de%20la%20UP.
    pdf. (site discontinued).

"Se iniciaron jornadas sobre la responsabilidad social de los medios de comunicación." 1970.
    El Mercurio, Santiago de Chile, November 26, 17.

Subercaseaux, Bernardo. 2010. *Historia del libro em Chile: desde la colonia hasta el bicentenario*.
    Santiago de Chile: LOM Ediciones.

Zárate, Verónica Valdivia Ortiz de. 2001. "Estatismo y neoliberalismo: un contrapunto militar.
    Chile 1973–1979." *Revista Historia* (34).

Zárate, Verónica Valdivia Ortiz de. 2010. "'¡Estamos en guerra, señores!'. El régimen militar
    de Pinochet y el 'pueblo', 1973–1980." *Historia* 1 (43).

Zarowsky, Mauricio. 2009. "Cultura y política en el laboratorio chileno. Un itinerario intelec-
    tual de Armand Mattelart (1962–1973)." Master's thesis, Universidad de Buenos Aires.

Part 2. Circulation

~~~~~~

Once comics are made, they must somehow find their way to readers. In traditional print media, circulation referred to how many copies of a periodical were sold and stood as a crude proxy for a publication's readership. But in recent cultural theory, circulation has also stood in for a way of understanding how the movement of objects configures social relations (Straw 2010). The publics organized around such "cultures of circulation" (Lee and LiPuma 2002) are important intermediaries who shape and are shaped by comics' circulatory matrix. By following comics and their publics in movement, we can see how any given part of a comics world is deeply embedded within larger structures.

This section opens with a consideration of comics journalism and criticism. In "Whatever Happened to the Comics Press?" Bart Beaty examines the rise and fall of the specialty comics press. Growing from roots in fanzines and amateur press associations, there was a brief moment when reporting on and reviewing comics was a viable business model for a handful of niche publications. That handful has been winnowed as new media and changing reading habits have cratered advertising revenues across legacy media. However, Beaty argues that the blogs and websites that replaced the dedicated comics press are too often mere appendages of media companies' PR departments and devote more space to covering the film, television, video game, and licensed merchandise industries than comics as such. Nonetheless, as some of the most prominent sources of information and opinion in the comics world, these websites shape the discourses that creators and audiences alike use to understand and frame contemporary comics.

While comic books have largely been imagined as entertainment commodities—not least by the vestigial comics press Beaty examines—this is obviously not the only use to which they can be put. Chapters by Shari Sabeti and Valerie Wieskamp discuss works that have been created for specific and distinctive purposes and circulate in spaces of education and gender-based violence activism, respectively. Sabeti's "All That Shakespeare Stuff" examines the producers of graphic-novel and manga adaptations of Shakespearean plays, arguing that producers embed conceptualizations of cultural value, "Shakespeare" and of education itself in their adaptations. In "Learning to 'Speak without Shame,'" Wieskamp discusses *Priya's Shakti*, a multimedia comic project intended as a culturally authentic response to and intervention in the problem of sexual violence in India. Here, we can usefully see how the orientation of one public (creators) towards another (specific audiences) shapes the social life of comic art.

The section's final chapter, "The Tribes of Comic-Con" by Rob Salkowitz, takes up what is undoubtedly one of the most salient scenes of comics' circulation today, the annual San Diego Comic-Con. Salkowitz, a business analyst with expertise in the pop-culture industries, uses social media data to suggest San Diego's unique profile among contemporary comic cons and looks at how distinct groups—divided into "builders" and "observers" with either an internal or external focus—make use of the event for their own purposes. This analysis reminds us that conventions and other intermediary institutions that serve as nodes in a circulatory matrix are not passive relays but dynamic, even contested, social spaces.

These examples demonstrate that comics' status as social objects means they never sit still. They move through various spaces and contexts, picking up new meanings in their interactions with the publics they thus encounter. The comics world is perpetually remade and redefined by the people who participate in its functioning.

References

Lee, Benjamin, and Edward LiPuma. 2002. "Cultures of Circulation: The Imaginations of Modernity." *Public Culture* 14: 191–213.

Straw, Will. 2010. "The Circulatory Turn." In *The Wireless Spectrum: The Politics, Practices and Poetics of Mobile Media*, edited by Barbara Crow, Michael Longford, and Kim Sawchuk, 17–28. Toronto: University of Toronto Press.

6.

Whatever Happened to the Comics Press?

~~~~~~~~~~~~~~~~~~~~~~~~~~~~~~~~~

THE SLOW RISE AND RAPID FALL OF A NICHE MEDIA INDUSTRY

Bart Beaty

I don't know why I spend time dreaming of doing sourced investigative
journalism when I should be concentrated on "HEY THIS IS COMING OUT"
—Tom Spurgeon (@comicsreporter), August 2016[1]

In spring 2016, Fantagraphics Books, the leading American publisher of
alternative or literary comic books and graphic novels, circulated an ad on
its website and on social media platforms drawing attention to *Patience,* the
newest book by acclaimed cartoonist Daniel Clowes.[1] At the time, Clowes's affiliation with Fantagraphics was entering its fourth decade. The artist released
his first title with the publisher, *Lloyd Llewellyn,* in 1986 before transitioning,
in 1989, to *Eightball,* the title for which he is much better known. By 2016,
the Clowes-Fantagraphics relationship had been on again/off again for many
years. Although the cartoonist continued to publish *Eightball* with the company semiregularly through 2004, works first serialized in that title had been
subsequently repackaged as graphic novels by Pantheon Books (*David Boring*
[2000], *Ice Haven* [2005]) and Drawn & Quarterly (*The Death-Ray* [2011]),
and Clowes had also produced nonserialized graphic novels for both of
those publishers (*Wilson* [2010] and *Mister Wonderful* [2011], the latter originally serialized in the *New York Times Sunday Magazine*). *Patience* marked
Clowes's return to the comic book company with whom he had begun his
career, and the book was a tentpole of its 2016 publishing season—a 180-page
graphic novel by one of the most celebrated of contemporary cartoonists.

Fantagraphics's ad for *Patience* relies on a simple appeal to collective authority. "The critics," it proclaims, "have spoken." Noting that *Patience* had now appeared on the *New York Times* Best Sellers list (in the unwieldily named category Hardcover Graphic Books) for fifteen consecutive weeks, Fantagraphics touted "rave reviews" from forty-four named sources ("and many more"), beginning with *NPR: Fresh Air*, the *Los Angeles Times, Publishers Weekly, Booklist,* and the *San Francisco Chronicle*. Among the critical sources cited are thirteen websites (including Salon, Slate, Longreads, and the AV Club), eleven print magazines (including the *New Yorker* and *Time*), eight daily newspapers (including the *Guardian* and the *Globe and Mail*), seven weekly newspapers, two radio broadcasts (both on NPR), two podcasts (*WTF with Marc Maron* and the *Dinner Party Download*), and one celebrity (Guillermo Del Toro). That the wall of text—which composes the bulk of the ad—is so overwhelming perhaps accounts for the fact that the ad designers and proofreaders did not notice that they had included the *New York Observer* twice in the list. The ad's logic is straightforward: these reputable establishments of middlebrow culture love *Patience*. What is somewhat surprising about the ad, in the context of a volume on the comics world, is that none of the magazines, newspapers, websites, or podcasts named is primarily concerned with comics.

Writing in the *Comics Journal* in May 1992, Fantagraphics publisher Gary Groth opined that, with regard to comics, "the media have to be watched like hawks; just when you think you've learned all their sleazy tricks, they come up with something like this" (4). The "this" that occasioned the writer's ire was a rave review in the *New Yorker* of Art Spiegelman's *Maus*. Groth's specific objection to the review by Ethan Mordden ("a nincompoop with [an] unlikely name") was the lack of historical understanding demonstrated in the *New Yorker*'s coverage of the landmark graphic novel. Groth argued that it was the role of the noncomics media to "trivialize, marginalize, and subvert cultural work[s] of distinction" (3). With their focus on "profit maximization," cultural outlets like the *New Yorker* could not be trusted to critique comics. Twenty-five years later, his company took exactly the opposite tack, touting reviews by noncomics media (including the *New Yorker*) in their own ads. What happened to bring about this complete reversal? In this chapter, I will consider the transformation of writing and reporting about comics in the United States over a fifty-year period in order to suggest that the desire to create an autonomous comics world with its own institutions that mirror those of better-established cultural fields (hinted at in Groth's editorial) has gradually, and perhaps not-so-reluctantly, given way to a new status quo. Today, comics journalism—to the extent that it can be said to exist at all—is fully embedded within larger structures of media reporting. Rather than an outsider trivializing, marginalizing, and subverting great comics, the *New Yorker* just might be the most powerful actor within an expanded notion of the comics press.

A BRIEF HISTORY OF WRITING ABOUT COMICS

Despite its centrality as an organizing institution within the comics world, very little scholarly work has been produced on the subject of comics journalism. Given the position he occupies in the collective imagination of the comics world, it is more than a little ironic that the first scholar to take a sustained interest in comics fanzines was Fredric Wertham, whose 1973 book, *The World of Fanzines: A Special Form of Communication*, was among the earliest significant analyses of the fan press. Wertham, like other historians of the format, traces the origins of the fanzine to science-fiction fans in the 1930s, noting the rapid expansion of fanzine publishing in the post–World War II era with a particularly pronounced acceleration in the 1960s. The origins of comic book fanzines are generally traced to the early 1950s and the publications that gathered around the output of EC Comics, notably Bhob Stewart's the *EC Fan Bulletin* and *Potrzebie*, Mike May's *EC Fan Journal*, Barry Cronin's *EC Scoop*, and the *EC Slime Sheet* by Ernie Crites, although the *Collector's News* (1947) predates those works as a comics-focused fanzine. These early comics fanzines, which rarely survived the death of EC Comics's comic book line in 1955, were followed, generationally, by the first fanzines focused specifically on superhero comics in the 1960s. Beginning with college professor Jerry Bails and teenager Roy Thomas's *Alter Ego* (1961) and Don and Maggie Thompson's *Comic Art* (1961), superhero fanzines rapidly developed a reputation among comic book nostalgists. With the creation of *CAPA-Alpha* in 1964, the first comic book-focused amateur press association, a distinct social network of comic books fans was created that would continue to grow over the course of the 1960s.[2]

In his book *Textual Poachers*, Henry Jenkins (2013, 159) notes, following the work of Constance Penley, that fanzine editors are torn between competing impulses toward "professionalism" and "acceptance," which is to say between high technical standards and the creation of a welcoming climate for inexperienced writers. This central tension helped define writing about comics during the fanzine era (and, notably, it continues to this day). Crucially, the earliest publications about comic books had a backward-looking point-of-view, addressing themselves to the history of the comic book format more strongly than they did to then-current debates within the industry.[3] An important outcome of this orientation was a focus within comics writing on the type of resource-building material that would later become invaluable for fans and scholars. It was fanzine writers (Michael Barrier, Don and Maggie Thompson, Malcolm Willits), for example, who discovered the identity of the "good duck artist" as Carl Barks and who put credits to his anonymously produced work. It was Jerry Bails who compiled lists of superhero comics produced during the industry's first decade in the *Collector's Guide: The First Heroic Age*. The earliest writing about comics tended to emphasize the compilation of data, including publishing credits on works that were frequently uncredited. To this end, the unpaid labor of fandom addressed itself to the support of the generally underpaid labor of comics production.

Contrary to some received understandings, the history of the comics press is not one in which an amateur enterprise slowly gives way to more professional efforts. The trajectory is not nearly so clear-cut. Indeed, in the most substantive analysis of the comics industry trade press, Alisa Perren (2016, 230) argues that within the "modestly sized American comic book industry," trade magazines function "more as hybrid fansites-PR venues than as official, legitimate sources of business information." The earliest efforts to monetize fanzine publishing occurred virtually simultaneously with the rise of organized fandom. In September 1961, the year that *Alter Ego* and *Comic Art* were launched, Jerry Bails published the first issue of *The Comicollector*, an adzine in which fans paid to advertise to buy and sell back issues. In December of that same year, Gordon Love launched a rival adzine, *Rocket's Blast*; the competing publications would merge into a single entity in 1964. The integration of fanzine and adzine publishing was always quite strong, and while fanzines allowed comic book fans to communicate information and opinions with one another, other institutions of the comics world actualized a growing fandom in ways that relied upon and bolstered the nascent comics press. In 1965, the first comic book price guide was published by the Argosy Book Shop, and, by 1968, the earliest American comic book specialty stores began appearing in California. By 1973, Phil Seuling had not only launched a monthly comic book convention in New York but had convinced DC Comics, Marvel Comics, and Warren Publishing to sell to him on a nonreturnable basis, thereby establishing the direct market. The social spaces of comic book stores and fan conventions quickly followed the creation of a fanzine-reading audience and were largely dependent upon them for drawing attention to them as opportunities for fans to meet and interact. To this end, the creation of fanzines and adzines drove the comics world towards more, if never fully, autonomous practices (the overlap between comic book fandom and science-fiction fandom, for instance, was quite strong during this period). Finding little coverage of their interests in the mainstream media, comics fans recreated the institutions of that media in miniature from 1953 through 1973.

The early 1970s marked a period of rapid professionalization for the comics press, as actors in the field were pulled in varying directions. Within a year of the creation of the direct market, Paul Levitz (the *Comic Reader*) had left fanzine publishing to work part time for DC Comics, Marvel Comics had launched its own fan publication (*Friends of Ole Marvel*), and the *Nostalgia Journal* began publishing (changing its name to the *Comics Journal*, under the editorship of Gary Groth, in 1976). By the mid-1970s, two ad-driven publications constituted the American comic book press: the *Comics Journal* (*TCJ*) and the *Comics Buyer's Guide* (*CBG*). (The two magazines would engage in an often-unfriendly rivalry for almost three decades.) With significant distribution through the direct market of comics specialty shops, *TCJ* and *CBG* were high-profile venues for advertising, news, reviews, and criticism. Over the course of the next two decades, they were joined in print by outlets including *Comics Scene*, *Nemo*, *Amazing Heroes*, *Wizard*, and *Hero Illustrated*. Various magazines catered to specific subsets of fandom, and each defined a portion of the comics-reading public around it. Notably, Fantagraphics published both the superhero-friendly *Amazing Heroes* and the superhero-skeptical *Comics Journal*. This period was marked by a rapid, if short-lived, professionalization of the comics press, as table 6.1 demonstrates. Even from this partial list of significant print publications, one can see the proliferation within the field over time and, more importantly, the precarious nature of the comics press. While the two most visible ad-supported publications begun in the 1970s had lengthy lifespans (forty-three years for *CBG*, thirty-eight years for *TCJ*), *Wizard* magazine survived for only twenty years before shifting its corporate emphasis to convention management, and most other magazines faltered much more quickly. Significantly, no major new comics magazines or newspapers have been created in the past decade, and the three longest lived all ceased print publication in the 2010s as the comics press gave way to the comics internet, though the *Comics Journal* returned to semi-annual print publication in 2019 following a six-year hiatus.

One argument about the internet's impact on the comics press is that it ushered in a return of the conditions that existed during the fanzine era of the 1960s. From a certain perspective, this is literally true. The introduction of email facilitated the recreation of former fan networks, including the reconstruction of amateur press associations as email discussion groups, with the speed of the internet fatefully displacing the post office. At the same time,

TABLE 6.1. LIFE SPAN OF SELECTED PRINT FANZINES, AD-ZINES, AND PRO-ZINES		
Title	**First Issue**	**Final Issue**
Alter Ego	1961	1969
Rocket's Blast Comicollector	1964	1982
Comic Buyer's Guide	1971	2013
The Comics Journal	1976	2013
Amazing Heroes	1981	1992
Comics Scene	1982	1983
Nemo	1983	1992
Comics Scene	1987	1996
Wizard	1991	2011
Hero Illustrated	1993	1995
The Imp	1997	2002
Comic Book Artist	1998	2005
Comic Art	2003	2007
Back Issue!	2003	N/A
Source: Wikipedia		

entirely new fora for the discussion of comics were introduced in the early 1990s as internet usage began to increase. Because the earliest internet users were often located at universities (some of the only institutions providing access), they fell into similar demographic groups as the fanzine creators of the 1960s. Usenet fora (in the rec.arts.comics and alt.comics areas) became active, as did closed, pay-for-access sites (CompuServe and Prodigy had the most noteworthy comics discussions groups). Like earlier fanzine traditions, the new internet discussion fora attracted a niche audience. Difficult to locate online in a pre-search-engine era and often closed or semiclosed to outsiders, early internet interactivity operated as a system of exclusion even while it continued some of the best traditions of fanzine culture, including efforts to identify and credit comics producers (the Grand Comics Database [www.comics.org], notably, was founded in 1994).

The introduction of the web as the dominant element of the internet had a transformative effect on the closed aspect of comics culture akin to the introduction of specialized comics magazines in the 1970s. As message boards grew in importance (Comiccon.com and *TCJ* message boards, for example), discussions moved into increasingly open public spaces. A consequence of this new openness could be seen in battles about the moderation of comments, with sites opting for different practices as they struggled to balance ideals of free speech against allowing the development of a public sphere deemed toxic by users (most message boards eventually collapsed in the face of this challenge). The widespread introduction of blogs and personal websites (many with comments sections) served to fragment message-board culture, permitting a higher degree of brand marketing (whether personal or corporate) and a more focused level of interaction among fans and creative personnel. The rise of social media such as Facebook, Twitter, and Tumblr further leveled the playing field, while fundamentally fracturing the notion of a unitary public sphere in the comics world. In April 2016, for instance, when comics journalist Heidi MacDonald ran a Twitter poll asking where her followers got their comics news, fifty-seven per cent chose "social media." The era of social media bolstered distinctions between the most popular comics creators (e.g., 2.8 million accounts following Neil Gaiman [@neilhimself] on Twitter) and the media that might ostensibly exist to cover them (276 thousand followers for @CBR; 81 thousand for @bleedingcool; 17 thousand for @comicsreporter).

Mapping the terrain of today's comics press is a challenging enterprise. While no significant news sources exist in print, sorting online press outlets is complicated by mission confusion. One effort to rank comics websites by Alexa rankings, Twitter followers, and Facebook friends placed The Nib at the top of the heap (Macdonald 2014). However, it was clear that the report had used the number for the top-level domain (medium.com) rather than the subsite specifically; moreover, the survey left out many of the best-known comics news sites but included webcomics, causing categorical uncertainty. The twenty sites most frequently visited featuring comics news according to Alexa ranking, as of July 2015, are listed in table 6.2. Of course, many of these sites are not properly termed comics news sites. Screen Rant, for example, bills itself as "The #1 Independent Movie and TV News Website," and What Culture places significantly more emphasis on film, television, and gaming than it does on comics. Further, as we shall see, even sites that are primarily focused on the comics world have strongly integrated coverage of movie and television adaptations into their mandates. Only a small number of the most popular comics news sites regularly deal with news from the comic book industry, and news from the comic strip industry is even less visible. This continues a long-term trend where, for decades, only *TCJ* and *CBG* could be consistently counted as comics news sources in print. The Eisner Award for Best Comics-Related Periodical, for instance, was won by only five publications between 1992 and 2007 (*CBG* [twice]; *TCJ* [four times]; *Hero Illustrated*; *Comic Book Artist* [four times]; and the revived *Alter Ego*). Since 2007, print magazines have won the award on only two occasions

TABLE 6.2. TWENTY-FIVE COMICS WEBSITES BY ALEXA RANKING	
Website	**Alexa Rank**
Screen Rant	1,312
What Culture	1,322
Comic Book Resources	1,394
Comic Book Movie	2,680
The Mary Sue	2,732
Crave Online	3,138
Bleeding Cool	3,476
Tastefully Offensive	5,412
Comics Alliance	8,020
Newsarama	15,700
The Beat	23,869
Geeks of Doom	29,960
ICv2	35,701
Major Spoilers	41,900
Hero Machine	63,881
Culture Japan	73,321
The Comics Journal	96,992
Omake Theater	103,080
Comics Reporter	107,964
Under Scoop Fire	111,152
Source: Alexa.com	

(*Hogan's Alley* [2016] and a tie between *Back Issue* and *PanelxPanel* [2019]), and the award has otherwise gone to the websites Newsarama, Comic Book Resources (three times), the Comics Reporter (three times), Comics Alliance, the AV Club, and the web version of *TCJ*. What these data make clear is that, over the course of five decades, reporting on comics has not significantly grown as a stand-alone enterprise; rather, discussion of comics has become increasingly integrated into reporting on other media (principally, film and television) and, as the example of reviews of *Patience* suggest, can be found in an ever-increasing number of noncomics world outlets whose coverage is expansive enough to include some coverage of the industry or high-profile releases to the extent that they are now even able to win comics-specific awards, as the AV Club did in 2017.

CHARACTERISTICS OF THE CONTEMPORARY COMICS PRESS

In August 2016, Augie De Blieck Jr., formerly a writer with Comic Book Resources, boldly proclaimed, "Big web comic book journalism is dead as an institution." Commenting upon the redesign of Comic Book Resources (rebranded as CBR.com the month that De Blieck wrote his essay), he suggested that comic books—the material that had previously figured so prominently in the name of the site—had become secondary to reporting on Hollywood. At the time of his writing, De Blieck noted, eight of the top ten stories on CBR.com were related to film or television, and only two to comic books. Readers familiar with the leading comics news sites will not be surprised by this finding. An analysis of the top ten sites on the same day that De Blieck's piece first appeared demonstrated that that site was hardly unique in its focus (table 6.3). That precisely half of the ten most popular comics news sites had no comic book content on their front page is indicative of the significant expansion of our conception of both the comics world and of comics journalism. Indeed, only three sites in the top twenty are primarily or exclusively devoted to news and reviews of comic books (twelve of the top thirteen stories in The Beat, all twelve for the Comics Reporter, and all thirteen for the *Comics Journal*), and those are the sites with the closest connections to the legacy comics press of the 1970s and 1980s (notably, Heidi MacDonald and Tom Spurgeon are former writers and editors of *TCJ*, and TCJ.com is the online continuation of that magazine).

TABLE 6.3. PROPORTION OF FRONT PAGE STORIES ABOUT COMIC BOOKS OR STRIPS, AUGUST 26, 2016	
Website	**%**
Screen Rant	0
What Culture	3
Comic Book Resources	25
Comic Book Movie	0
The Mary Sue	0
Crave Online	0
Bleeding Cool	33.3
Tastefully Offensive	0
Comics Alliance	10
Newsarama	75

Crucially, as the example of the comics press so ably demonstrates, the so-called comics world is not a world exclusively—or even primarily—concerned with comics. When sites like CBR.com dedicate seventy-five per cent of their coverage to film and television, it is not to film and television generally (as in the case of *Variety* or the *Hollywood Reporter*), but to a specific slice of Hollywood production that is derived from comic books. Articles on the Marvel Cinematic Universe, the *Riverdale* television show based on Archie Comics properties, or casting on *Supergirl* crowd out reporting on the source material in a manner that is akin to the transformation of comic cons by the promotional culture of Hollywood. As numerous bloggers responding to De Blieck's complaints rightly noted, this is a simple example of websites following consumer demand. *Supergirl*, for example, was shifted from CBS television to the CW after its first season due to poor performance in the ratings, when its season finale drew a mere 6.2 million viewers. At the same time, the sixth issue of the then current print version of the *Adventures of Supergirl* sold only 10,982 copies (Kissell 2016; Miller 2016). While both versions of the character would be regarded as performing below the expectations of their media, the fact remains that the television version of the character is watched by almost six hundred people for every one that purchases the comic book version. To this end, the comics press—driven, like virtually all online media, by close attention to website analytics—reflects the domination of the comics world by film and television. As comic books became a content provider for Hollywood blockbusters in the twenty-first century, the comics press shifted its focus to the engines that drive success within the comics world.

The comics press's domination by coverage of non-comic book material is suggestive of social and economic relations within the field, but further insight can be found by examining exactly what kinds of coverage comics actually receive. Among the ten most popular comics news sites listed in table 6.3, the top thirty comic book stories included only two articles that could reasonably be termed "news": a Newsarama story on the relocation of Image Comics to Portland, Oregon, and a Newsarama story on the cancellation of Marvel Comics's *Nighthawk*. The vast majority of the comics content on the sites consisted of comic book previews supplied to the sites by publishers (particularly to CBR.com), notices of creators moving to and from various titles, and comic book reviews. Comics Alliance offered three light essays (e.g., "The Legion of Super-Heroes Top Ten Villains") but nothing that would qualify as news analysis. For the most part, the leading comics news websites are extremely implicated in the promotional strategies of the leading comic book publishers. In this way, as Perren (2016, 229) notes, they are no different from sources covering other media industries: "trades are especially dependent on advertising revenue from the specific industries they cover, and will do what they can to curry favor from the biggest players (and often heaviest advertisers) in that industry." This is particularly striking when sites simply provide links to preview pages from current or forthcoming comic book titles but can also be seen in the coverage of publishing announcements. CBR.com, Newsarama, and The Beat, for example, each hosted articles stating that Marvel Comics had released a teaser ad for a project named *MU* and that they were expected to reveal more information about the project at a forthcoming Diamond Retailer Summit—no further analysis or information was provided. In essence, the news carried on the sites was an announcement that a corporate press release would be forthcoming.[4] In cases like these, the distinction between the comics press and the promotional arm of Marvel Comics is exceedingly difficult to discern. The comics press is not simply dominated by Hollywood but is subservient to the promotional engines of the largest publishers because, as Tom Spurgeon lamented on Twitter, previews drive clicks.

The near-total absence of an autonomous comics press was also highlighted by a lengthy—and snarky—2015 year-in-review article series written by Abhay Khosla and published by *TCJ*.[5] Across thousands of satirical words, Khosla recounted the major news stories covered by the comics press in 2015. These included the assassination of the *Charlie Hebdo* editorial team in January, arguments about sexualized and racialized imagery in certain comics, DC Comics's decision to include half-page ads for Twix in their comics, and a large number of sexual harassment cases in the industry. While Khosla's take on this coverage is far from neutral, the most striking elements of his piece highlight systemic issues within the comics press. The *Charlie Hebdo* attacks, for example, were far more comprehensively covered outside the comics press than they were within it. This, of course, reflects the reality of budgets—large news operations with foreign offices could dramatically out-compete small ones on a story with such global significance. At the same time, the top stories demonstrated the way that news sites had fallen dramatically behind social media. The stories about objectionable content in comics, a recurrent theme throughout the year, had their fullest expression not in the news sites but across Twitter, where debates involved dozens or hundreds of commentators (indeed, much of the coverage of, for example, the Raphael Albuquerque's *Batgirl* cover simply compiled Twitter messages into an easily readable format; see, e.g., Cowden [2015]). Similarly, the harassment scandals recounted accusations made most forcefully and clearly on Twitter, where individuals involved in the events—or close to them—argued amongst themselves about issues of guilt and innocence. Twitter took on a heightened role in these controversies precisely because the comics press was so reluctant to investigate claims of harassment at companies like DC, Marvel, and Dark Horse, who supply content, in the form of previews and access to creators, and whose advertising budgets directly support the sites. Given such remarkable synergy between publishers and the trade press, Twitter could be seen as the only viable outlet for volatile claims. Not surprisingly, the lack of coverage—or conflicts of interest within the coverage that did occur—became a secondary aspect of the scandals (Macdonald 2015; Terror 2015).

That the contemporary comics press is dominated by comic book previews and Twitter recapping is not surprising given that it is, for the most part, not a domain of professional journalists. The epigraph for this chapter is a tweet from Tom Spurgeon, former editor of the print edition of *TCJ* and driving force behind the four-time Eisner-winning website the Comics Reporter until his passing in 2019.[6] One of the most acclaimed journalists in the history of the comics press, Spurgeon launched a Patreon account in 2015 to underwrite his dream of a more substantial form of comics reporting. As of October 2018, that fund had 301 supporters pledging $436 per month, or $5,232 annually. This amount was $6,908 below the 2018 poverty line in the United States (Department of Health and Human Services 2018). Heidi MacDonald's Patreon generated $813 per month from 155 supporters in 2016 (she discontinued her Patreon after her site was acquired by Lion Forge in 2017 and resumed it in 2020 when The Beat went independent again), while Noah Berlatsky, who ran the comics-related essay site Hooded Utilitarian until 2016, had a failed Patreon campaign that was unable to garner the requested $150 per month (Berlatsky now generates $421 per month in support of his e-book publishing).[7] Writing on this issue in The Beat, MacDonald (2016) put her case bluntly with a piece occasioned by the cancellation of Sktchd, a comics essay site run for a year by David Harper before the workload became overwhelming for him and he reprioritized his full-time job. For MacDonald, "there is obviously a huge world of comics news out there that should be covered that isn't Marvel and DC. And that's what most sites cover, because it's the bread and butter, traffic wise." In an era of instantaneous data analytics, the comics press—to the degree that it still exists—is driven to tailor coverage towards stories that most clearly drive traffic. In the absence of any ongoing institutional support for comics coverage, independent reportage is necessarily curtailed. In hindsight, it seems almost miraculous that Fantagraphics Books would, for so long, employ full-time staff to edit the *Comics Journal*, including a news editor whose job was to do investigative reporting. Now, comics journalism is an exponential amplification of trends in other forms of journalism—unmoored from any sort of capital that might underwrite and support it and desperately seeking revenue streams in an increasingly fragmented media market.

Given the obvious resource shortcomings of the comics press today, it is worth asking how far—if at all—writing about comics has traveled since the days of fanzines produced in short runs on mimeographs. Certainly, the internet has facilitated an expansion of scale; there are far more comics bloggers than there ever were comics fanzine publishers, and far more readers as well. Nonetheless, for the vast majority of these individuals, writing about comics is an avocation—very few have been able to professionalize their hobby, and most never will. As with fanzine publishers of an earlier age, writing about comics is a hobby that will eventually be abandoned for different pursuits. MacDonald (2016), writing about the failures of the comics press in reporting "very complex stories of sexual harassment that have recently rocked the comics industry," observed that she had "yet to see a substantive report on the matter that wasn't written by someone who was actually involved in the situation (myself included), which is mind boggling." The reality is that the comics world lacks anything that might accurately be called comics reporting. The most successful news outlets are not focused on comics themselves, except in passing, and the most profitable sites that actually have been concerned with comic books primarily existed as dot-com start-ups to be purchased by larger media companies. Notably, Comic Book Resources, which began life as a spin-off from a discussion board focused on the DC Comics mini-series *Kingdom Come*, was sold by Jonah Weiland to Valnet Inc., a media holding corporation that also owned rival news site Screen Rant. Similarly, Newsarama, which traces its origins to Mike Doran's news postings on the Prodigy message boards, outlived that internet service provider and was sold to Imaginova, a media company founded by CNN's Lou Dobbs in 2007, and then again to TopTenReviews (now the Purch Group) in 2009. In the end, as with fanzine publishing, the success stories in comics journalism concern those that have been able to get out of comics journalism—either by transitioning to an editorial or creative role at a comic book publisher or by selling a site to a media holding company looking to broaden its advertising reach. In both cases, the full-scale assimilation of the press to the revenue-maximizing interests of the comic book industry (now multimedia industry) is taken for granted.

CONCLUSION

In the 1990s, Gary Groth could dream in the pages of *TCJ* of an autonomous comics press that might someday rival the *New Yorker* in terms of
its influence on the development of the art form. Groth supported his vision by subsidizing an economically precarious magazine for nearly four
decades before conceding the inevitable outcome of the print magazine
industry. While other art world institutions have come into being in the
quarter-century since Groth lambasted the mainstream reception of *Maus*
(consider academia, which has developed dozens of conferences, half a
dozen professional organizations, several peer-refereed journals, and even
degree-granting programs over this time period), the comics press has, if
anything, taken steps away from autonomy and is now almost completely
tied to the promotional culture of the comics industry. Indeed, such is the
level of integration that contemporary comic book creators feel free to criticize the performance of the comics press when a title is unsuccessful and
subsequently canceled. Yet for the most part, there is no outlet of the comics
press that can single-handedly make or break a comics project with a review
or a preview. In the social-media era, discussion of comics has become too
fragmented for individual considerations to hold sway. Not for nothing did
Fantagraphics cite forty-four different reviews to sell *Patience*—the logic of
comics criticism is buckshot, not sniper fire. The effect of this change, ironically, has been to make the mainstream press the substitute for the comics
press. At a time when Art Spiegelman (1999) is able to pen long-form essays
on Jack Cole for the *New Yorker*, and the most prominent of literary comic
books are regularly reviewed in the quality press of the *New York Times* or
The Guardian, the comics press no longer apes the mainstream in miniature. It has become a small part of the larger whole, and all of those comics
journalists are reduced to the status of freelance aspirants.

Acknowledgments

This chapter was strongly influenced by discussions over many years with Tom Spurgeon,
who gave me my first paid writing position in comics journalism in 1997. Tom was a dear
friend and a steadfast colleague. I dedicate this chapter to his memory.

Notes

1. http://fantagraphics.com/flog/patience-new-york-times-best-seller-15-weeks-counting/.
2. The history of comic book fanzines in the 1960s has been recounted in several volumes
by Bill Schelly (1999, 2010; Thomas and Schelly 2008), a participant during that period.

3. The essays collected in Dick Lupoff and Don Thompson's *All in Color for a Dime*, a 1970 compilation of the "best" writing from a range of comic book fanzines, are almost exclusively aimed at the nostalgic comics reader.

4. See, for instance, http://www.cbr.com/new-marvel-mu-teaser-spotlights-cullen-bunn-and-leinil-yu/; http://www.newsarama.com/30834-marvel-s-mystery-mu-project-adds-new-wrinkle.html; http://www.comicsbeat.com/marvel-to-announce-mu-by-bunn-and-mcniven-at-diamond-retailer-summit/.

5. "The TCJ 2015 Year-in-Review Spectacufuck": http://www.tcj.com/the-tcj-2015-year-in-review-spectacufuck-part-i/; http://www.tcj.com/the-tcj-2015-year-in-review-spectacufuck-part-ii/; http://www.tcj.com/the-tcj-2015-year-in-review-spectacufuck-part-iii/; http://www.tcj.com/the-tcj-2015-year-in-review-spectacufuck-part-iv/.

6. Disclosure: Spurgeon is the editor who first hired me to write for *TCJ*, and for several years I was a paid contributor to the Comics Reporter. I have not been a supporter of his Patreon account, nor of any others described in this chapter.

7. Patreon is a platform for crowdfunding on an on-going basis, rather than being tied to discrete projects, as in a Kickstarter campaign. Support levels are accurate as of October, 2018, and can be accessed from the respective Patreon pages: https://www.patreon.com/comicsreporter; and https://www.patreon.com/noahberlatsky. See also Berlatsky (2016).

References

Berlatsky, Noah. 2016. "What I Learned from My Failed Patreon Campaign." The Kernel, February 28. http://kernelmag.dailydot.com/issue-sections/staff-editorials/15941/failed-patreon-curse-of-the-mainstream-writer/.

Cowden, Catarina. 2015. "The Batgirl Cover Controversy, Explained for Casual Fans." Cinema Blend. http://www.cinemablend.com/celebrity/Batgirl-Cover-Controversy-Explained-Casual-Fans-70807.html.

De Blieck, Augie, Jr. 2016. "The End of Big Comic Book Journalism." Pipeline Comics, August 26. http://www.pipelinecomics.com/the-end-of-big-comic-book-journalism/.

Groth, Gary. 1992. "A Case of Complex Ignorance." *The Comics Journal*, May: 3.

Jenkins, Henry. 2013. *Textual Poachers: Television Fans and Participatory Culture*, 20th anniversary ed. New York: Routledge.

Kissell, Rick. 2016. "Ratings: No Finale Boost for CBS' 'Supergirl'; NBC's 'The Voice' Tops Night Despite Low." *Variety*, April 19. http://variety.com/2016/tv/news/ratings-cbs-supergirl-down-in-finale-monday-1201756535/.

MacDonald, Heidi. 2014. "What Is the #1 Comics Blog?" The Beat, October 27. http://www.comicsbeat.com/what-is-the-1-comics-blog/.

MacDonald, Heidi. 2015. "It's About Disclosure in Comics Journalism." The Beat, November 3. http://www.comicsbeat.com/its-about-disclosure-in-comics-journalism/.

MacDonald, Heidi. 2016. "Comics Journalism: You Get What You Pay For." The Beat, June 10. http://www.comicsbeat.com/comics-journalism-you-get-what-you-pay-for/.

Miller, John Jackson. 2016. "July 2016 Comic Book Sales Figures: Estimated Comics Sold to North American Comics Shops as Reported by Diamond Comic Distributors." Comichron: The Comics Chronicles. http://www.comichron.com/monthlycomicssales/2016/2016-07.html.

Perren, Alisa. 2016. "The Trick of the Trades: Media Industry Studies and the American Comic Book Industry." In *Production Studies, the Sequel! Cultural Studies of Global Media Industries*, edited by Miranda Banks, Bridget Conor, and Vicki Mayer, 227–37. New York: Routledge.

Schelly, William. 1999. *The Golden Age of Comic Fandom*, rev. ed. Seattle, WA: Hamster Press.

Schelly, William. 2010. *Founders of Comic Fandom: Profiles of 90 Publishers, Dealers, Collectors, Writers, Artists and Other Luminaries of the 1950s and 1960s*. Jefferson, NC: McFarland.

Spiegelman, Art. 1999. "Forms Stretched to Their Limits." *The New Yorker*, April 19, http://www.newyorker.com/magazine/1999/04/19/forms-stretched-to-their-limits-2.

Terror, Jude. 2015. "Fanboy Rampage: Hanna Means Shannon Hired at Dark Horse, Rich Johnston Celebrated with Blowout Twitter Fight." The Outhousers, October 31. http://www.theouthousers.com/index.php/news/133666-fanboy-rampage-hannah-means-shannon-hired-at-dark-horse-rich-johnston-celebrates-with-blowout-twitter-fight.html.

Thomas, Roy, and Bill Schelly, eds. 2008. *Alter Ego: The Best of the Legendary Comics Fanzine*, 2nd ed. Raleigh, NC: TwoMorrows.

Wertham, Fredric. 1973. *The World of Fanzines: A Special Form of Communication*. Carbondale: Southern Illinois University Press.

7.

"All That Shakespeare Stuff"

COMIC BOOKS AND THE PUBLIC PEDAGOGY OF ADAPTATION

Shari Sabeti

One of the "publics" increasingly identified for comic books in recent years has been students and teachers. Comic books and education, of course, have a history—and not always a positive one. In the 1950s, commentators in both the United Kingdom and North America such as George Pumphrey (1954, 1955, 1964) and Fredric Wertham (1954) identified some comics as a threat to both literacy and morality (for further details see Barker 1989; Nyberg 1998; Beaty 2005). Yet, even against this backdrop, a series such as *Classics Illustrated* gained popularity as a way of wooing young children to great works of literature through a medium they found attractive.

Now it seems that this once uneasy relationship between educators and comics has blossomed. Graphic novels and comic book adaptations are being increasingly employed by teachers to address a changing literacy landscape dominated by visual and digital forms of knowledge. Multimodal texts such as comic books appear to bridge home and school practices, appealing to young people's new ways of knowing (Kress 2005; Ito et al. 2010; New London Group 1996). They have the aesthetic appeal of a computer screen while retaining features of a conventional book (Tabachnik 2010), and they communicate meaning through a variety of modes simultaneously, making them potentially more inclusive of a variety of learners (Schwartz 2002; Jacobs 2013). While research to date has tended to focus on the reception of comic books in classrooms (Cary 2004; Frey and Fisher 2008; Pantaleo 2011, 2015), very little attention has been paid to the *production* of comics aimed specifically at schools. In this chapter, I focus on literary adaptations into the comics medium, and specifically on that most challenging of verbal texts taught in schools, Shakespeare. In what follows, I foreground the insights of adaptors themselves, how *they* perceive the pedagogical work they are doing in adapting Shakespeare into the comic book form, and their reflections on its relative success. I take as my theoretical frame the idea of "public pedagogy" (Giroux 2000; Sandlin et al. 2011), positing the "educational" comic book and indeed "Shakespeare" as sites where pedagogies are enacted between adaptors, text, and the reading public.

THE "EDUCATIONAL COMIC BOOK"

This project sought to explore the underlying assumptions about readers, education, schooling, and "Shakespeare" that went into the production of comic book and graphic-novel adaptations of the plays of William Shakespeare. I was interested in what knowledge of and about Shakespeare was being implicitly valued, mobilized, or omitted. I was also concerned with what this told us about the aims and values underpinning literature education more broadly—sometimes these were conservative, sometimes more revolutionary. For example, Graham, the managing director of Classical Comics, told me that the adaptations were conceived by his brother, who founded the company, in order to "promote classic literature to school children . . . to make a child want to read Shakespeare rather than have a groan go up in class." High production values were strategic in this sense, meant to draw in young readers with glossy pages and bright colors. Behind this desire was a fervent belief that reading classical literature was important; speaking of his brother, he said: "He really thought . . . you could help change a child's character through appreciating classical literature because the reason it's classic is that it's so profound . . . that person would go on to read more and more classic literature. It would aid learning and appreciation of the world and just build a fuller character." There is a strong—if traditional—pedagogical intention here, but other adaptors also expressed a desire to communicate and inspire. Asked about his enthusiasm for the texts, David, one adaptor who had been working within the comics medium for a number of years, told me: "I suppose there's this pedagogy somewhere in me . . . I get excited about ideas, I suppose, and I want to communicate them to people . . . And maybe it goes together with being an editor, which is another form of pedagogy in a way, doctoring other people's prose." As a founding member of the Writers and Readers Publishing Co-operative (WRP Co-op), he was introduced by Ivan Illich, the author of *Deschooling Society*, to the work of the famous Mexican comic artist Rius (Eduardo del Rio). Rius had begun to make overtly didactic comic books such as the Para principantes (For Beginners) series—clear, intelligent, and witty introductions to present-day politics and problems aimed at the general public (see Rubenstein 1998 for further details). Rius's second book in the series, *Marx para principantes* (1972), was translated into English in 1976 as *Marx for Beginners* by the WRP Co-op (the For Beginners series was subsequently revived as "Introducing" and "Introducing Graphic Guides"). Some of the adaptations of Shakespeare I am focusing on follow in this more radical tradition and see comic books as communicative, pedagogic, political, and anti-elitist. Furthermore, their status as popular culture is assumed to be the source of their pedagogical strength.

For this project, I focused on four different series of Shakespeare comics, two based in the United Kingdom (Manga Shakespeare and Classical Comics) and two based in the United States. (No Fear Shakespeare Graphic Novels and Shakespeare: The Manga Edition). I will cite examples from all of these publishers, but there is a greater focus on the work of Manga Shakespeare adaptors because this series is the largest, and I was able to gain access to a greater number of artists, providing a better insight into their working processes. The research involved a series of semi-structured interviews with comic book artists, textual adaptors and Shakespeare scholars who worked on producing these texts depending on their availability and accessibility at the time of the research. Prior to each interview, I ensured that I had read the texts carefully and refreshed my knowledge of the original play, making note of any particular questions or pages I wished to ask them about. I also took care to look up their other work as artists and to ask them questions about their artistic practices and approach more generally. Given my position both as an *educational* researcher and a previous high school teacher of English, I wanted to ensure that they knew I had no particular agenda. Because of the potentially controversial nature of the adaptations, I ensured that my interview questions were focused around the adaptation *process* and their reflections on this as artists/scholars, rather than on the debates surrounding Shakespeare, comic books, and pedagogy more broadly. We met in public spaces such as cafés, and I would place my copy of their text (usually with several Post-it Notes protruding from its pages) on the table so that they could identify me. They were extremely generous with their time, despite busy schedules and deadlines, and I am grateful to them for this. These interviews were recorded using a digital voice recorder with the permission of the participants and subsequently transcribed. While I am aware that the participants are published authors and artists, and hence clearly identifiable, I have followed the ethical guidelines of the UK universities, funders of the project, and the British Educational Research Association in using pseudonyms throughout, and participants were made aware of my intention to do so. The adaptations themselves vary in terms of the representational and aesthetic choices made, and it is worth briefly surveying these here.

Manga Shakespeare is produced by a small UK-based publishing company called SelfMadeHero. Originally commissioned in 2007, there are now fourteen titles in the series. They are designed to resemble publishing formats and visual styles associated with manga, or Japanese comics. Hence, the books are reduced to about two hundred pages of black-and-white images with colored plates only at the start to introduce the characters. Manga Shakespeare is, economically speaking, the most successful of the series I looked at. Its bestselling title, *Romeo and Juliet*, has sold nearly 100,000 copies around the world. The comics have been translated into Italian, Spanish, Portuguese, Turkish, Hungarian, Arabic, Czech, and Slovakian and have even been used to teach Japanese university students Shakespeare. They are marketed at both schools and individual teenage readers and manga fans. The adaptations keep the original Shakespearean language but cut it radically to fit the form and length of the book. Apart from two history plays (*Richard III* and *Henry VIII*), they reset the plays in different contexts—usually a contemporary or futuristic one, though *King Lear* has been recontextualized in a colonial *Last of the Mohicans*–style America. There is a dynamic style of presentation (see figure 7.1) with uneven panel cuts, images that bleed to the edge of the page, and a suggestion of temporal, spatial, and emotional movement characteristic of manga. For this series, I interviewed the chief adaptor, David, who worked on the textual redaction and storyboarding and who liaised with the artists; the artists responsible for various plays; and a Shakespeare scholar, John, who was employed by the publisher to check the final manga edition for grammatical and narrative sense and authenticity.

There is also a manga version produced by Wiley in the United States, again first commissioned in 2007. These use black-and-white images on rough pulp paper and also employ Shakespeare's original language. The language is abridged much less radically than the British versions, and the pages still look quite "text heavy" (see figure 7.2). The plays are set in their original historical contexts, or, as one of the adaptors told me, "as Shakespeare would have intended." The four titles in this series—*Hamlet, Macbeth, Romeo and Juliet*, and *Julius Caesar*—are also the four Shakespeare plays most often taught in US high schools. I interviewed the textual adaptor, Allen, and two of the artists involved in the adaptations.

No Fear Shakespeare Graphic Novels, similarly published in the United States and aligned with popular school texts (though there is no adaptation of *Julius Caesar*), chooses to employ the simplified modern English text from

Figure 7.1. Romeo and friends arrive at the Capulet party. From *Manga Shakespeare—Romeo and Juliet* by Sonia Leong and Richard Appignanesi, 2007. Reproduced with permission of the publisher.

Figure 7.2. "To be or not to be" soliloquy from *Hamlet: The Manga Edition* by Tintin Pantoja and Adam Sexton, 2007. Reproduced with permission of the publisher.

their No Fear Shakespeare series. They are also black and white but use the more regular panel sequences and grids we might associate with American comics. These guides are marketed very specifically at school students and are to be found in the "study guide" sections of chain stores such as Barnes and Noble (which owns Spark Notes, the publisher of No Fear Shakespeare). Act and scene numbers are indicated to readers using page breaks and signs, and subplots (a casualty of some of the other adaptations) are generally retained. For this series, I was able to interview one of the artists and used the blog of another for evidence of working processes.

Finally, Classical Comics is a small UK-based publisher set up by an enthusiast in 2007 with the main aim of engaging children in classic literature. There are five adaptations in all—*Macbeth, Romeo and Juliet, The Tempest, Henry V,* and *A Midsummer Night's Dream*—and there are currently two others in process (*Hamlet* and *Julius Caesar*). The publisher also commissions other literature in adaptation, making e-books, CD-ROMs, and interactive motion comics. Classical Comics markets exclusively to schools and probably has the highest production values of the four publishers in focus here. The comics are always in color, the pages thick and glossy, and well-known (but expensive) comic artists do the work. Three versions of each play are produced with a different text: full and unabridged, which is called "Original"; a "Plain Text" version, which is modernized English and adapted by English teachers; and a "Quick Text," which is abridged and in modern English. The latter, I was told, sell more to primary/elementary schools. Plays are set in their original contexts, and characters appear in period costume. Classical Comics has a market in the United Kingdom, Canada, Australia, and the United States. For the latter, it produces American English versions of the "Plain" and "Quick" texts. I spoke to the managing director of this series, Graham, in detail about the aims and processes involved.

The very existence of these comic book adaptations is based on an assumption that Shakespeare needs to be mediated for younger audiences. While they go about doing this in different ways—simplifying the language, visualizing the plot in glossy color pages, or recontextualizing the story into more familiar settings—they all attempt to make Shakespeare's work more relevant or engaging than it supposedly is. As my interviews go on to show, however, the business of disentangling Shakespeare from the institution of schooling proved difficult.

SHAKESPEARE AND PEDAGOGY: THE ADAPTORS' PERSPECTIVE

Henry Giroux (2000) has argued that all culture is inherently pedagogical and operates as a site where dominant ideologies are both reproduced and resisted. It is worth pausing for a moment then to consider how these processes play out in the case of Shakespeare. Why, after all, do we continue to teach his work despite the difficulties of doing so in a contemporary context? The arguments often put forward by educationalists and policy makers range from his importance as part of our national culture and linguistic heritage to the more mundane "critical thinking skills" (for a discussion of such debates see Cunningham 1998; Coles 2004, 2013; Ward and Connolly 2008). There are also philosophical arguments about the educational potential of Shakespeare's work and the beneficial effects of literary study more generally (Cavell 2003; Nussbaum 2010). First, appreciating and enjoying the language and dramatic aspects of his work occasion an *aesthetic* response. Second, his plays explore the complexities of being human and, in doing so, elicit an empathy and understanding that bring about an *ethics* of response. Both of these make a contribution, perhaps, to what Graham called the building of "character." If all culture is, as Giroux argues, pedagogical, then what kinds of ideologies are being reproduced and resisted in the site of adaptation?

The adaptors that I worked with were both receivers *and* producers of such pedagogies. They were receivers in terms of their understanding of Shakespeare and his cultural value; they were producers because they adapted and repackaged his work in order to teach and explain it. These adaptors felt this tension keenly, and they were aware of how their adaptations might alter what it was that readers actually learned about Shakespeare—in some cases, in ways that were unintended. All of them saw what they were doing as *pedagogic work*, even if some of them were not always sure whom it was that they were teaching. However, when I asked them the question, "What does Shakespeare mean to you?" the vast majority replied with the monosyllable "school." Allen, speaking of how he was approached by US publisher Wiley and Sons to adapt Shakespeare's text, told me: "I don't think he even specified who the intended audience was. I mean I always assumed that it was high school, junior high and high school, but I don't think that was ever explicated." However, many of them saw what they were doing as an antidote to the traditional desk-bound study of Shakespeare's work that they themselves had experienced. Indeed, despite the development of a plethora of resources for teaching Shakespeare in more active and engaging ways (most notably perhaps Rex Gibson's *Teaching Shakespeare*), assessment practices often dictate how his works are taught (see Kress et al. 2004). Peter (the comic artist who adapted *The Tempest* for Manga Shakespeare) asked: "Can you imagine, let's say for example, if two hundred years in the future, James Cameron films weren't watched but were just read as scripts? He'd probably flip out if he knew it." So, while they were aware of their public as a school one for the most part, many of them were also interested in using the comic form, and their adaptation, as a way of rectifying some of the problematic ways that Shakespeare's work is taught. In Peter's comment, there is also the assumption that Shakespeare *himself* would not have approved of what his work had come to mean in the context of modern schooling. In a sense then, it is not the adaptors—cutting, tampering, drawing, and editing Shakespeare's work—but teachers and the practices of the classroom that do the most damage to his plays and reputation.

In the next section, I draw out from my interview material the main ways that adaptors saw their task (and the comic book adaptation) as pedagogically useful. I then go on to consider the ways in which they reflected on what might have been lost in the adaptation process. In the interests of space, I have had to select only a few of the "gains" and "losses" identified. It is worth noting also that my interview questions never *directly asked* about losses and gains; instead, as I mentioned earlier, those conversations tended to explore artistic processes, which resulted in reflections on what they considered to be the successes and limitations what they were able to achieve. I am also aware that in choosing to structure the material in this way I run the risk of oversimplifying it, but I do so partly for the sake of clarity and partly in order to open up further questions about the potentials and pitfalls of comic book adaptations.

Comic Book Shakespeare: Pedagogical Gains

The first positive outcome of the comic book versions of Shakespeare, as identified by adaptors, was the fact that Shakespeare's text was visualized and performed. The experience of a reader would therefore be much closer to that of a theater-goer and more appropriate, given the original purpose of these texts. Allen (the textual adaptor for the US Manga Edition series) said of his work on the project: "It seemed very valid to me pedagogically. We all know that it's easier to understand the language of a Shakespeare play when you're actually watching a performance rather than just reading the text."

David (the textual adaptor for the UK Manga Shakespeare) called these texts "a form of pocket-book theater." Here the adaptors identify a gain that is actually recouping something essential about Shakespeare that schooling seems to have lost. It interested me how much the adaptors referenced

Shakespeare himself in justifying their choices; to them, the comic book adaptation was not a marketing ploy but an intentional, thoughtful, and ethical decision to communicate and convey the plays to a younger audience. Another important advantage they noted was the way in which readers of comic books could themselves dictate the pace at which they read. Allen, who had argued that these adaptations "approximated the dynamic of a performance," also said that they were

> in some ways . . . even better because when you are watching the performance you can't stop it . . . you can't stop it and say, "woah, woah, woah, hang on . . . what's Hamlet saying here?" and take it line by line, but I thought this in some ways *would* provide one with the opportunity to do both those things: to see an image of the scene but also to take time pulling stuff apart.

Of course, "pulling stuff apart," as well as allowing space and time for understanding, is what English teachers ask their students to do. So not only is the comic book true to the spirit of Shakespeare the dramatist, but it also respects and aids the demands of literature education in analyzing, close reading, and deconstructing of texts.

Another advantage of these adaptations was that they foregrounded and explained the plot. John, who was a Shakespeare scholar employed by Self-MadeHero to check their completed adaptations for sense and "authenticity" told me:

> What you gain is a very sharply profiled sense of the plot which actually is surprisingly hard to grasp . . . I mean actually when you have to sit down and work out the plot of *Much Ado About Nothing*, it's extraordinarily difficult, complicated . . . And in that sense to pare the text down in that way, you're actioning the script. Peeling away the accretion of the beautiful poetic detail but in the name of getting to the . . . core of what's physically going on.

Again, here the metaphors draw on the theater and acting—the original context of the writing itself—as if to imply that we are somehow doing the right things with these plays. David, who redacted the text before John checked it, called his job one of "filleting," a metaphor that suggests he is retaining what is of value, but also removing what is hard or tough. Part of their pedagogic task then was to make the plays palatable. They use metaphors related to food preparation: to pare down (trim, peel, cut away outer edges) and fillet (remove the bones and keep the flesh to make it go down more easily). These metaphors are also suggestive of skill, care, and respect for the original material itself. The removal of difficult bits of Shakespeare is not seen as an act of desecration; indeed, John told me, "Shakespeare was difficult, even to the people who first went to see the plays when he was writing them." Shakespeare himself was aware of this double audience in his writing, often saying something in complex poetic language and then repeating it in more straightforward terms. The comic book, with its double narrative of images and text, then presents a perfect alternative.

When I asked Mark about how he chose to split the text of *Romeo and Juliet* up across panels for his adaptation in the No Fear Shakespeare series, he spoke about a particular scene where Lady Capulet is trying to convince Juliet to marry Paris. Mark, whose beautiful and detailed drawings are set in a traditional early Renaissance Verona, decided to cut the text up into several consecutive panels that show the Nurse "fixing Juliet's hair and attempting to mold her into the image of a young lady." The point is, he told me, that "she just sits there" passively (figure 7.3). Here he is clearly using the comics medium to communicate a particular theme he understands to exist in the play, namely, the way Juliet is continually constructed by others. This is not stated explicitly but rather demonstrated through the particular way he designs his page. And if this "theme" is successfully conveyed, then there is another pedagogy at work that is worthy of our attention. It may be that these multimodal texts have something in common with video games and convergence culture. Speaking of the Yu-Gi-Oh! franchise, Hayes and Gee write: "When a word is associated with a verbal definition, we say it has a verbal meaning. When it is associated with an image, action, goal, experience, or dialogue, we say it has a situated meaning. Situated meanings are crucial for understandings that lead to being able to apply one's knowledge to problem solving" (2010, 187). Children are able to understand quite complex and sophisticated relations between different modes and media because these worlds are designed with a lucidity and forethought that enable them to decode them. In this way, Hayes and Gee argue, "a very arcane vocabulary becomes lucidly meaningful to even small children" (Hayes and Gee 2010, 187). Indeed, Gee and Hayes go so far as to argue that this kind of learning process, a problem solving, is much more applicable to daily life than some of the more traditional content and modes of school teaching. Complex language, if inserted within a "lucid design" and fully situated, is easily grasped or learned. Matt's attempts to convey an interpretation of *Romeo and Juliet* is lucid because he has designed the comic book in a particular way and situated the language and characters in it so that their meanings become

Figure 7.3. From *Romeo and Juliet* (No Fear Shakespeare Graphic Novels) by Matt Wiegle, 2008. Reproduced with permission of the publisher.

clear. This, of course, takes us back to our starting point, the justification of the comic book as a kind of "pocket-book theater." In a play, Shakespeare's language is *always* situated in action and is visually performed.

We can see these all as examples of what Gaztambide-Fernández and Arráize-Matute have defined as the relational and ethical dimensions of pedagogical work:

> Pedagogy does not refer to just any encounter, but an encounter that is always already defined by hierarchical structures that position one as the one that influences and the other as the one to be influenced, even as contextual factors may shift who inhabits one position or the other. Any definition of pedagogy must begin with the intention of one subject to influence the life of another—to "push against," in a manner of speaking, another's subjectivity. (2014, 56)

In helping young people come to know Shakespeare, these texts are "relational" as well as "intentional." Through the practice of textual and visual adaptation, the adaptors imagine and enact how they might bridge the world of Shakespeare and the world of contemporary teenagers. That bridge conveys the knowledge they envisage those teenagers needing. Gaztambide-Fernández and Arráize-Matute stress the "desires" of human agents behind texts and places and distinguish between "pedagogy" and "curriculum," arguing that, "while one can certainly learn from viewing a film, it is not the film—in and of itself—that teaches" (2014, 57). However, this misses something, I think. In the interview material, it was easy to discern moments where the artists/adapters were interpreting the play themselves and then working these interpretations out pedagogically as objective truths. Their own learning about Shakespeare (either old or new) therefore found its way into the text as a form of teaching. This wasn't rationally intended in the way that Gaztambide-Fernández and Arráize-Matute would argue. The comics medium (like all media) also has its own rules, and these inevitably altered the pedagogic possibilities of the text. It is these *unintended* pedagogies that I wish to focus on now, some of which the adaptors were aware of at the time and some which were reflected on in hindsight.

Comic Book Shakespeare: Pedagogical Losses

The first casualty identified by adaptors was Shakespeare's poetic language. Clearly, this is lost in versions where the text has been modernized. But even in those that use Shakespeare's own text, the very fact of redacting the text into speech bubbles seemed to do away with the poetry, as John suggested:

> I suppose the chief loss is you lose the sense of the driving force of all Shakespeare's plays, which is iambic pentameter. And you lose the extraordinary vitality of the imagery, of the way the language is fluid and the internal jokes, all that Shakespeare stuff, you know. All that texture. And especially in a rhyming play. Although a few rhymes were kept, obviously. You lose that sense of its poetry.

Arguably, this poetry is an important aspect of teaching a Shakespeare play and, given that most of Shakespeare's plots were derived from other sources, the language is ultimately what makes Shakespeare "Shakespeare." The pleasure that might come from experiencing the words and complex imagery begins to disappear in these versions. One of the artists, who had done some acting in her past, told me that "you lose the rhythm of it, and that made me very sad." While the artists were skilled at bringing out the comic lines, using a variety of strategies for making things explicit or letting the reader know that something was intended to make them laugh (for example, using manga tropes such as *chibis* or background toning), there was some anxiety about the tragedies. John, the scholar, reflected in this way:

> I wonder if readers will read them as adventures and as stories rather than as tragedies. Yeah, I've always remembered something that someone pointed out which is at the end of a comedy in the theater, an audience that had been laughing all the way along, when the lights go up, they're very distant. They get up in their own little world, they've enjoyed it and they go home. Whereas after a really harrowing tragedy, the lights go up and there's a sense of collective solidarity in one's fellow humans sort of thing, which I think is very true actually.

This perhaps is more to do with an ethics of response—the supposed capacity of literature to alter individual subjectivity and to bring about solidarity. Is it possible that the comics medium cannot handle this gravitas, or was it simply not prioritized?

There was also a concern about the historically situated nature of some of the more controversial and racially sensitive stories, *The Merchant of Venice* and *Othello*. The challenges of fixing a visual representation of a character were particularly prominent for the Manga Shakespeare artists working on these texts, two plays not adapted by the other publishers perhaps for this

Figure 7.4. Representations of characters from Manga Shakespeare: *Othello* (left) and *Merchant of Venice* (right). Reproduced with permission of the publisher.

reason, though both are widely taught. Both artists responded by turning the world of Venice, the setting of both plays, into something quite fantastical (figure 7.4). In the case of *Merchant of Venice*, this became a world populated by elves. In *Othello*, which was adapted by a Japanese manga artist, a fairytale dream world was realized through the pictures: "So our Japanese friend certainly dealt with that in a bizarre way. He turned him [Othello] into an angel! And it breaks the stereotype, doesn't it? A pretty white angel too if I remember correctly ... [O]ne of the characters is a dog" (David).

Such decisions have pedagogical consequences, transforming knowledge in unanticipated ways because the images themselves act and have agency on readers that were not necessarily intended by the producers. John said:

> After all the plays are about the fact that Othello is Black and that Shylock is a Jew. Obviously, these are very sensitive and controversial subjects, but nevertheless they are facts of the plays. And if you make everyone a bit weird and abnormal, deviate from the norm that one expects, then perhaps the force is lost. So they become fantasies about malignancy as opposed to being focused on hate figures—the Jew, the Moor.

Clearly, what is gained and lost will, in the end, depend on the unforeseen pedagogies enacted around the texts themselves—how a teacher uses them, what status he or she gives them, and what a particular learner takes from the text and images.

PEDAGOGIES OF THE "IMAGE TEXT": SOME CONCLUDING THOUGHTS

It is clear that these texts are able to teach students certain things. They teach the teenage reader Shakespeare's plots, the themes and characters of the plays, and in some cases his language. They teach this *through the medium of comics*, and hence they also must teach (or the teacher must teach) the student *how to read* a comic book. In two of the cases that I've looked at, this is a particular tradition of comics—manga—with its own distinctive conventions. They also teach through what Gee has called "design" because they are multimodal and situate Shakespeare (and Shakespeare's language) in relationship to images and actions. In the case of radical visual adaptations, such as the Manga Shakespeare series, the texts are also multireferential and situate Shakespeare within other cultural symbols and genres that students may already be familiar with, such as science fiction, fantasy, anime, and so on. But do they also teach teenagers that Shakespeare wrote action-adventure stories rather than tragedies of human failure? Do they take away the poetry and linguistic richness of his work? Are they only teaching those aspects of Shakespeare, in fact, that can be easily measured by the apparatus of modern schooling and assessment?

Shakespeare's tragedies arguably rest on soliloquies—moments of inaction—for their psychological and thematic depth. When I spoke to David about the medium of the comic book, he told me: "The comic book—the graphic novel—doesn't like dwelling too long on the text. You've got to move on. It's got to move on at a particular pace. If you are sitting there for even one minute looking at this long speech going, 'Yeah, okay, so what's happening already? Come on!' That won't do." So what does an adaptor do then with long soliloquies (Hamlet's "To be or not to be" probably being the most extreme example)? While comics open the way for students to dwell on images, dwelling on the text may be more difficult. This presents a particular dilemma in the case of Shakespeare, as many of these soliloquies are ascribed with a cultural value and cannot be edited out (see Sabeti 2014 for an extended discussion of how "To be or not to be" was adapted in two comic book versions). Scott McCloud argues that most American and European comic books generally employ action-to-action transitions between panels, whereas Japanese manga tend to use aspect-to-aspect transitions (figure 7.5). The latter enables the reader to contemplate aspects of a particular scene, rather than being forced to move on in narrative action (McCloud 2004, 74–80). Aspect-to-aspect transitions can build atmosphere, both of place and feeling. They are able to convey profound emotions such as suffering, loss, distress, and horror. McCloud identifies the early work of Art Spiegelman as employing a broader range of transitions and techniques than many American comics, something Spiegelman went on to exploit in his explorations of trauma and grief in *Maus* (77). Indeed, Jeff Adams (2008) argues that Spiegelman's "pedagogic contribution" is—like W. G. Sebald and Keiji Nakazawa, two other artist/writers who employ what Adams calls the "pedagogy of the image text"—to inform future generations about social and historical catastrophes. Spiegelman does this in *Maus*, Adams writes, by pulling "the narrative out of the private sphere . . . Vladek's (Spiegelman's father who experienced the Holocaust) memory is made available through narration of his experiences, each packed with a specificity of events" (2008, 46).

Have the comic book artists I spoke to missed an opportunity to teach something more profound than plot, character, and the basics of theme? Given that comic books *are* able to convey tragedy and horror, is there a tendency to avoid doing so? Even when aspect-to-aspect transitions are

Figure 7.5. From *Understanding Comics* by Scott McCloud (2004, 74).

employed, as they are by many of the manga artists I spoke to, they are used
to engage readers in a scene or construct the fictional world of the adaptation.
Here is Nina speaking of her adaptation of *Twelfth Night* and the introduction of Count Orsino: "It's boring just having him walk into a scene . . . you
have to set it up. I think I was showing you a little bit of the garden to give the
reader a sense of being there. Then a little detail showing the car and stuff. I
think it all helps to build the world." Such techniques are employed to bring
a sense of immediacy and immersion in a fantasy world, not to bring about
empathy or feeling with a character's emotional predicament.

In an article discussing Art Spiegelman's graphic work *In the Shadow of No
Towers* (his coming to terms with the tragic events of 9/11 by "putting grief
into boxes"—Spiegelman's own phrase), Karen Espiritu (2006) cites Judith
Butler's remarks about the political potentials of "tarrying with grief," rather
than translating it into retaliatory action as the Bush administration did:

> Is there something to be gained in the political domain by maintain-
> ing grief as part of the framework within which we think our inter-
> national ties? If we stay with the sense of loss, are we left feeling only
> passive and powerless, as some might fear? Or are we, rather, returned
> to a sense of human vulnerability, to our collective responsibility for
> the physical lives of one another? (Butler 2004, 29–30)

As John identified, this feeling of collective loss and the human solidarity that
comes with it should be the outcome of watching a tragedy in the theater.
My meaning here is not to criticize or evaluate the work of the adaptors but
simply to note this as an interesting feature of the adaptations. It perhaps
tells us more about schooling, or the assumptions about schooling and what
is valued there, than it does about anything else. What is arguably missing is

the "ethical" dimension of pedagogy highlighted by Gaztambide-Fernández and Arráize-Matute, the desire to "push against" and "provoke a particular kind of change or a different kind of experience on another" (2014, 59). These adaptations might inform students, or explain Shakespeare's work, but can they shift their subjectivities in the way that the theatrical experience of a Shakespeare play may be able to do? Lisa Zunshine (2011), writing of Marvel's adaptation of Jane Austen's *Pride and Prejudice*, highlights another "loss" in school-oriented adaptations. She has noted that the Marvel version downplays the socio-cognitive complexity of the original text. It does so, she writes, by "dispensing with, or at least streamlining, the individual writing style of an author. After all, it is individual style that brings in complex mental states . . . This is, in effect, what study guides do, and this is, to some extent, what Marvel's *Pride and Prejudice* does" (2011, 126).

Zunshine, aware that the comics medium is perfectly capable of representing such states of mental complexity (she too references Spiegelman's work), puts this down (as I have suggested) to the demands of the "education" and "study guide" market, which tends to simplify texts. However, gaining insights into the processes of these particular adaptors has highlighted the care they took over their task, the intelligence they applied to it, and the responsibilities they felt in bridging the worlds of comic books and schools. The nuanced way in which they articulated both the gains and losses inherent in the adaptation process shows an understanding of their readers as a "public" that is more sophisticated and less cynical than Zunshine's analysis of Marvel might suggest.

Acknowledgments

I would like to thank all of the adaptors I spoke to during the course of my research. They were generous with their time and thoughtful in their comments. I am also grateful to the publishers of the editions for their permission to reproduce images, and particularly to Emma Hayley at SelfMadeHero for her support. My thanks go to the two anonymous reviewers of this chapter for their comments and insights, which have strengthened the argument and methodological reflection. Finally, I would like to acknowledge the financial support of the Carnegie Trust for the Universities of Scotland and the British Academy and Leverhulme Trust who have funded parts of this project.

References

Adams, Jeff. 2008. "The Pedagogy of the Image Text: Nakazawa, Sebald and Spiegelman Recount Social Traumas." *Discourse: Studies in the Cultural Politics of Education* 29 (1): 35–49.

Barker, Martin. 1989. *Comics: Ideology, Power and the Critics*. Manchester: Manchester University Press.

Beaty, Bart. 2005. *Fredric Wertham and the Critique of Mass Culture.* Jackson: University Press of Mississippi.

Butler, Judith. 2004. *Precarious Life: The Powers of Mourning and Violence.* London: Verso.

Cary, Stephen. 2004. *Going Graphic: Comics at Work in the Multilingual Classroom.* Portsmouth, NH: Heinemann.

Cavell, Stanley. 2003. *Disowning Knowledge in Seven Plays of Shakespeare.* Cambridge: Cambridge University Press.

Coles, Jane. 2004. "Much Ado about Nationhood and Culture: Shakespeare and the Search for an 'English' Identity." *Changing English: Studies in Culture and Education* 11 (1): 47–58.

Coles, Jane. 2013. "'Every Child's Birthright'? Democratic Entitlement and the Role of Canonical Literature in the English National Curriculum." *Curriculum Journal* 24 (1): 50–66.

Cunningham, Karen. 1998. "Shakespeare, the Public and Public Education." *Shakespeare Quarterly* 49 (3): 293–98.

Espiritu, Karen. 2006. "'Putting Grief into Boxes': Trauma and the Crisis of Democracy in Art Spiegelman's *In the Shadow of No Towers*." *Review of Education, Pedagogy, and Cultural Studies* 28 (2): 179–201.

Frey, Nancy, and Douglas Fisher, eds. 2008. *Teaching Visual Literacy: Using Comic Books, Graphic Novels, Anime, Cartoons and More to Develop Comprehension and Thinking Skills.* Thousand Oaks, CA: Corwin Press.

Gaztambide-Fernandéz, Rubén A., and Alexandra Arráiz Matute. 2014. "'Pushing Against': Relationality, Intentionality, and the Ethical Imperative of Pedagogy." In *Problematizing Public Pedagogy*, edited by Jake Burdick, Jennifer A. Sandlin, and Michael P. O'Malley, 52–64. London: Routledge.

Gibson, Rex. 1998. *Teaching Shakespeare: A Handbook for Teachers.* Cambridge: Cambridge University Press.

Giroux, Henry. 2000. "Public Pedagogy as Cultural Politics: Stuart Hall and the 'Crisis' of Culture." *Cultural Studies* 14 (2): 341–60.

Hayes, Elisabeth R., and James Paul Gee. 2010. "Public Pedagogy through Video Games: Design, Resources and Affinity Spaces." In *Handbook of Public Pedagogy: Education and Learning beyond Schooling*, edited by Jennifer A. Sandlin, Brian D. Schultz, and Jake Burdick, 185–93. New York: Routledge.

Ito, Mizuko, Sonja Baumer, Matteo Bittani, danah boyd, Rachel Cody, Becky Herr-Stephenson, Heather Horst, et al. 2010. *Hanging Out, Messing Around and Geeking Out: Kids Living and Learning with New Media.* Cambridge, MA: MIT Press.

Jacobs, Dale. 2013. *Graphic Encounters: Comics and the Sponsorship of Multimodal Literacy.* New York: Bloomsbury.

Kress, Gunther. 2005. "Gains and Losses: New Forms to Texts, Knowledge and Learning." *Computers and Composition* 22: 5–22.

Kress, Gunther, Carey Jewitt, Jill Bourne, Anton Franks, John Hardcastle, Ken Jones, Euan Reid. 2005. *English in Urban Classrooms: A Multimodal Perspective on Teaching and Learning.* Abingdon and New York: Routledge.

McCloud, Scott. 2004. *Understanding Comics: The Invisible Art.* New York: Harper Perennial.

New London Group. 1996. "A Pedagogy of Multiliteracies: Designing Social Futures." *Harvard Educational Review* 66 (1): 60–92.

Nussbaum, Martha. 2010. *Not for Profit: Why Democracy Needs the Humanities.* Princeton, NJ: Princeton University Press.

Nyberg, Amy Kiste. 1998. *Seal of Approval: The History of the Comics Code.* Jackson: University Press of Mississippi.

Pantaleo, Sylvia. 2011. "Grade 7 Students Reading Graphic Novels: 'You Need to Do a Lot of Thinking.'" *English in Education* 45 (2): 113–31.

Pantaleo, Sylvia. 2015. "Exploring the Intentionality of Design in the Graphic Narrative of One Middle-Years Student." *Journal of Graphic Novels and Comics* 6 (4): 398–418. doi:1 0.1080/21504857.2015.1060624.

Pumphrey, George H. 1954. *Comics and Your Children.* London: Comics Campaign Council.

Pumphrey, George H. 1955. *Children's Comics: A Guide for Parents and Teachers.* London: The Epworth Press.

Pumphrey, George H. 1964. *What Children Think of Their Comics.* London: The Epworth Press.

Rubenstein, Anne. 1998. *Bad Language, Naked Ladies, and Other Threats to the Nation: A Political History of Comic Books in Mexico.* Durham, NC: Duke University Press.

Sabeti, Shari. 2014. "The 'Strange Alteration' of Hamlet: Comic Books, Adaptation and Constructions of Adolescent Literacy." *Changing English: Studies in Culture and Education* 21 (2): 182–97.

Sandlin, Jennifer A., Brian D. Schultz, and Jake Burdick, eds. 2010. *Handbook of Public Pedagogy: Education and Learning beyond Schooling.* New York: Routledge.

Sandlin, Jennifer A., Michael P. O'Malley, and Jake Burdick. 2011. "Mapping the Complexity of Public Pedagogy Scholarship: 1894–2010." *Review of Educational Research* 81: 338–39.

Schwarz, Gretchen E. 2002. "Graphic Novels for Multiple Literacies." *Journal of Adolescent and Adult Literacy* 46 (3): 262–65.

Tabachnik, Stephen E. 2010. "The Graphic Novel and the Age of Transition: A Survey and Analysis." *English Literature in Transition* 53: 3–28.

Ward, Sophie C., and Roy Connolly. 2008. "Let Them Eat Shakespeare: Prescribed Authors and the National Curriculum." *Curriculum Journal* 19 (4): 293–307.

Wertham, Fredric. 1954. *The Seduction of the Innocent.* New York: Rinehart.

Zunshine, Lisa. 2011. "What to Expect When You Pick Up a Graphic Novel." *SubStance: A Review of Theory and Literary Criticism* 40 (1): 114–43.

8.

Learning to "Speak without Shame"

A FEMINIST RESPONSE TO GENDERED VIOLENCE IN *PRIYA'S SHAKTI*

Valerie Wieskamp

The multimedia comic book *Priya's Shakti* features a tiger-riding heroine. In the first chapter, when readers meet Priya, she is alone and in despair after a brutal gang rape. With some help from the Hindu goddess Parvati, Priya eventually overcomes her fears and learns to speak of her rape "without shame." Then she travels the lands astride a tiger to spread her message of hope and gender equality. According to the comic's producers, she becomes a superhero of a sort by helping to initiate conversations on sexual violence.

This compelling character is the response of a group of artists to a public tragedy in India. On December 16, 2012, a group of young men gang-raped twenty-three-year-old medical student Jyoti Singh Pandey, who later died as a result of her injuries. Though sexual violence in India and around the world is often cloaked in silence, the "Delhi bus rape" incited an abundance of public discourse (Roychowdhury 2013). From local protests in India to Western newsrooms, folks around the globe listened to and participated in conversations about the brutal attack (Simon-Kumar 2014).

Amidst this sweeping public outcry, Indian American documentarian Ram DeVineni recognized the need to intervene in the cultural norms that exacerbate gendered violence. In response, he created *Priya's Shakti* with a transnational team of artists, writers, producers, and gender-based violence experts. These creators felt the comics medium ideal for its ability to render a heavy topic more accessible, especially for preteens just beginning to learn about sexuality and gender roles (Martinez 2014). Through this accessible narrative, the graphic novel exposes the gender discrimination Priya confronts throughout her life, her encounter with sexual violence, and the social shame and rejections she experiences after her rape.

Priya's Shakti represents an important case study for exploring comics' impact upon public culture. It marks a discourse distinct from mainstream responses to the Delhi bus rape both within India and around the world. Through a rhetorical analysis of *Priya's Shakti (Chapter 1)*, I argue that the comic book models important feminist and postcolonial interventions in rape culture and represents new publics that dominant discourses have excluded. The creators of *Priya's Shakti* aim to change perceptions of sexual violence in particular and gender relations in general. By foregrounding the cultural dynamics at the root of gender-based violence, the comic initiates an essential strategy that, according to feminist activists and scholars, is essential for combatting rape culture. Even as the international public depicts sexual violence as a consequence of Indian culture, the internationally circulated comic book utilizes Indian cultural traditions as a resource for social change across the globe. Though produced by Indian Americans, the comic reverses the neocolonial tendency to privilege Western-centered responses to social issues by showcasing elements of Indian heritage as a solution to the problem of rape culture. Finally, *Priya's Shakti* begins to address publics excluded from both international and Indian discourses by representing rural, lower-class, and disadvantaged women, thus proliferating a variety of voices.

INTERVENTIONS IN INDIAN PUBLIC CULTURE

Priya's Shakti (Chapter 1) initiates a discourse that counters dominant discussions about sexual violence in India, which have emphasized punitive measures and victim-blaming. In the wake of the Delhi bus incident, protestors blamed the Indian government for its failure to adequately prevent and prosecute rape (Simon-Kumar 2014). Through these protests, the state was imagined "as a sovereign entity capable of enacting top-down change" (Kapur 2014, 9). In alignment with this authoritarian imaginary, public demands emphasized punitive measures such as "the death penalty, chemical castration, and death by stoning" (Dutta and Sircar 2013, 295). The Indian government responded in kind, introducing a host of new legislation and security measures that included harsher punishment for rapists. The new legislation focused exclusively upon punishing attackers, ignoring the Indian women's movement's recommendations to address the cultural factors contributing to gender-based violence (Dutta and Sircar 2013, 301). Despite the legislative changes made in India after the attack, according to Indrani Bagchi (2014, 147), "insensitivity regarding rape survivors continues." Conservative voices within India called for restrictions on women's mobility and circulated victim-blaming discourses. Phadke, Ranade, and Khan (2013, 41) assert "the policing of girls and women of all ages . . . has acquired an unprecedented justification" in the aftermath of the Delhi bus rape. Such responses reflect a worldwide pattern. Too often, gender-based violence is blamed on women and used to justify both restrictions on women's mobility and increased government intervention.

Left out of these discourses are resources to shift the gendered norms that exacerbate rape culture not only in India but also around the world. Indian feminists have argued the necessity of articulating women's rights in a "language that moved beyond women's protection and toward freedom of movement" (Amrute 2015, 331). Dutta and Sircar (2013) contend that laws that strengthen state power and discipline women's sexuality do not sufficiently counter rape culture. Scholars of gendered violence in various contexts similarly argue that culturally constructed gender norms, especially those that position women as weaker and more vulnerable than men, exacerbate rape culture (Barnett 2008; Murnen, Wright, and Kaluzny 2002; O'Toole, Schiffman, and Edwards 2007). According to these feminist activists and researchers, neither punitive measures against attackers nor the containment of women successfully addresses rape culture at its roots. Instead, they call for cultural responses that address gender inequality and stigma.

Heeding this call, a team of creators worked together to produce *Priya's Shakti*. Inspiration for the comic came from Ram Devineni, an Indian-born documentarian who had been living in New York City and working as a bank technologist at Citibank (Mahajan 2014). By chance, Devineni was visiting India when the 2012 Delhi bus rape occurred. While attending protests after the incident, he spoke to a police officer about the attack. "Basically the officer's response," he recalls in an interview, "was that 'no good girl walks home at night,' implying that she probably deserved it, or at least provoked the attack" (Rehman 2015). Devineni then recalls realizing that "the problem of sexual violence in India was not a legal issue; rather it was a cultural problem. A cultural shift had to happen . . . Deep-rooted patriarchal views needed to be challenged." He spent a year traveling through India and Southeast Asia, "learning from poets, philosophers, activists, and sociologists working for NGOs focused on gender-based violence" and talking to rape survivors (Rehman 2015). Over the course of his travels, Devineni began to understand that the lack of social support created a major barrier in addressing the problem. He determined that stricter laws would be useless if social stigma continued to prevent sexual violence survivors from reporting. After receiving a layoff notice and a severance package from Citibank in October of 2013, he decided to use the severance to fund a creative response to the problem (Mahajan 2015).

Devineni had a funding source and the desire to tell a story about gendered violence but was not yet set on a form. He created a short film cut from old 1970s Bollywood films and headed to New York for a meet-up gathering for those interested in cross-platform storytelling (Mahajan 2015). There, he met Ignatz and Eisner Award–nominated illustrator Dan Goldman. With an interest in using art for activist purposes, a profound respect for Indian and Hindu culture, and expertise in multimedia comics, Goldman was eager to work with Devineni (Schlaikjer 2015). It was Goldman who ultimately recommended that Devineni develop his project into a comic book. Devineni also partnered with Vikas K. Menon to coauthor the story. Menon is a poet, playwright, and songwriter, as well as a board member of Kundiman, an organization dedicated to supporting Asian American literature (Kundiman). In what they describe as a highly collaborative process, Devineni and Menon spent a year developing the storyline before sharing it with Goldman to illustrate (Salian 2015).

To ensure that the comic book would serve the interest of those affected by sexual assault and to overcome the challenge of having men write and illustrate a comic about a woman's encounter with sexual violence, they consulted with several women and organizations experienced in addressing sexual assault in South Asia (Red Elephant Foundation 2016). Though Priya is a fictional character, the story Menon and Devineni wrote together is based on the experiences of real survivors of sexual violence Devineni had previously interviewed in India (Mullin 2015). Additionally, Devineni and Menon sought the help of women from India with expertise in working with gendered violence on a transnational level: Shikha Bhatnagar, who has worked on behalf of underserved communities in both India and the United States (Bhatnagar 2013), acted as their gender-based violence advisor, and Lina Srivastava worked as their transmedia producer and impact strategist. Srivastava worked as an attorney before founding a social innovation strategy group in New York. She is experienced in working with worldwide social justice organizations, in developing projects that use narrative and cultural expression to address social issues, and in addressing the issue of gendered violence (Srivastava n.d.). To develop community outreach and engagement, the creators partnered with one of India's leading NGOs, Aapne Aap Women Worldwide, a grassroots organization that empowers women and girls to end sex trafficking (*Sutra Journal* 2015). After the release of the first chapter, the

Priya team worked with Mumbai-based filmmaker Paromita Vohra—famous for her Bollywood films—to publish a second chapter that addresses acid attacks against women (Shah 2015). These creators share a commitment to social justice, expertise in leveraging art for social change, and a cultural background from or appreciation for South Asia.

Priya's Shakti begins with rape survivor Priya's appeal for help from Parvati—a Hindu goddess known as the embodiment of creative force (Kingsley 1988). The comic is illustrated with vibrant iconography of Hinduism, the dominant religion of India, and a comic illustration style that relies on realism, an approach that is the specialty of illustrator Dan Goldman (Mullin 2015). In an eight-panel sequence, the story of Priya's assault is told efficiently, with minimal text and imagery. Ensuring that the comic book remained appropriate for young people, Goldman aimed to depict the sexual violence as "scary and awful" but not "graphic" (Seervai 2014). Readers see an ominous group of men following Priya as she walks home, we see Priya's attempt to run thwarted as one of the men throws a stone at her head, and finally we see Priya frightened, lying on the ground as men's hands grab her and tear her clothes. The final frame depicts Priya leaning against a post outside her family farm, accompanied by the thought bubble, "What will I tell my family?" Priya's concern, unfortunately, is warranted. Her family shames her and banishes her. Upon witnessing Priya's suffering, Parvati incarnates into Priya. With bright green tears streaming down her cheeks—indicating Parvati's habitation of Priya's body—she appeals for justice both to local government and one of the attackers. When the attacker, who had known Priya from school, begins to assault Priya/Parvati again, the goddess becomes angry. She reveals herself to the attacker, cursing the frightened man. This turmoil awakens Parvati's husband, Lord Shiva—a central god in Hinduism known for "effecting periodic destruction of the universe" (Dimmitt and Buitenen 1978, 148). Enraged and wreaking havoc on his mountain home, Shiva calls an assembly of Hindu gods. There, his face contorted in anger, Shiva decrees that humans "will no longer be able to procreate." Shiva's command polices the sexuality of both men and women, resembling government and conservative voices that called for stricter punishment of offenders and restrictions in women's mobility in response to gender-based violence.

Parvati challenges Shiva's patriarchal intervention, offering a distinct counter to punitive measures to address sexual violence. While Shiva's response mirrors the Indian government's aforementioned legislative intervention, Parvati's response mirrors feminist discourse that iterates the social ills of patriarchal hierarchy. Shiva approaches the problem with anger, looking upon the world with his arms rigidly folded, inciting authoritarian measures.

Parvati, in contrast, examines the issue with empathy and understanding. Priya looks upon the saddened and panicked people of the earth, observes the chaos, and asserts that Shiva "doesn't realize that rape is an act of violence and domination." She concludes that rape "cannot truly be opposed with more of the same!" Indeed, Shiva's destructive decree results in additional violence, causing a "great war across all the worlds." Such authoritarian action is also a form of traditional masculinist power. By relying exclusively on punitive strategies, states imply that violence is inevitable and overlook cultural interventions. Shiva's proclamation follows this pattern. Through his all-encompassing punishment, he imagines sexual violence as endemic to humankind. As with so many nation states, Shiva, too, fails to notice opportunities for education and cultural change.

Parvati's response, in contrast, demonstrates a commitment to egalitarian and culturally empowering modes of addressing sexual violence. Realizing that outside forces are necessary to shake Shiva's resolve, Parvati transforms into the warrior goddess, Kali. In Hindu scripture, Kali often represents Parvati's fierceness and is nearly always shown as the dominant figure in interactions with Shiva (Kingsley 1988). True to form, the comic depicts her dancing wildly above Shiva. Her twelve arms raised, her tongue characteristically lolling, and face enlivened by the goddess's typical vigor, Kali calls upon him to stop the war. "Transfixed by the great goddess' energy," Shiva agrees on a pardon. This, again, is typical of Kali, known for wielding her very strangeness to shake naïve assumptions and allow fresh perceptions of the world to restore balance in the universe (Kingsley 1988). Notably, she does not meet Shiva's warlike stance and domination with "more of the same." Rather than coercing him with her wrath, she persuades him to change through her "energy." Continuing the note of egalitarianism, a compromise is made once Kali transforms back into Parvati. The goddess leans calmly over Shiva, who is recumbent against a mountainside. The pair agrees that if Parvati demonstrates to him that humans are capable of change, Shiva will rescind his decision.

Countering discourse that represents women as weak and endangered, *Priya's Shakti* emphasizes feminine strength and empowerment. Feminist scholarship on rape culture reveals the importance of such a strategy. Measures toward gender equality that empower women are essential in combatting the cultural influences that exacerbate rape culture (Hall 2004; Heberle 1996). In Indian cosmology, "Shakti" is a source of feminine primordial energy, a creative power through which all existence evolves (Jamuna 2010). Befitting its title, the comic's narrative develops through Priya's empowerment. According to the creators of *Priya's Shakti*, rather than focusing on perpetrators or punitive action, the comic book is about "a woman honing her own voice" in order to challenge oppression (Srivastava 2014). Parvati proves to Shiva that humans may change by empowering Priya to overcome her fears so she may advocate for social change.

The goddess returns to Priya, who, after having been rejected from her family home, had been living in the jungle. Her arm outstretched in a comforting welcome, Parvati now appeals to her devotee for help, positioning the common rural woman as the superhero of the comic. Parvati provides Priya with the mantra, "Speak without shame and stand by me, bring about the change we want to see." After conquering her fear, Priya returns to her village and gathers a "force of allies through love, song, and connection." Her bravery convinces Shiva that humans possess the capacity to change. She travels through India, calling upon people to better support survivors of sexual violence and to change their perceptions of gender by treating women with respect, by educating children of different genders equally, and by speaking out against the mistreatment of women. The method of addressing sexual violence inspired by Parvati models feminist ideals of collective empowerment.

INTERVENTIONS IN INTERNATIONAL PUBLIC CULTURE

Internationally, discourses about sexual violence in response to the Delhi bus rape tended to exhibit a neocolonial mindset that blamed sexual violence on India itself, overlooking how similar perceptions of gender exacerbate sexual violence globally. Such imperialist representations have recurred throughout history. Gayatri Chakravorty Spivak (1988, 296) critiques the neocolonial collective fantasy that Western intervention is necessary to rescue "brown women from brown men." Through this fantasy, the protection of women signifies the establishment of a "*good* society," and a nation's inability to protect its women is depicted as demonstrative of inferiority. In such discourses, developing nations must adopt Western cultural ways to progress toward modernity and solve social ills. This pattern appears in international reporting of the Delhi incident. Kapur (2014, 10) asserts that "some of the Western press implicitly claimed a position of cultural superiority by representing Indian men as more prone to rape" and by "representing Indian society as more violent, aggressive, and hence primitive." Dutta and Sircar similarly describe global media as "recreating the colonial imagery of premodern victimhood" (2013, 295). Amrute (2015, 331) observes that international press accounts emphasized "India's 'rape culture,' explaining the attack in terms of prevailing cultural attitudes toward women ... police collusion in rape, and cultures of shame that blame women for their own violation." Though Western news sources present rape culture as unique to India, victim-blaming and problematic gender roles appear to varying degrees around the world.

The creators of *Priya's Shakti* address sexual violence in ways markedly distinct from the imperialist mindset found in Western discourse. Though it has been produced by individuals living in the United States and, thus, could *seem* to be a neocolonialist intervention, this comic differs from such discourse. The creators of *Priya's Shakti* explicitly draw from iconography and narratives central to Indian culture for the solution to the problem. This counters Western-centered interventions that imagine non-Western cultures as the *cause* of the problem rather than a potential *cure*. Through the comic book, the answer to sexual violence is found within Hindu culture and within common Indian people themselves. Mehta and Mukherji (2015, 3) assert that comics may serve as effective postcolonial texts by placing local signs within the global public sphere so that they may no longer be perceived as "obsolete authenticities." Rather than introducing Western solutions in response to the problem, the comic book utilizes Indian culture to change public discourse about sexual violence. Indian culture, in this way, may no longer be perceived as the antiquated root of sexual assault, but a resource for better addressing gendered violence.

The creators emphasized tropes and styles unique to Indian culture, drawing from a rich public tradition of Indian comics. Both Devineni and Goldman cite Anant Pai's *Amar Chitra Katha* (*ACK*) series, which depicted stories from Hindu mythology in comic book form, as inspiration for the mythological aspects of *Priya's Shakti* (Dasi 2015). Devineni recalled from his childhood in India: "I remember reading these mythological comic books," he states in an interview, "They were read by every kid. It was the way I learned about Hinduism" (Mullin 2015). This series has been a cultural and educational phenomenon in India since its inception in the late 1960s (Stoll 2014). McLain (2009) notes that the *ACK* comics played an important and sometimes problematic role in establishing national identity as India was developing as a newly independent nation after British colonial rule.

The creators have situated Priya within matriarchal traditions of Hinduism, thus depicting Indian heritage, not as warranting replacement by Western cultural ways, but as a potential solution. Impact strategist Lina Srivastava (2014) explains the use of Hindu mythology as a source of empowerment: "Our narrative dives into the matriarchal origins of Hinduism from millennia ago, mining that narrative to understand that Hinduism and Hindu-based cultures which affect millions of people does not support the subordination of either women or men and does not need to be interpreted as such." These traditions, the comic's website reads, "have been displaced in modern representations of Hindu culture." Indeed, Jamuna (2010) observes that women in ancient India held higher status in the public imagination. Bose (2000) also notes the appreciation for women's religious and intellectual activities in early Indian history.

The return to India's feminine-positive tradition appears directly in the comic's text through references to empowered goddesses and women activists in India's history. As Parvati contemplates an alternative to Shiva's punitive solution, she says, "Humans must learn *again* that the divine lies within women and men equally." That gender equity must be learned "again," situates the resources to combat sexual violence as already within Indian culture. Additionally, the comic features empowered Hindu goddesses, such as Parvati and Kali. The story also alludes to the goddess Durga, who was a central figure in Tantric practices of Hinduism—a tradition that featured goddess worship (Khanna 2000). Durga rode a tiger and created a collective of sisters to assist her in fighting demons. Priya represents the goddess Durga. Riding a tiger and singing her mantra throughout her own and other villages, she amasses followers to help spread her message of women's empowerment. To help Priya find courage, Parvati recalls for her other women of India's recent past who advocated for social change: "Like Savitri [a Hindu goddess] who outwitted death. Like the women who helped India gain independence, and continue to vote their conscience, and the women who have taken on the struggle." Accompanying panels depict the goddess Savitri, urban women supporting Mahatma Gandhi in the fight for Indian independence, women voting, and women in the countryside dressed in the pink saris characteristic of the Gulabi Gang, who fight against gendered violence in rural India. In this way, Priya is included within an impressive lineage of empowered Indian women.

In contrast to neocolonialist discourses—in which Western nations aim to "rescue" those in developing nations while ignoring similar problems at home—*Priya's Shakti* reaches toward a global public. *Priya's* creators describe the comic book as decidedly global. The impact strategist for the project, Lina Srivastava, explains in an interview that "as a feminist and a person of Indian origin" it was important to her that the project did not contribute to the narrative that "India has a rape problem." The goal, Srivastava says, is to reach young people in "India, the US and worldwide" (Jenkins 2016). Elsewhere, she writes that the producers aimed to "encompass both the specificity of the situation in India, as well as make a sweeping critique of the structures that buttress gender-based violence everywhere" (Srivastava 2014). Similarly, the visual artist Dan Goldman has stated, "We know rape is a problem in India, but it is not an Indian problem, so the idea was to create a movement that is not only about India but comes from India to the rest of the world" (Shah 2015). *Priya's Shakti*, thus, differs from neocolonialist discourses. It defies imperialist patterns in which white men rescue brown women. Accordingly, at present, the comic book is available in Hindi, English, Portuguese, Italian, and Spanish.

ADDRESSING ALTERNATIVE PUBLICS

Discourses attempting to publicly address sexual violence often focus upon those who fit the mold of ideal womanhood. Public response to the Delhi bus rape followed this pattern. Dutta and Sircar (2013) detail numerous rapes that were not granted significant public consideration compared to the Pandey case, asserting that class filters which rapes receive mass outcry. According to Rao (2014), television outlets in India narrowly limit coverage of sexual violence to attacks against middle-class and upper-caste women in urban areas.[1] Western discourse exhibits similar exclusionary filters. Roychowdhury (2013) asserts that the Western media emphasized Pandey's upward mobility, framing her as an emblem of the modern Indian woman. That she was a successful medical student returning from watching a movie when attacked rendered her more relatable to Western audiences. Discourses both within India and around the world emphasize modern, upper-class/caste women.

The creators of *Priya's Shakti* instead focus on common women. Srivastava (2014), the comic's transmedia producer, describes Priya as both an "everywoman and a superhero." She explains that this was an intentional departure from dominant discourse: "Priya is not docile, light-skinned, hyper-sexualized or objectified in the way mainstream Indian or global media often presents women." Priya hails from rural India, where women suffer the most from gendered violence (Richards 2016). Priya had to forgo education to work on the family farm, where she and her family reside in a modest wooden hut with a thatched roof. Priya represents the poor and rural rape victims glaringly absent from dominant public discourse.

The creators of *Priya's Shakti* highlight the capacity for strength and empowerment in everyday people by positioning Priya, rather than Parvati, as the ultimate hero of the story. Devineni notes that despite the story's divine intervention, ultimately it is "up to Priya, the rape survivor to motivate and challenge people. The Gods get involved, but she's the real agent of change in the story" (Mullin 2015). This aim appears readily throughout the book. While in the jungle, shortly before being approached by Parvati, Priya encounters a tiger and, terrified, climbs a tree for shelter. After conquering her fears through the mantra she receives from Parvati, she descends from the tree and approaches the animal, gradually realizing that the tiger is her "Shakti," or divine cosmic energy. She then mounts the tiger and proudly returns to the village that shunned her, singing her mantra along the way. The allusion to Durga in this scene illustrates the sense of divine within Priya. This is a common feature in the matriarchal tradition of Tantric Hinduism, in which all women "irrespective of their caste, creed, age, status, or personal accomplishment" are regarded as the physical of incarnation of the goddess's Shakti (Khanna 2000, 114). A panel in which Priya speaks to villagers from atop her tiger emphasizes this Tantric sense of power. Priya's speech balloons read, "I am not divine, no more than you. But all of us are part of the divine." She then travels the lands joyfully singing her mantra, inspiring a diverse collective of voices to join her cause.

In addition to the book itself, the creators used new media to incorporate stories of real sexual-assault survivors and reach an expanded public. The final pages feature four illustrations of women of diverse backgrounds alongside the words: "Survivors of gender-based violence tell their true stories." Readers may interact with the text by scanning the images with an "augmented reality" application from Blippar. Having just opened an office in Delhi in 2013 and having an interest in social sector work, Blippar was the perfect partner for the new media component of the comic (Mahajan 2015). The app connects readers to video clips of the stories of survivors of sexual violence who, like Priya, have joined the fight for justice despite their struggles. Each video features an audio track of a rape survivor narrating her own experience, in her own language, without shame. To ensure the anonymity of each survivor—an important safety measure—the videos contain a stylized comic illustration of the woman. Accompanying speech balloons caption the woman's experiences in various languages, allowing a diverse viewership to connect to the story. The abstracted illustrations allow survivors to remain anonymous, while the use of survivors' voices contributes a simultaneous sense of authenticity.

The videos augment Priya's message that cultural change is necessary and further highlight institutional barriers and stigma faced by sexual violence survivors. At the time this essay was written, two of the stories had been completed. The first video highlights both caste bias and the failures of India's criminal justice system in responding to matters of gender-based violence. The narrator describes being raped and brutally beaten by her attackers, who instructed her to "keep quiet, or we will kill you and your lower caste family." This story not only grants voice to lower-caste and rural publics typically excluded from mainstream discourse, but also reveals that some individuals may be targeted *because of* their class. The young woman's story also illuminates the resistance survivors face from law enforcement. When police reluctantly visited her home to investigate, they concluded that her injuries appeared to be from a "normal domestic fight." Instead of taking her statement, they scolded her and refused to investigate the case, even though her injuries were so severe that she was bedridden for an entire month.

By scanning the illustration in the lower right corner, viewers access a similar story that highlights issues of impunity and the cultural barriers in reporting sexual violence. While walking to her grandmother's home, this young woman was kidnapped by a group of boys, taken to an "isolated place," and raped. The boys sedated her and made a video of the rape with which to blackmail her. Unlike the rural migrant attackers in the Pandey case, these boys were politically connected and considered themselves "untouchable by the law." Though the woman in the video initially remained silent, she decided to speak out after another girl was raped the following week. After filing a report, she and her family received death threats, and the village threatened to banish them. Though India and the world demanded the punishment of Pandey's attackers, this young woman faced social repercussions for reporting.

Both videos highlight the survivors' Shakti, providing viewers with real-life models of Priya's message to "bring about the change we want to see." The comic illustrations of these survivors emphasize this by positioning them in visual alignment with Priya. It is also apparent in the words of the survivors themselves. The young woman in the first video assertively states that she intends to "fight the battle for justice." For her, justice means that "culprits should be punished & boys educated about gender issues." By emphasizing educational interventions, this story invites cultural responses to gender-based violence. Similarly, in the second video, the woman explains that she intends to help fellow survivors of sexual violence. She states that when she meets other survivors, she tries to support and inspire them: "I tell them that I too am a survivor, and you need courage. I am also fighting." As the video concludes, she explains that she presently volunteers and hopes to eventually found an NGO to help more survivors of gendered violence.

These real-life, illustrated stories supplement the message of empowerment and cultural intervention initiated by the comic book and help circulate Priya's message on social media. At the end of the videos as well as the end of the comic book itself, viewers are asked to "#StandWithPriya" by using the

Blippar app to photograph themselves with the heroine and post it to social media channels. Between Twitter and Instagram, this hashtag has been used over a thousand times. Priya's Shakti has over 11,000 likes on Facebook and over 1,400 Twitter followers as of this writing. As did Durga in fighting the demon, Priya has created a collective of supporters through social media to help her bring about change.

RECEPTION

The comic book reached out to a worldwide public. *Priya's Shakti (Chapter 1)* "achieved viral status" even before it was "officially launched" (Biswas 2014). The book is freely available in every digital format—as a PDF from the comic's website or through platforms such as Apple's iBooks, comiXology, BitTorrent, and Amazon, among others. As of August 2015, the comic had been downloaded over 560,000 times. The website received over 999,000 visits in December 2014—the first month the comic was launched—and received over 3,927,000 visits from January to August of 2015 (Devineni, pers. comm.). This consumption has been on a global level. Fifty percent of the PDFs of the comic book downloads have been from outside of India, with a large number being downloaded in Brazil (*"Priya's Shakti:* The Magical Comic Book" 2015).

The comic has been well received by the media and global organizations.[2] *Priya's Shakti (Chapter 1)* was featured in over 400 news stories around the world and in every major news publication within India (India.com 2015). Over 250 news outlets have reached out to Ram Devineni for interviews (Mullin 2015). English-language news sources in India and South Asia have described the comic as an "innovative" and "groundbreaking" book with a "global impact" (Ansar 2014; Mehta 2015; Salian 2015). News sources from outside India have described the book as an "innovative" approach to break the "Rape-Talk Taboo" (Bhalla 2014; Chowdhury 2014). The United Nations has honored the book's heroine, Priya, as a "Gender Equality Champion," commending the book for contributing to the national debate about sexual violence in India and also citing the comic as a "global phenomenon" (UN Women). Of the comic, Oisika Chakrabarti, UN Women senior communications and media specialist, says: "To deliberately flip the usual narrative and show a survivor of sexual violence as a superhero is commendable" (Goldberg 2015). The creators also received a prestigious grant from the Tribeca Film Institute's New Media Fund, which supports social impact projects that integrate media platforms (Tribeca Film Institute n.d.).

The creators of the comic book have increased the reach of Priya by circulating her tale in myriad formats. They have commissioned street artists to paint murals with imagery from the book around Delhi and Mumbai, which have inspired conversations about "female power and strength" (Rao 2015). Viewers can scan these images with their smart phones to reveal additional animations and stories from the comic (Al Jazeera 2014). Though the technology necessary to download the comic book and interact with images through Blippar certainly excludes those across the digital divide, the producers are also circulating other "low-tech" forms. They are working with Aapne Aap Women Worldwide to bring the printed comic to communities and schools as an educational tool (Pandey 2014). In partnership with Aapne Aap, the creators launched an Indiegogo crowdfunding project that achieved its fundraising goal in just five days. The donations were used to print 30,000 copies of the comics. As Aapne estimates that each copy will be read by three to five children, this greatly furthers Priya's reach (Buchanan 2015). Devineni has developed comic book writing workshops to help children strengthen their voices. World Bank's WEvolve program has also stepped in to support circulation of the comic in schools and communities (World Bank 2015). Additionally, Priya has circulated worldwide through exhibits. In the summer of 2015, an interactive exhibit of the comic book was installed in New York's City Lore Gallery. Following the exhibition in New York the comic will be presented in such locations as Italy, Spain, London, and Dubai (Reuters 2014).

Though the comic's scope is certainly an important step in proliferating the empowerment of girls and women, there are some gaps. *Priya's Shakti* relies upon Hindu goddesses and gods. According to Devineni, "The comic book doesn't preach or go into Hinduism at all, it's really more about the mythological stories" (Mullin 2015). The Hindu icons embedded in the book thus serve as metaphors to advance a story. Still, the iconography used throughout the book may exclude adherents of non-Hindu religions. In addition, with the emphasis on the heterosexual love between Shiva and Parvati, queer sexual orientations are left out of the story—an issue that has gone thus far without comment from the creators. Since 2015, the creators have created additional chapters but have yet to engage with these issues.

CONCLUSION

The creators of *Priya's Shakti (Chapter 1)* produced a strong counter to discourses that developed in response to the Delhi bus rape. The comic book exhibits its pedagogical salience by establishing survivor Priya as an easily identifiable role model with an accessible message of gender equity. The book also presents an important postcolonial intervention by rejecting Euro-American master narratives of ideal civil society. It also avoids focusing on prosecution and punishment as the means to address the problem, focusing instead on educational and cultural modifications rooted in Indian culture. The creators of the comic position Hindu iconography and Indian cultural traditions as a global vehicle for addressing gender-based violence, thus recognizing the reality that the solution to sexual assault cannot simply be found through modernization. The representations of rural, lower-caste, and disadvantaged women featured differ drastically from the emphasis on idealized victims found in dominant discourse.

Though comics in India have arguably been historically oriented towards male audiences, this trend has been shifting (Jamuna 2010). *Priya's Shakti* is part of a growing body of feminist comic art that counters rape culture and dominant patriarchal narratives in this comics world. The book *Drawing the Line: Indian Women Fight Back*, published in 2014, is based on themes and illustrations created during a comic book workshop. It addresses themes of rape reporting, arranged marriages, and female solidarity (Kuriyan, Bertonasco, and Bartscht 2015). Amruta Patil created one of India's first graphic novels, *Kari*, about a queer young woman in love, and explores feminist identity politics in her adaptation of the *Mahabharata* beginning with *Adi Parva* (Mukherji 2015). In other nations, several comic strips tackle issues related to rape culture: Kate Leth, the Canadian artist of *Kate or Die!*, illustrated a comic strip in which the protagonist has a heated discussion about rape culture with an anonymous disbelieving man (2012); to intervene in the stigma around women's bodies and sexuality, Japanese artist Megumi Igarashi created a comic book memoir depicting her experience of being arrested for obscenity for creating art sculpted in the image of her own vagina (Rokudenashiko 2016); and American artist Alli Kirkham (n.d.) has illustrated several comics dealing with issues of sexual violence and consent. *Priya*, however, has become the first book to develop an iconic superhero to battle gendered violence.

Priya's Shakti is an example of how comics worlds overlap and address the realm of political public life. It arose from a specific public problem, responding to the smoldering discourse about sexual violence in India surrounding the infamous bus rape. The creators conditioned it on women's lived experiences, as the narrative draws from and even includes Devineni's interviews with rape survivors. Priya's team of creators has since worked with public advocacy organizations like Aapne Aap Women Worldwide to bring the comic book into schools, and the heroine has even received accolades from the United Nations. Through museum installations, workshops, murals, and online videos, comic superheroine Priya and her message of gender equality fluidly move beyond the printed pages of the comic book and show how comics worlds influence and exist within larger publics.

Notes

1. The caste system in India is a hierarchy in which people are divided into rigid social groups.

2. Due to the difficulty in tracking the use of a text that has been downloaded from the internet on a global scale, the majority of my sources for measuring the comics reception in this paragraph rely upon institutional actors.

References

Al Jazeera. 2014. "Indian Comic Features Rape Survivor as Hero." The Stream, December 9. http://stream.aljazeera.com/story/201412081620-0024417.

Amrute, Sareeta. 2015. "Moving Rape: Trafficking in the Violence of Postliberalization." *Public Culture* 27 (2): 331–59.

Ansar, Humaira. 2014. "*Priya's Shakti*: A Comic on Rape That's More Than a Book." *Hindustan Times*, December 14. http://www.hindustantimes.com/books/priya-s-shakti-a-comic-on -rape-that-s-more-than-a-book/story-OwQ1KfGvRiHQmkzkzjYJqN.html.

Bagchi, Indrani. 2014. "The Struggle for Women's Empowerment in India." *Current History* 113 (762): 144–49.

Barnett, Barbara. 2008. "Framing Rape: An Examination of Public Relations Strategies in the Duke University Lacrosse Case." *Communication, Culture & Critique* 1 (2): 179–202.

Bhalla, Nita. 2014. "Rape Survivor Turns 'Superhero' in India's First Digital Comic." *Reuters*, December 17. http://in.reuters.com/article/india-comic-rape-idINKBN0JV22Q20141217.

Bhatnagar, Shikha. 2013. "About." Shikha Bhatnagar: Global Social Impact Consultant. http:// www.shikhabhatnagar.com/about/.

Biswas, Sreejita. 2014. "Superwoman of Substance." *Bangalore Mirror*, December 21. http:// www.bangaloremirror.com/columns/sunday-read/Superwoman-of-substance/article show/45587640.cms.

Bose, Mandakranta. 2000. *Faces of the Feminine in Ancient, Medieval, and Modern India*. New York: Oxford University Press.

Buchanan, Rose. 20015. "Priya: The Comic about a Rape Victim Challenging India's Attitude to Sexual Violence." *Independent*, March 19. http://www.independent.co.uk/arts-enter tainment/books/features/priya-the-comic-about-a-rape-victim-challenging-indias -attitude-to-sexual-violence-10120229.html.

Chowdhury, Jennifer. 2014. "India's Newest Heroine Breaks Rape-Talk Taboo with Comic Book." NBC News, December 16. http://www.nbcnews.com/news/asian-america/indias -newest-heroine-breaks-rape-talk-taboo-comic-book-n268481.

Dasi, Suna. 2015. "*Priya's Shakti*: Comics, Justice and the Indian Way, Part II." Sci-fi Fantasy Network, October 5. http://www.scififantasynetwork.com/priyas-shakti-comics-justice-and -the-indian-way-part-ii/.

Dimmitt, Cornelia, and J. A. B. van Buitenen. 1978. *Classical Hindu Mythology: A Reader in the Sanskrit Purānas*. Philadelphia: Temple University Press.

Dutta, Debolina, and Oishik Sircar. 2013. "India's Winter of Discontent: Some Feminist Dilemmas in the Wake of a Rape." *Feminist Studies* 39 (1): 293–306.

Goldberg, Eleanor. 2015. "Indian Comic Book Superhero Who Survived Rape Fights Stigma, Gets UN Women on Her Side." Huffpost Impact, February 10. http://www.huffingtonpost .com/2015/02/10/priya-shakti_n_6647464.html.

Hall Rachel. 2004. "'It Can Happen to You': Rape Prevention in the Age of Risk Management." *Hypatia* 19 (3): 1–18.

Heberle, Renee. 1996. "Deconstructing Strategies and the Movement against Sexual Violence." *Hypatia* 11 (4): 63–76.

India.com. 2015. "*Priya's Shakti*: Groundbreaking Augmented Reality Art Exhibition in New York City," May 4. http://us.india.com/arts-and-culture/priyas-shakti-groundbreaking -augmented-reality-art-exhibition-in-new-york-city-372973/.

Jamuna, B. S. 2010. "Strategic Positioning and Re-presentations of Women in Indian Comics." *International Journal of Comic Art* 12 (2–3): 509–24.

Jenkins, Henry. 2016. "Telling Stories: Lina Srivastava Talks About Transmedia Activism (Part Three)." Confessions of an Aca-Fan, January 26. http://henryjenkins.org/2016/01/ telling-stories-lina-srivastava-talks-about-transmedia-activism-part-three.html.

Kapur, Ratna. 2014. "Brutalized Bodies and Sexy Dressing on the Indian Street." *Signs* 40 (1): 9–14.

Khanna, Madhu. 2000. "The Goddess-Women Equation in Śākta Tantrism." In *Faces of the Feminine in Ancient, Medieval, and Modern India*, edited by Mandakranta Bose, 109–23. New York: Oxford University Press.

Kingsley, David R. 1988. *Hindu Goddesses: Visions of the Divine Feminine in the Hindu Religious Tradition*. Berkeley: University of California Press.

Kirkham, Alli. n.d. Everyday Feminism. Accessed December 11, 2020. http://everydayfemi nism.com/author/allik/.

Kundiman. n.d. "About Us." Accessed January 28, 2016. http://kundiman.org/.

Kuriyan, Priya, Larrisa Bertonasco, and Ludmilla Bartscht, eds. 2014. *Drawing the Line: Indian Women Fight Back*. New Delhi: Zubaan Books.

Leth, Kate. 2012. Kate or Die! http://kateordie.tumblr.com/post/24988635952/sometimes-i -have-the-time-and-patience-to-get-from.

Mahajan Jaya. 2015. "The Making of *Priya's Shakti*." PBS.org, January 22. http://www.pbs.org/ pov/blog/news/2015/01/the-making-of-priyas-shakti/.

McLain, Karline. 2009. *India's Immortal Comic Books: Gods, Kings, and Other Heroes*. Bloomington: Indiana University Press.

Mehta, Binita, and Pia Mukherji. 2015. *Postcolonial Comics: Texts, Events, Identities*. New York: Routledge.

Mehta, Foram. 2015. "India's New Comic Book Superhero Gives a Voice to Victims of Gender-Based Violence Everywhere." India.com, January 7. http://www.india.com/lifestyle/

indias-new-comic-book-superhero-gives-a-voice-to-victims-of-gender-based-violence
-everywhere-239645/.

Mukherji, Pia. 2015. "Graphic Ecriture: Gender and Magic Iconography in Kari." In *Postcolonial Comics: Texts, Events, Identities*, edited by Binita Mehta and Pia Mukherji, 157–69. New York: Routledge.

Mullin, Kyle. 2015. "Tiger Tamer & Comic Book Heroine Raises Rape Awareness in *Priya's Shakti*." *Paste Magazine*, April 20. http://www.pastemagazine.com/articles/2015/04/raising-rape-awareness-with-tiger-tamer-comic-book.html.

Murnen, Sarah K., Carrie Wright, and Gretchen Kaluzny. 2002. "If 'Boys Will Be Boys,' Then Girls Will Be Victims? A Meta-Analytic Review of the Research That Relates Masculine Ideology to Sexual Aggression." *Sex Roles* 46 (11): 359–75.

O'Toole, Laura L., Jessica R. Schiffman, and Margie L. Kiter Edwards. 2007. *Gender Violence: Interdisciplinary Perspectives, Second Edition*. New York: New York University Press.

Pandey, Geeta. 2014. "India's New Comic 'Super Hero': Priya, the Rape Survivor." BBC News, December 8. http://www.bbc.com/news/world-asia-india-30288173.

Phadke, Shilpa, Shilpa Ranade, and Sameera Khan. 2013. "Invisible Women." *Index on Censorship* 42 (3): 41–45.

Priya's Shakti. n.d. "Get Comic Book." Accessed February 22, 2016. http://www.priyashakti.com/comic/.

"*Priya's Shakti*: The Magical Comic Book That Takes on Rape." *Metro*, May 18, 2015. http://www.metro.us/entertainment/priya-s-shakti-the-magical-comic-book-that-takes-on-rape/.

Rao, Mallika. 2015. "Here's Why the Biggest Slum in India Is Honoring a Fictional Rape Victim." Huffington Post, May 26. http://www.huffingtonpost.com/2015/05/26/priyas-shakti-street-art_n_7294470.html.

Rao, Shakuntala. 2014. "Covering Rape in Shame Culture: Studying Journalism Ethics in India's New Television News Media." *Journal of Mass Media Ethics: Exploring Questions of Media Morality* 29 (3): 153–67.

Red Elephant Foundation. 2016. "Shakti." http://www.redelephantfoundation.org/2016/01/shakti.html.

Richards, Matthew S. 2016. "The Gulabi Gang, Violence, and the Articulation of Counterpublicity." *Communication, Culture & Critique* 9 (4): 558–76.

Rokudenashiko [Megumi Igarashi]. 2016. *What Is Obscenity? The Story of a Good for Nothing Artist and Her Pussy*. Toronto: Koyama Press.

Roychowdhury, Poulami. 2013. "'The Delhi Gang Rape': The Making of International Causes." *Feminist Studies* 39 (1): 282–92.

Salian, Priti. 2015. "Literary Interview: *Priya's Shakti*." *Anokhi Media*, June 24. http://anokhimedia.com/magazine/literary-interview-priyas-shakti.

Schlaikjer, Erica. 2015. "Interview Series: Dan Goldman." *Live FAST Magazine*, December 17. http://livefastmag.com/2015/12/interview-series-dan-goldman/.

Seervai, Shanoor. 2014. "Indian Comic Book Features Gang-Rape Survivor as Hero." *The Wall Street Journal*, December 24. http://blogs.wsj.com/indiarealtime/2014/12/24/indian-comic-book-features-gang-rape-survivor-as-hero/.

Shah, Jinal. 2015. "*Priya's Shakti*: When Technology Meets Art and Social Issues in NYC." India.com, June 17, http://www.india.com/arts-and-culture/priyas-shakti-when-technology-meets-art-and-social-issues-in-nyc-418712/.

Simon-Kumar, Rachel. 2014. "Sexual Violence in India: The Discourses of Rape and the Discourses of Justice." *Indian Journal of Gender Studies* 21 (3): 451–60.

Spivak, Gayatri Chakravorty. 1988. "Can the Subaltern Speak?" In *Marxism and the Interpretation of Culture*, edited by Cary Nelson and Lawrence Grossberg, 271–313. Chicago: University of Illinois Press.

Srivastava, Lina. 2014. "An Interactive Fight against Gender-Based Violence: *Priya's Shakti.*" Huffington Post, December 17. http://www.huffingtonpost.com/lina-srivastava/priyas -shakti_b_6336632.html.

Srivastava, Lina. n.d. "About." Strategy for Social Impact. http://www.linasrivastava.com/ about/.

Stoll, Jeremy. 2014. "Telling Stories and Building Community: Making Comics in India." *Marg: A Magazine of the Arts* 66 (2): 16–25.

Sutra Journal. 2015. "*Priya's Shakti*: Addressing Gender Imbalance through Religious Art." November. http://www.sutrajournal.com/ram-devineni-on-priyas-shakti.

Tribeca Film Institute. n.d. "Priya's Shakti." Accessed December 6, 2020. https://www.tfiny .org/films/detail/priyas_shakti.

United Nations Entity for Gender Equality and the Empowerment of Women (UN Women). n.d. "Gender Equality Champions." *The Beijing Platform for Action Turns 20*. http:// beijing20.unwomen.org/en/voices-and-profiles/champions#ram.

World Bank. 2014. "Using the Power of Fashion to Counter Gender Violence." July 27. http://www.worldbank.org/en/news/feature/2015/07/27/using-power-fashion-counter -gender-violence.

9.

The Tribes of Comic-Con

CONTINUITY AND CHANGE IN THE TWENTY-FIRST-CENTURY FAN CULTURE

Rob Salkowitz

Conventions have always occupied a unique and important space within the culture of fandom and the creative enterprises of comics, gaming, and genre-based media (Sassaman and Estrada 2009; Bolling and Smith 2014; Salkowitz 2012). Cons began as niche gatherings but in the past fifteen years have become sprawling spectacles, mirroring the general mainstreaming of fandom from subculture to mass culture. Today, the burgeoning industry of fan conventions is integral to global entertainment, technology, media, and marketing, as well as a multi-billion-dollar business in and of itself. The rapid growth of fandom as being a mass-market phenomenon raises questions about the integrity and authenticity of fan culture. Can a movement defined by idiosyncratic tastes, insularity, and high barriers to entry survive a vast influx of less committed members and the arrival of economic actors eager to exploit them as a mass audience?

Conventions are at the center of this question. Conventions have almost always had a commercial component and featured celebrity guests, but until recently, those commercial and celebrity activities were tied directly to the interests of hardcore fans. Today, big brands and celebrities with little or no connection to fan culture are as likely to be present at conventions as artists and publishers. Many attendees of these shows are familiar with comic book and game properties principally through mass-media adaptations rather than the original versions, while others are there purely because pop culture cons have become media events themselves and a good place to attract attention.

Many of these changes to the structure and character of fan conventions, and thus fan culture, derive from the massive popularity of Comic-Con

International: San Diego (hereafter referred to as "San Diego Comic-Con," "SDCC," or "the Con"). Beginning in the 1990s, San Diego Comic-Con emerged as the largest and most prominent pop culture convention in North America and among the largest in the world. The Con had been the focus of fandom and the industry for decades; as comics culture moved to the center of entertainment and media, so too has SDCC. And yet, San Diego Comic-Con has found a way to retain its unique position at the top of the convention industry and the locus of fandom, balancing the powerful forces of commercialization against its original mission to champion comics and the popular arts and, implicitly, an older conception of fan identity. How does it sustain that equilibrium?

My goal in this chapter is to examine the structure and appeal of SDCC as it is perceived by its longtime attendees and organizers, its online fan base, the community of scholars and analysts who use it as a backdrop for their studies, and the media who represent the Con to the wider world. For the purposes of this analysis, I have identified various subsegments as "tribes," a common ethnographic formulation denoting ethnic and kinship-based affinity groups, which has come into usage in consumer research to refer to social units that bond around shared interests, consumption patterns, behaviors, and passionate attachment to content (Mamali, Nuttall, and Shankar 2018, 6; see also Cova and Cova 2002; Cova, Kozinets, and Shankar 2007; Mitchell and Imrie 2011). Each of these tribes not only uses the Con as a platform for its own interests and agendas but also contributes something unique to SDCC that allows the show to maintain integrity despite the market forces driving it—and the culture of comics fandom—toward commercialization and hollow spectacle. I draw on a range of documentary sources, including interviews with a dozen key influencers ranging from early SDCC founders to fans, community managers, and authors. I have also supplemented the research done specifically for this chapter with my work over the past three years looking at the economics and demographics of fan conventions in North America, my personal experience attending SDCC since 1997, and some emerging tools for social media analysis.

COMIC-CON AND THE CULTURE OF FANDOM

SDCC began is a fan event, drawing hundreds, then thousands, then tens of thousands through its first thirty years. But starting in the early 2000s, SDCC experienced a quantum leap in size, attendance, scope and media attention, maxing out at a staggering 135,000 unique attendees—the capacity of its venue, the San Diego Convention Center (see figure 9.1 below). It became the first genre show to attract A-list Hollywood celebrities, exclusive media previews, exclusive merchandise, and respectful coverage from the press. It was the first to experience a "feeding frenzy" from fans desperate for tickets and hotel accommodations. Its exhibit floor hosts gigantic booths from game developers and film studios alongside artists, collectibles dealers and publishers.

The Con's success has inspired large events companies like Reed Exhibitions and Informa to spin up new divisions exclusively dedicated to mounting pop culture shows around the world. It's led to a gold rush of independently organized conventions, including many long-running comic and gaming conventions, which have experienced nearly universal growth at staggering rates. Professional organizers have become experts at separating fans from their cash, threatening the ecological balance of commerce, content, and community that makes fan conventions so appealing. While the popularity of cons has brought new blood into fandom, overcommercialization has also made it more difficult and less appealing for long-time members of the community to participate. Without an audience willing to actively cocreate the experience or customers with sufficient interest to support specialty vendors, fan conventions risk hollowing out into colorful consumer shows of no particular character or interest. Some would say this is already the case at some larger fan-branded events.

SDCC is importantly different from its peers in several respects. First, it is organized as a 501(c)3 nonprofit educational corporation, with a mission to "create awareness of, and appreciation for, comics and related popular artforms."[1] The organizers, most of whom have been in place for decades,

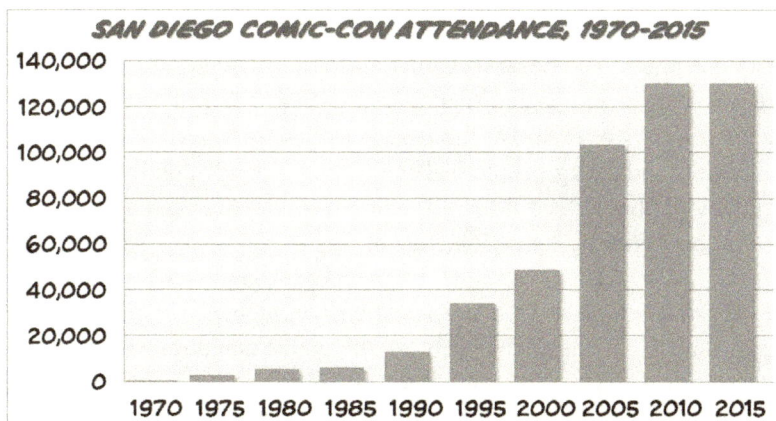

Figure. 9.1. San Diego Comic-Con attendance, 1970–2015. Source: SDCC.

do not report to outside shareholders and can ignore pressures to maximize short-term gains. They can also lawfully use volunteer labor. Second, SDCC has benefited from its proximity to Hollywood, attracting show business talent since its earliest days. Third, its longevity—continuously operating since 1970—makes it an institution, and its economic impact—generating upwards of $140 million in revenue for the city of San Diego—helps its relationship with local businesses and government. All of this keeps SDCC in the game. But its culture keeps it on top.

MACROCULTURE AND MICROCULTURE

Social media give us a window into the culture of SDCC at a macro, quantitative level. While the sample of fandom that uses social media is not a perfect proxy for the audience as a whole, it provides useful insights into the attitudes, behaviors and preferences of a vast and vocal community of self-identified fans. Advanced social media analytics tools give us a way to segment and analyze the mass social media fanbase using machine learning, pattern recognition and data visualization, revealing a wide range of distinct interests and affinities that lurk beneath the topline metrics. Data cited in this paper was generated using Affinio (affinio.com), a social analytics platform used by brands and marketing professionals to identify and target consumer subsegments.

Among the more than 135,000 who attend SDCC every year and the million who follow its Twitter account, you can find distinct fan audiences for mainstream (superhero) comics, alternative art and literary comics, science fiction, fantasy, media properties, animation, horror, manga and anime, tabletop and hobby gaming, videogames, collectible toys, fashion and merchandise, fine art and dozens—if not hundreds—of other sub-genres. There are people there for one thing and for many things. There are attendees who come primarily or exclusively to engage in cosplay. There are families and singles, old and young, people of all ethnic backgrounds, political views, and gender identities.

An analysis of the 825,173 followers of the SDCC's official Twitter account (@comic_con) retrieved on June 16, 2016, produced a diverse cross-section of subgroups. As seen in figure 9.2, their biographies not only included predictable fan identities but also categories that could only be parsed by demographics and location (e.g., moms, teen girls, creators, fans from Mexico, people with a civic interest in San Diego). SDCC's followers also demonstrate a high degree of overlap and clustering, with only a handful of subgroups

Figure 9.2. Word cloud analysis of most-used terms in the biographies of followers of the @comic_con (San Diego) account, retrieved June 16, 2016. Note preponderance of general terms "life," "lover," "music," and other non-fandom-specific identifiers.

Figure 9.3. Word cloud analysis of most-used terms in the biographies of followers of the @NY_comic_con (New York) account, retrieved June 20, 2016. Note preponderance of fandom-specific identifiers including variations on "gaming," and "comics."

showing significant disconnection from the overall community. By comparison, the 152,677 followers of New York Comic Con (@ny_comic_con) were much easier to fit into classic fan taxonomies, with over 30% showing a strong interest in videogaming and esports, 30% calling themselves fans of mainstream, independent or manga-style comics, and about 20% identifying with geek culture in general (see figure 9.3). NYCC fans also tend to cluster more tightly within these subgroups, with much clearer lines of demarcation between subgroups and fewer opportunities for overlap and affiliation. San Diego Comic-Con's greater reach provides more opportunity for commingling between subgroups, and the large percentage of its followers who don't identify themselves in terms of a specific interest are presumably potential customers for all kinds of different entertainment experiences.

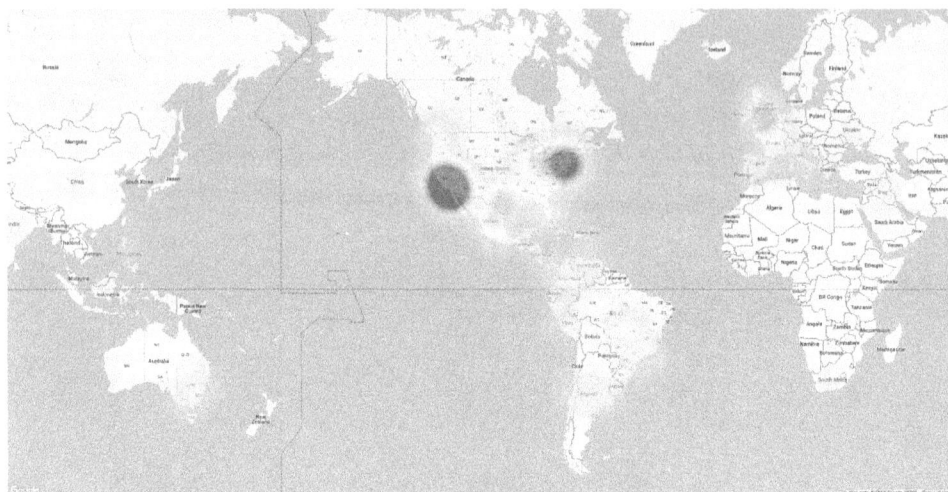

Figure 9.4. Geographical heatmap of followers of @comic_con.

A final important differentiator between the community that follows SDCC online and that of almost every other comic and pop culture convention in the world is its international reach. As of 2016, New York Comic Con's fanbase was heavily weighted to the northeastern United States, centered on the New York, New Jersey, and Connecticut tri-state area, with smatterings of fans from elsewhere in the US and the United Kingdom. SDCC also has its largest hotspot of followers in California, but it also includes significant footprints in the northeastern United States and Gulf of Mexico, western Europe, Latin America as far south as Argentina and Brazil, the Philippines, and the southeastern quadrant of Australia.

Analysis at this level provides some quantitative insight into the interests and affiliation of the largest communities that follow conventions on social media, which are, to some extent, a proxy for the audience that attends the shows in person. However, it falls short of helping us understand the mechanisms by which SDCC, and all comic/pop culture conventions to some extent, create formal and informal structures that bind these subgroups together into a vast collective. To understand those dynamics, we need to shift analytical frameworks from macro to micro and examine four structural groups that cut across taxonomies of fan interest and geography. These tribes are best understood according to their functional roles within the Con ecosystem and the reciprocal relationship they have with SDCC as an institution.

THE TRIBES DRIVING SDCC'S DISTINCTIVE IDENTITY

SDCC has uniquely managed to mobilize support across four key groups: the professional community, fandom, the academy, and mass media. Working individually and in relationship with one another, these different groups operate both internally and externally to augment the convention experience for attendees, publicize the convention to the non-fan audience, and give SDCC a mystique and aura that elevates it above superficially comparable events, conferring an enormous competitive advantage. These groups function not as "gatekeepers" that use artificial standards of authenticity to preserve the exclusivity of fandom but as conservators of the best traditions of fan culture to ensure they are there to be enjoyed and built upon by succeeding generations.

The tribes line up according to criteria that fit their roles and functions in the cultural ecosystem of the Con. Because I am a business analyst by trade, I tend to view these sorts of things as quadrant charts, with the four key groups as "driving forces" (a term I am borrowing from the management technique called scenario planning; see Wilkinson 1995), in that they operate according to internal logics and produce predictable outcomes. In this framework, the groups align along two different axes based on their objectives and their audience.

In figure 9.5, the *x* axis describes whether the culture is primarily interested in creating structures that add to the convention experience ("builders") or describing and explaining that experience ("observers"). The *y* axis describes whether the audience for the groups' activities is primarily the wider public and popular, accessible activities ("external focus") or elites and specialists interested in the less obvious dynamics of the convention ("internal focus").

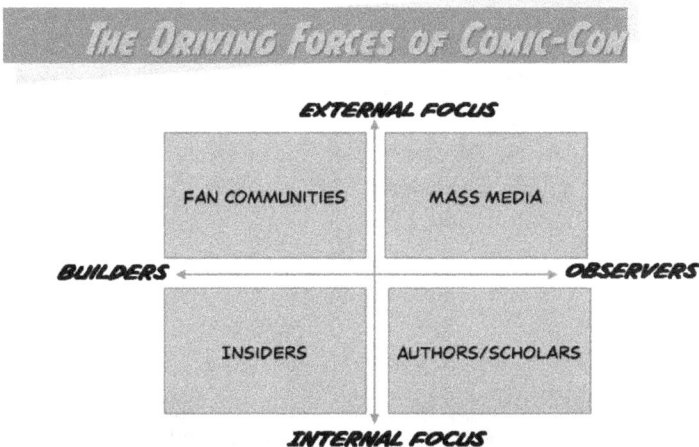

Figure 9.5. The driving forces of Comic-Con.

- **Insiders** (*internally focused builders*) maintain traditions, events and activities that preserve the SDCC experience they recall from years' past. Their efforts keep the spirit of early fandom alive underneath the hype and glitz, tethering SDCC to an authenticity that differentiates it from conventions that are purely about commerce and spectacle.
- **Fan communities** (*externally focused builders*) have built networks around SDCC, creating content and events that celebrate the convention itself. This helps attendees better manage their experience at an event that has become nearly unmanageable. They also contribute to the mystique of SDCC as a unique destination for fans.
- **Authors and scholars** (*internally focused observers*) study aspects of SDCC from either an academic or economic perspective. By making the Con an example of social and business trends, they establish it as a unique ecosystem worthy of study.
- **Mass media** (*externally focused observers*) use SDCC as the subject or backdrop for widely distributed works (films, documentaries, TV programs, new media), helping to cement it in the popular imagination as the center of all things geek.

These four groups are not mutually exclusive. Sometimes their objectives overlap, and membership in one culture does not preclude membership in others.

Insiders: The Foundations of Comic-Con

Insiders have typically attended SDCC for many years—some since the very first Con. Most have progressed beyond amateur fandom and work (or worked) professionally in the comics, publishing or entertainment industries. Some work for Comic-Con itself. Others are longtime exhibitors: sellers of old comic books or original artwork, purveyors of merchandise, or mainstays on the show floor, greeting their fans and selling original art and sketches. Because these insiders grew up in an older fan culture, their expectations of a comic convention differ significantly from attendees whose first exposure was to the larger, more multimedia-style events of recent years. Insiders struggle against the tide of commercialization and scale to maintain the SDCC experience that they value. Their connections, professional status and decades-old social network afford them the opportunity to keep a foothold in the world of the Con, where they continue to exert a strong influence.

Insiders perpetuate many of the rituals and institutions that differentiate SDCC from other large pop culture conventions. At the deepest layer, the board of directors and most of the paid management structure of Comic-Con International (CCI) are composed of people who have been with the organization since the 1980s or before, including executive director Fae Desmond, chief communication and strategy officer David Glanzer, Eisner Awards administrator Jackie Estrada, and John Rogers, who served as CCI's President from 1986 until his death in 2018 at age 57. "With regard to our event, I think our strength is that we're fans ourselves," said Glanzer. "We try to produce the type of event we would like to attend ourselves."[2] Their commitment to the educational mission of SDCC is evident in the list of special guests invited to the Con each year, the makeup of the programming, the continued presence of Artists Alley, and similar actions.[3]

Many insiders who are not formally affiliated with CCI take San Diego Comic-Con's mission to celebrate the popular arts seriously by contributing their time to programming during the show. A group including artist Scott Shaw, writer Mark Evanier, cartoonist Sergio Aragonés, and a handful of others who have attended SDCC since the 1970s hosts panels that focus on the history of comics culture rather than current products. Longtime members of the fan community are routinely honored as guests of the convention, along with elderly professionals unknown to most current-day attendees. The Will Eisner Awards, honoring the best work of the year, have been an SDCC mainstay since 1988. The Comic Arts Conference (CAC) offers a four-day track of programming devoted to comics scholarship and the presentation of research papers, serving as an academic conference running within and parallel to the consumer activities of the convention. With the rush of entertainment companies, publishers, celebrities and others clamoring for programming slots, many larger conventions have curtailed or eliminated this sort of programming. At San Diego, through the influence of the Insiders, they persist, giving the show a connection to the history of comics and the history of fandom that is increasingly unusual in the modern convention world.

Beyond their contributions to programming, insiders have also built up a number of social traditions to maintain personal connections as the Con has grown in size and become more hectic. Throughout the weekend, various parties, annual dinners and innocuous-sounding events on the schedule mark the moments when this tribe comes together to affirm its identity and maintain the cultural continuity of SDCC at its very core.

Fan Communities: Apostles of Comic-Con

SDCC has always been a popular topic on blogs and social media. Most of the top comic and fan blogs devote coverage to news and programming as soon as it becomes available. Some routinely post lengthy guides and tip sheets for prospective attendees, gathering all the folk wisdom: "wear comfortable shoes, drink lots of water, wash your hands a lot . . ." (Spurgeon 2014). However, there is a group of sites and social resources that came into existence solely to cover—and thereby promote—San Diego Comic-Con.

The most prominent and long-standing of these is the San Diego Comic-Con Unofficial Blog (sdccblog.com), launched by Zack Young in 2009. In the intervening years, the Unofficial Blog has grown into a community site with a team of a half-dozen editors, writers, and designers. The site spends the entire year gearing up for the five days in July when Comic-Con takes place. It posts announcements from the Con organizers, important dates, tips, rumors, and analysis. It also posts content from previous years' conventions, such as video clips, interviews, and photos. In the two to three months leading up to the Convention, the Unofficial Blog kicks into high gear, with as many as a dozen new posts per day. Because of its traffic, the Unofficial Blog has become a hot destination for advertisers trying to reach Con attendees ahead of the show. It has also become the hub of a huge fan community both on the site and on Twitter, where people can ask questions, complain, and generally get themselves psyched up for attending the convention.

Friends of Comic-Con (friendsofcc.com) is a community forum site started in November of 2011 by Alyssa Franks. As of 2015, the site's membership exceeds 4,500, and Franks runs it with a small team. Franks (2013) describes the site's origin as follows:

> The Friends of Comic Con International (CCI) Forum started with a group of fans who congregated daily on the CCI Facebook page to meet, chat, ask & answer questions, and have fun. . . . It is a place that was created with a lot of pain and even more love by fans of Comic Con International for fans of Comic Con International where people can continue to meet, chat, ask & answer questions, and have fun.

Conversations center on topics such as obtaining badges and hotel rooms, as well as programming. "The folks who repeatedly visit the site are interested in the experience of cons, not just comics," said Franks. "Our members are interested in making connections with other forum members attending the show." "Conventions are key to the tribe of geeks," said Franks. "They allow for a meeting of minds, a celebration of what makes our tribe unique. Cons help attendees realize how many other folks enjoy the same things as they do . . . Cons give someone who self-identifies as a geek a place they can go and be themselves. Sometimes for the first time, they feel like they are finally among others who feel the same as they do."[4]

Another fan-created resourced dedicated to providing information about SDCC is the *San Diego Comic-Con Survival Guide* by Douglas Kline. When I spoke with him, Kline, a comics and Star Wars fan since the 1970s, explained that he founded several geek blogs for "the fun and connections." He attended his first SDCC in 2004 and was overwhelmed by the size and scale. The experience was powerful enough that he returned every year. "I don't ever plan not to go," he said. Eventually, his knowledge and enthusiasm for the event made him a resource for his circle of friends and fans. "I had a lot of people asking me questions online and in person on how to 'beat the system' when it came to the basics of SDCC. One even suggested I write a book, so I did." Kline published the first edition of the *SDCC Survival Guide* in 2010, along with a website and a mobile app. It was updated and fully rewritten in 2014. Running more than 100 pages, the guide provides practical tips and guidance about every aspect of the experience. The book is "unauthorized" and has no affiliation with the convention, but it has helped many people get more out of their SDCC experience.

The con fan sites and resources serve several purposes in creating a cohesive and distinct fandom around the convention experience in general and SDCC in particular. First, they are an informal source of news and rumors, providing free publicity around the event. Unlike the official SDCC website, the community sites post this information from a fan level rather than institutional perspective, with a more conversational voice. In the lead-up to the Con, the sites offer countdowns, breaking news announcements and a steady stream of "can't wait for the big show!" posts that stoke anticipation. Attendees who have been to SDCC before typically look forward to a return visit but are surrounded by friends and coworkers who have no way to relate to their experience or enthusiasm. Fan sites aggregate this collective anticipation and excitement, building it to a fever pitch. They also help first-timers get a sense of what to expect and how the actual experience may differ from media accounts.

Because the practicalities of attending SDCC have become so complex and fraught with uncertainty in recent years, the sites serve another critical function in the months leading up to the Con. They allow people to vent their excitement, expectations, and frustrations over everything from guest and program announcements to the anxieties of getting a room during "Hoteloween" in a kind of group therapy. During the event(s), the sites and their associated social media feeds serve as a real-time newsroom, conveying information about schedule changes, lines to get into certain panels, unexpected celebrity sightings, and events in the exhibit hall, which can be too vast and crowded to keep track of even when you are in the midst of it.

Finally, fan sites often organize face-to-face meetups at the convention where people who have only met and conversed online can get together in person. Comic-Con is a very busy and crowded place, where even well-organized professionals are wary of scheduling meetings too tightly or "hoping to run into" a friend or colleague as one might do at a less enormous trade show. For far-flung fans hoping to connect, an organized and preplanned meeting is a huge benefit.

Authors and Scholars: Validators of Comic-Con

In addition to the internal and external communities that build institutions that strengthen and differentiate SDCC from other conventions, the Con benefits from a singular reputation in both scholarship and media as the epicenter of fan culture. Academic scholars, business analysts (including myself), and popular historians have all contributed to the body of literature surrounding the convention.

Perhaps the definitive "insider" account of SDCC was produced by two veteran staffers, Gary Sassaman and Jackie Estrada, to commemorate the fortieth anniversary of the event in 2009. *Comic-Con: 40 Years of Artists, Writers, Friends and Fans* was initially published as a limited edition for Comic-Con by Chronicle Books, but it has long been available through trade booksellers such as Amazon. Featuring an introduction by Ray Bradbury, the large-format hardcover runs over 200 pages and is richly illustrated with photographs and incidental artwork from the program guides produced for the event each year. The text includes reminiscences from longtime attendees and industry professionals, a complete official history of the event, notes from each year's show, and overviews of the trends that characterized each of the Con's four decades.

Estrada also produced two volumes of photographs she made over her long association with SDCC as an attendee, exhibitor, and staff member. *Comic Book People: Photographs from the 1970s and 1980s* (2014) and *Comic Book People 2: Photographs from the 1990s* (2015) were published via Kickstarter and then sold through retail channels. The photos in the books are mostly snapshot portraits or candid shots of individual creators, special guests, convention organizers, exhibitors, and prominent members of early fandom, mostly taken at SDCCs over the years. Estrada's curatorial approach emphasizes how central the Con has been to fandom and the entertainment industry.

Both volumes of *Comic Book People* and the fortieth anniversary book embody the Insider cultural perspective and narrative about the Con, offering newcomers a glimpse at the event's rich heritage, which may not be immediately obvious to the modern audience, while reifying the long-timers' cherished memories of the Con's—and their own—importance to the history of comics and fandom. They can also be read as an implicit rebuttal to criticism that the modern version of Comic-Con has "sold out" to Hollywood and/or is "no longer about comics." Estrada's work makes the case that SDCC was an eclectic show from the start, comprising Hollywood, science fiction, horror, fantasy, illustration, and comics and has simply expanded, not abandoned, its mission as it has grown.[5] Starting in the 2010s, critics and writers not formally affiliated with the convention began using the event as a springboard for broader observations about fan culture, contemporary art, and entertainment, business, and social behavior.

One of the first of these works to appear was *Comic-Con Strikes Again!* (2011) by Douglas Wolk, a longform monograph that was one of the first titles curated as part of Amazon's Kindle Singles program. Wolk emphasizes the color and spectacle of the event while giving a panoramic view of Comic-Con's vast scope and scale. He said his intended audience was not necessarily longtime attendees or insiders but anyone who may have heard about Comic-Con through the media and was curious as to what actually took place there. It is important to the broader narrative and perception about SDCC in its current incarnation as a must-attend event for fan elites, industry professionals, and cultural observers in general.

My own *Comic-Con and the Business of Pop Culture* (2012) used the same 2011 SDCC as a lens and organizing model for discussing trends in technology, media, communication, entertainment, and marketing from the perspective of a business analyst. At the time *Comic Con and the Business of Pop Culture* came out in 2012, there was some coverage of SDCC in the entertainment business press, mostly as an event and spectacle, and some writing in various trade presses as it related to tactical issues like guerilla marketing and product promotion. In the years that followed, almost all the forward-looking business press such as *Wired* and *Fast Company*, online media like Slate, Salon and Vox, and eventually even staid traditional business publications like the *Wall Street Journal* and *Forbes* began featuring coverage of comics and geek culture as a regular business beat.

SDCC is also fertile ground for academic study, particularly in fields like ethnography and cultural studies. Since 2007, Dr. Matthew J. Smith has led annual field trips to Comic-Con for students from around the country, and his student researchers traditionally present their work in the final session of CAC on Sunday afternoon. An edited collection of essays produced from the field school was published in 2014 (Bolling and Smith 2014). The book contains thirteen essays in five topic areas: identity and play, gendered fandom, negotiating fandom through communicative practices, technology and participation, and attending con, as well as several introductory and concluding essays by the editors and other scholars. "As a lifelong reader, I was well aware of the significance of Comic-Con," Smith (2014, 10) writes in his introduction. "Trade publications, letter pages, even sly nods to it in some of the comic book stories themselves all underscored the centrality of the one event to the industry, and communicated to a reader born and raised in West Virginia just how magical a place this must be." For Smith, Bolling, and other field school participants, SDCC offers a microcosm of comics culture, where students in a variety of disciplines can find meaningful and valid examples of fan behaviors, attitudes, and practices. It is a living data set where hypotheses about group dynamics and subcultures, such as those laid out in a more general way by scholar Matthew Pustz (2000) in his foundational work, *Comic Book Culture: Fanboys and True Believers*, can be applied and extended to a new and evolving fan culture.

Media Representations of Comic-Con

The fourth pillar of institutional support for Comic-Con is not a tribe in the ethnographic sense, although it functions according to an identifiable set of logics and motives and produces an important—perhaps decisive—component of SDCC's advantage. For those reasons, I include the media in my framework as an "externally facing observer," even though media representations of the Con need to be examined with a slightly different set of analytical methods.

SDCC, with so many unusual items for sale, celebrities on stage, and the colorful attire of many of the fans, has always been a photogenic event. However, for most of its history, the media coverage it received has been characterized by a tone of condescension, derision, or simple lack of understanding. Most media reports boiled down to a variation of "Hey look—grownups dressed as superheroes!" or "nerds gather to do nerdy things." The famous *Saturday Night Live* skit in which William Shatner tells a bunch of fans at a Star Trek convention to "get a life!" ("Trekkies" 1986) was perhaps the iconic distillation of this mode of criticism, giving generations of mainstream reporters permission to treat geek culture gatherings as unserious. But as Comic-Con became central to the economics of the entertainment industry, the tone of media coverage began to shift. Studios brought their

A-list stars to Comic-Con to court the influential alpha fans who lined up to attend the panels in Hall H and quickly discovered that a respectful, even reverential tone toward fandom would serve them better than treating them as freaks and geeks.

Starting in 2006, the cable network G4, whose programming focused on millennial-era gaming and geek culture, began doing live broadcasts from SDCC. The editorial focus and target audience of G4 ensured that these reports celebrated Con culture as cool and of-the-moment. It also provided a platform for a new class of celebrities—young stars, early social media sensations, or B-list actors from genre films and shows—to strut their geek bona fides and demonstrate a new model of media-friendly fandom to supplant, or at least supplement, the old stereotypes. Other youth-oriented media like MTV followed suit. The changing representation of fan culture applied generally across comics, gaming, cosplay, manga/anime, and other fandoms and fan events, but it was driven by the inescapable importance of SDCC in the converging entertainment, technology, publishing, and marketing industries. In 2016, CCI launched its own media channel, Comic-Con HQ, in collaboration with the entertainment studio Lionsgate, to capitalize on this for its own brand development.

All this hype succeeded in changing perceptions. By the mid-2000s, Comic-Con lost its old reputation as "nerd prom" and became, in the eyes of the press, some combination of the Super Bowl, Mardi Gras, the Academy Awards, and Woodstock: an elite annual celebrity-studded cultural milestone whose fundamental weirdness made it cool. Hollywood itself even started using SDCC as shorthand for "fan central" in mainstream feature films like *Paul*, a science-fiction comedy directed by Greg Mottola (2011) and written by and starring Simon Pegg and Nick Frost; a feature length documentary *Comic-Con Episode IV: A Fan's Hope* (Spurlock 2011); and on the CBS situation comedy show *The Big Bang Theory*, where it exists as an object of reverence for the four lead characters and was the centerpiece of a 2014 episode called "The Convention Conundrum."

CONCLUSIONS

The rise of fan conventions as star-studded celebrity events has gone hand in hand with the changes to fan culture brought about by social media, technological innovation, evolving popular taste, and demographic factors. This is both empowering for fandom, in that it brings it out of the shadows to be recognized as an important driver in the economics of the media and entertainment industry, but also a threat to the unique, quirky factors that gave it coherence as a social phenomenon in the first place.

The dramatic spike in attendance for SDCC that began in the early 2000s was an early harbinger of this trend, making it at once a template for other business entities seeking to engage fans at the same level of scale and intensity, and also a cautionary example about the ecological fragility of subcultures that are suddenly "discovered" and thrust into the onrushing currents of mainstream tastes. The integrity of conventions in general, and SDCC in particular, is central to fandom because they provide a kind of comradery and peak experience that's impossible to reproduce online or in smaller settings. The risks posed to the comics world and comics culture by their over-exploitation could permanently alter the unique sense of community that gives fandom coherence and meaning.

SDCC enjoys several significant institutional advantages that allow it to resist this dynamic, at least at its core levels, even as it grows and adapts in the face of a changing entertainment and media landscape. At the innermost level, it retains the loyalty of longtime members of its community who explicitly perpetuate the legacies of older fan culture. That's reflected by the management team of the convention, by SDCC's structure as a nonprofit, and by a tight-knit group of insiders who contribute to the show in various ways. The show has also managed to attract a superstructure of external institutions such as fan sites and communities who support the Con, stoke enthusiasm, and acculturate first-time attendees into the rituals of attending (and surviving) SDCC. Scholars and authors make SDCC the subject of works that underscore its social, economic, and cultural value in much the same way as UNESCO might designate a World Heritage Site. They confer on SDCC unique prestige and legitimacy that enables the show to differentiate itself from competitors and retain its characteristics. Finally, the mass media, driven by its own dynamics and priorities, carries the word out to the world about the centrality of Comic-Con, making its preeminence in the economic and cultural space a self-fulfilling prophesy.

The success of these efforts working individually and in tandem is reflected in the distinct nature of SDCC's fan base compared to other large conventions. The social media analytics presented earlier in this chapter, while not complete and conclusive, demonstrate that the SDCC audience is fundamentally different in character and composition, as well as in scale, to that of its nearest competitor. So long as these factors remain in effect, SDCC has the potential to keep its place at the center of fan culture, anchor that culture in the continuities of its past, and point the way toward whatever the future holds.

Notes

1. "About Comic-Con International," on the SDCC official website, http://www.comic-con .org/about.
2. David Glanzer, email exchange with the author, July 1, 2016.
3. For fuller discussions of this, see Salkowitz (2016a, 2016b).
4. Alyssa Franks, email exchange with the author, October 20, 2015.
5. Estrada has unambiguously expressed this opinion in many conversations with the author over the years.

References

Bolling, Ben, and Matthew J. Smith, eds. 2014. *It Happens at Comic-Con: Ethnographic Essays on a Pop Culture Phenomenon*. Jefferson, NC: McFarland.
Cendrowski, Mark. 2014. "The Convention Conundrum." *The Big Bang Theory*, season 7, episode 14. CBS. Originally broadcast January 30.
Cova, Bernard, and Véronique Cova. 2002. "Tribal Marketing: The Tribalisation of Society and Its Impact on the Conduct of Marketing." *European Journal of Marketing* 36: 595–620.
Cova, Bernard, Robert V. Kozinets, and Avi Shankar, eds. 2007. *Consumer Tribes*. Oxford, UK: Butterworth-Heinemann.
Estrada, Jackie. 2014. *Comic Book People: Photographs from the 1970s and 1980s*. San Diego, CA: Exhibit A Press.
Estrada, Jackie. 2015. *Comic Book People 2: Photographs from the 1990s*. San Diego, CA: Exhibit A Press.
Franks, Alyssa. 2013. "Introduction to the Staff and Why the Forum Is the Way It Is." Friends of Comic-Con (discussion forum), January 20, http://friendsofcc.com/forum/index .php?topic=1208.msg16797#msg16797.
Mamali, Elizabeth, Peter Nuttall, and Avi Shankar. 2018. "Formalizing Consumer Tribes: Towards a Theorization of Consumer-Constructed Organizations." *Marketing Theory*. doi:10.1177/1470593118767723.
Mitchell, Cleo, and Brian C. Imrie. 2011. "Consumer Tribes: Membership, Consumption and Building Loyalty." *Asia Pacific Journal of Marketing and Logistics* 23: 39–56.
Mottola, Greg (dir.). 2011. *Paul*. DVD. Universal City, CA: Universal Studios Home Entertainment.
Pustz, Matthew J. 1999. *Comic Book Culture Fanboys and True Believers*. Jackson: University Press of Mississippi.
Salkowitz, Rob. 2012. *Comic-Con and the Business of Pop Culture: What the World's Wildest Trade Show Can Tell Us about the Future of Entertainment*. New York: McGraw-Hill Professional.
Salkowitz, Rob. 2016a. "San Diego Comic-Con Guest List Paints a Broad Picture of Geek Culture." *Forbes.com*, May 10. http://www.forbes.com/sites/robsalkowitz/2016/05/10/san -diego-comic-con-guest-list-paints-a-broad-picture-of-geek-culture/#6c9bd2d05cb5.

Salkowitz, Rob. 2016b. "How Comic-Con Became Fandom's Super-Brand." *Forbes.com*, July 1. http://www.forbes.com/sites/robsalkowitz/2016/07/01/the-business-of-comic-con-sdccs-david-glanzer-on-branding-and-expanding/#433a63ab2f7a.

Sassaman, Gary, and Jackie Estrada. 2009. *Comic Con: 40 years of Artists, Writers, and Friends*. San Francisco: Chronicle Books.

Smith, Matthew J. 2014. "Introduction: The Pilgrimage to Comic-Con." In *It Happens at Comic-Con: Ethnographic Essays on a Pop Culture Phenomenon*, edited by Ben Bolling and Matthew J. Smith, 9–14. Jefferson, NC: McFarland.

Spurgeon, Tom. 2014. "Welcome to Nerd Vegas: A Guide to Visiting Comic-Con International 2014 (The Placeholder Edition)." The Comics Reporter, May 25. http://www.comicsreporter.com/index.php/briefings/commentary/.

Spurlock, Morgan (dir.). *Comic-Con Episode IV: A Fan's Hope*. DVD. Toronto, ON: Entertainment One.

"Trekkies." 1986. *Saturday Night Live*, season 12, episode 8. NBC. Originally broadcast December 20.

Wilkinson, Lawrence. 1995. "How to Build Scenarios." *Wired*, Nov. 1. https://www.wired.com/1995/11/how-to-build-scenarios/.

Wolk, Douglas. 2011. *Comic-Con Strikes Again!* Kindle Single. https://www.amazon.com/Comic-Strikes-Again-Kindle-Single-ebook/dp/B005FHHFQ0.

Part 3. Reception

Whether because of comics studies' origins in connoisseurist fandom or its contemporary relationship to literary studies, comic scholars have long focused on producing sophisticated interpretations of the comics form and individual graphic narratives. While there is always much that can be learned from a virtuoso reader, the scholar is only one reader among many and has no special status as an arbiter of a text's meaning. In any case, no reading is truly "individual" but results from myriad social processes working directly and indirectly to form the reader's perceptual apparatus (Bourdieu 2010; Fish 1980). Comics studies could certainly learn much from empirical studies of various kinds of comics readers, but the moment of reception is not limited to reading in the narrow sense. After all, as Nick Couldry (2004, 125) has observed, "in many cases, 'media consumption' . . . can only be understood as part of a practice that is not itself 'about' media." To interrogate comics' reception is to ask how they enter into ordinary people's lives and the uses to which they are put.

Accordingly, contributions in this section incorporate a range of understandings of reception, with reference to several different publics and contexts. Picking up where Salkowitz left off in the last section, T. Keith Edmunds also examines comic conventions as key institutions within the comics world. In "Comics and Comic Cons," he attempts to determine how a psychological "sense of community" is produced among participants at con events and who they see as their main community. Understandings of self and group are also the focus of Christopher J. Galdieri's "Follow the Readers." Galdieri argues that DC Comics's tradition of allowing the readers of their Legion of Super-Heroes comics periodically select the team's leader involved readers in the text in ways that both prefigured later attempts to involve enroll audiences' immaterial labor in the creation of storyworlds and revealed how contemporary readers were defining the superhero. People's engagements with comics also extend beyond the page. Adriana Estrada

Wilson's chapter, "Not Just Superhero Stories," provides an update on the classic comic-shop ethnography, exploring how forms of fandom nurtured there serve as "cultural tools" in the rest of participants' lives. Reception can also be creative, as Kalervo A. Sinervo argues in "Pirates and Publishers." Sinervo analyzes the relatively brief heyday of illicit comics scanning and distribution over peer-to-peer networks to show some of the limits of the discourses of "piracy" promoted by rent-seeking media industries. On this view, the comics scanner operates as both an audience member and a quasi author. Finally, as editors, we felt it was important to address comics scholars' own participation in comics worlds. We often imagine ourselves as outside observers on the scene, but our work as researchers and teachers also has effects on the comics world. Thus, the book closes with an interview with Charles Hatfield and Franny Howes about the field of comics studies and the professional status of comics scholars in the academy as one last public for comics and graphic novels.

This final set of publics illustrates the many potential reworkings of comics and their worlds at the level of reception. Such work is not inherently separate from—and indeed often overlaps with—production and circulation as equal realms within their ecosystems. These social worlds within the worlds of comics are interconnected, and, as scholars, we should recognize how all such social contexts are interconnected, including our own.

References

Bourdieu, Pierre. 2010. *Distinction: A Social Critique of the Judgement of Taste.* Translated by Richard Nice. Abingdon, UK: Routledge.

Couldry, Nick. 2004. "Theorising Media as Practice." *Social Semiotics* 14: 115–32.

Fish, Stanley. 1980. *Is There a Text in This Class? The Authority of Interpretive Communities.* Cambridge, MA: Harvard University Press.

10.

Comics and Comic Cons

FINDING THE SENSE OF COMMUNITY

T. Keith Edmunds

Imagine a crowded hall in a convention center. In this hall, vendor booths ranging from the very simple to the elaborate exist side by side, staffed by business owners, volunteers, and employees. It is not the vendors and the incredible array of wares for sale that one first notices, however, but the throngs of people filling the aisles that threaten to overwhelm.

No single demographic dominates the cavernous hall—seniors wander aimlessly alongside preteens darting enthusiastically from one end of the exhibits to the other, as young couples pushing strollers and holding toddlers' hands slowly find their way through the mass of bodies. Middle-aged men wearing t-shirts featuring superheroes examine goods on display as a group of young women clad in steampunk cosplay gear brush past. Everywhere, people point and smile and grumble and talk to strangers—about products, people, and pop-culture properties. Although the bulk of the people in this convention hall are strangers, there is an undeniable sense that they are, beneath the surface, very similar to one another.

Comic book fandom appears to be a well-defined community (Brown 1997). This nongeographic community (or community of interest) becomes most visible when it gathers together at conventions—events like the one described above. These comic cons are an opportunity for fandoms to gather in a safe arena and enjoy shared values and experiences (Fiske 1992), similar to those seeking social connections in comic book stores (Woo 2011). Scholars examining these events have noted the dramatic growth of these events, with some attracting over 100,000 attendees, and others increasing their attendance numbers over twentyfold in less than twenty-five years (McCain Gentile, and Campbell 2015; Salkowitz 2012), yet, despite this increase and the development of fan studies as an academic field, there are still very few studies focusing on fan conventions (Kington 2015, 225).

Even a cursory examination of the participants at a comic book convention (comic con) reveals that there are multiple communities that gather at these events; however, there nevertheless appears to exist a sense of community among the diverse attendees (Salkowitz 2012). Pustz (1999) suggests that comic book-reading communities themselves are many and varied and that what is shared between these distinct groups is not community but culture. Conversely, groups with similarly diverse interests have been identified as having a strong sense of community under a shared, broad category such as science fiction (Obst, Zinkiewicz, and Smith 2002). Looking at comic cons, then, one may ask if these events exist as a consequence of preexisting communities, such that diverse (if overlapping) communities gather in a single location for face-to-face contact, or if these events act as catalysts to create a sense of community among the participants, regardless of the particular fandoms to which they belong.

This chapter will examine the sense of community in the "event community" of comic cons and compare it to the sense of community in the "comic book community." Social identity theory and psychological sense of community, as theoretical underpinnings, will be used to examine how people perceive these communities. By examining any differences between the event and comic book communities—and the people that constitute them—the role of comic book conventions in relation to individuals' identities as fans may be further illuminated.

IDENTITY AND COMMUNITY

Because a person's fandom is inevitably connected to their social identity (Reysen and Branscombe 2010; Laverie and Arnett 2000), the connection between the self and comic book conventions can be viewed through the lens of social identity theory (SIT). Applied to fandoms, this theory holds that when individuals identify as members of a fan community, they construct an aspect of their identity based in part on the fan object, in part on the shared identity with the community, and in part through their interaction with others in this community (Pearson 2007). The association individuals have with the community helps form a common understanding of a shared identity (Muñiz and O'Guinn 2001). While individual identity and social (or collective) identity are certainly entangled concepts (Jenkins 2008), the focus here is on social identity.

Succinctly, social identity can be defined as "the individual's knowledge that he belongs to certain social groups together with some emotional and value significance to him of this group membership" (Tajfel 1972 qtd. in Hogg 2006). In other words, one's self-concept is in part defined by the social groups to which one belongs. As membership in a fan community is typically freely chosen by the individual (Groene and Hettinger 2015) in order to acquire an emotional connection or fulfill particular needs, the act of being a fan within a fan community (imagined or real) plays a role in the individual's identity (Laverie and Arnett 2000). Because individuals often belong to multiple communities and therefore have multiple, separate senses of community (Brodsky and Marx 2001), individuals' self-concepts may be envisioned as collections of identities, each reflecting a group or community to which they belong (Terry, Hogg, and White 1999). These different identities interlock and overlap with one another, often in socially meaningful ways (Phillips 2002). The application of SIT to media fandoms has been supported by research, the findings indicating that these fandoms operate consistently with the basics of SIT (Groene and Hettinger 2015; McCain, Gentile, and Campbell 2015).

While individuals belong to a number of groups (not all of which may be classified as communities), it is unlikely that the resulting identities are all of equal psychological importance to them (Cameron 2004; Laverie and Arnett 2000). According to SIT, people not only categorize themselves and others based on the groups to which they belong, but groups are also evaluated as being superior or inferior to one another (Trempte 2006). These groups, too, are defined in terms of the individual's self-perceptions as a group member—if three or more people perceive themselves as sharing particular attributes, those individuals may construe themselves as a group and distinguish themselves from others who do not belong (Hogg 2006); conversely, the identification of these individuals as a group sharing certain attributes may be imposed upon them. In other words, individuals tend to belong to many communities, not only related to those groups with which an individual identifies and defines themself (including interests, occupations, or any other collectivity with which one chooses to identify) but also those categorizations by which one is identified and defined by others. Therefore, individuals have many social and personal identities. In the case of the comic book community, the cultural stigma that has historically been attached to comic book fandom informs members' social identity (Lopes 2006; Brown 1997) and may lead to the desire to seek the company of likeminded others. It is important to note, however, that based on the principles of social identity theory, no direct social interaction is required for people to develop a sense of community.

The importance and value of one's social identities is highly subjective. This high degree of variability impacts how immediately accessible these identities are to an individual in everyday life (chronic accessibility) and in particular environmental conditions (situational accessibility). As a result, an individual's salient identity may change with the situation or context (Hogg 2006); therefore, in any given situation, the individual has several options as to how to categorize themselves. How it is done depends not only on the situation and context, but also on the individual's most salient goals and motives at the moment (Ashmore, Deaux, and McLaughlin-Volpe 2004). As stated by Laverie and Arnett (2000), "the self is composed of 'multiple selves,' some of which are more important than others" (227). In contexts where individuals with particular interests (such as comic books) feel they will be accepted for their interests, they are likely to access the relevant identity and form attachments to those individuals with the same specific or related interests (McCain, Gentile, and Campbell 2015).

Because fan behavior related to these identities frequently takes place in social settings or otherwise involves relationships to others in contexts referred to as "fan communities," it becomes important to understand what exactly is meant by the term "community." Puddifoot (1995) suggests that the use of definitions that are so broad as to encompass all aspects of what might be termed "community" has led to a dilution of core meaning of the concept. This concern is echoed by Cohen (2002) who highlights the issue facing many scholars working with the idea of community: "'Community' is used so variously, even inconsistently, and so loosely that, paradigm considerations apart, it has ceased to be of any obvious analytical use as a category in social science" (165). Regardless of these dismissals of the term, community is a useful and evocative descriptor for a particular type of social grouping. Further, many definitions used for community may also apply to culture—two concepts that overlap in their meanings (Kral et al. 2011). It is far beyond the intentions of this chapter to attempt to operationally define these terms and instead uses them in their commonly understood definitions, while acknowledging the existing difficulties in the language. Despite the problematic terminology, community remains an issue of academic interest, though the formation of community appears to have moved, due in part to technological advances in transportation and communication, from traditional place-based formations to developing around interest (Tyler 2013; Obst, Zinkiewicz, and Smith 2002).

The study of fans and fandom has been dominated by this interest-based view of community (Sandvoss 2005). A "fan" can be defined as an individual who is actively engaged with a particular interest (Groene and Hettinger

2015), and communities of these like-minded individuals tend to develop independent of a fixed geographical location (Sandvoss 2005; Ito et al. 2010). In fact, fans engaging in solitary activities—reading comics, for example—often perceive themselves as part of a community even if they are not explicitly interacting with other members of the same fandom (Busse and Gray 2011). This lack of direct communication or physical interaction does not preclude the fan from being a member of an imagined community (Wertsch 2002) that shares common beliefs and values (Groene and Hettinger 2015). The idea of an imagined community is far different from that of an *imaginary* community (Jenkins 2008). Benedict Anderson (2006) famously argued that imagined communities, of which the nation was the exemplar, could arise despite individual members never knowing one another. So, despite never interacting with many of their fellow members, individuals belonging to imagined fan communities may develop a shared sense of identity (Busse and Gray 2011; Sandvoss 2005; Carlson, Suter, and Brown 2008), and the communities themselves have a "very real social and cultural impact" (Sandvoss 2005, 55). An interesting consequence of such imagined communities was identified by Burke (2015), whose study of superhero movie audiences found "that little more than half of the self-described comic book fans actually still read comics" (120).

However, this sense of belonging to a community is not necessarily present in every case. Fans can engage in their solitary activities without experiencing (or even desiring) a sense of community. Fandoms, therefore, may consist of both individuals who feel a sense of community and those who do not. A distinction thus emerges: whereas *fandoms* focus on the connection of individuals to the fannish object, *fan communities* relate to the connections between individuals (real or imagined) around the fannish object.

The psychological sense of community (PSOC) an individual may feel about any particular group is primarily dependent upon that individual belonging to that community. In other words, one cannot have a sense of community without belonging to that community (Obst, Zinkiewicz, and Smith 2002). As a measure, PSOC indicates the connections felt between the individual and the community (Mannarini, Rochira, and Talo 2012), and a strong PSOC can occur in communities of interest where there is no regular physical interaction (Obst, Zinkiewicz, and Smith 2002)—as is the case with imagined communities—precluding the need for individuals to like other individuals within the community.

McMillan and Chavis (1986) are widely regarded as having laid the foundation for studying PSOC, and, although there are several models for sense of community, theirs is the primary theoretical model used (Mannarini and Fedi 2009). According to this model, four elements comprise PSOC:

- *Membership* is the understanding of the in-group versus the out-group. It is a matter of boundaries demarking who is a member of the community and who is not (McMillan and Chavis 1986), and the element of PSOC focused on the individual's own sense of belonging. Fans identify the fandoms to which they belong as distinct from other fandoms, clearly indicating that there is a boundary to membership—an in-group and an out-group (Groene and Hettinger 2015; Fiske 1992). Membership in a community with a distinct in- versus out-group leads to a collective identity where all in-group members have, or are believed to have, some characteristic or characteristics in common (Ashmore, Deaux, and McLaughlin-Volpe 2004). The importance of this collective identity extends beyond the simple function of categorization, however, as cognitive beliefs are also attached to this identity. That is, the sense of collective identity is not dependent solely on being an in-group member, as being considered a member of a group carries with it a set of particular characteristics. Hogg (2006, 117) underscored the importance of individuals internalizing this sense of identity: if individuals "have no sense of belonging, do not identify, and do not define and evaluate self in terms of the properties of the group, then they are unlikely to think, feel, and behave as group members."
- People are attracted to communities where they feel influential. The concept of *influence* focuses on both the individual's ability to have an impact on the community and community issues as well as the community's ability to influence its members (McMillan and Chavis 1986; Coffman and BeLue 2009).
- *Integration and fulfillment of needs* refers to those aspects of the community that act as motivation for individuals to remain as members of the community. McMillan and Chavis (1986) suggest that some of the common motivators provided by community are "status of membership, success of the community, and competence of capabilities of other members" (13). The assumption here is that community members are comparable in their desires, values, and needs (Coffman and BeLue 2009), resulting in similar motivational drives.
- A *shared emotional connection* between community members is based on the degree to which an individual feels that whatever impacts the community also impacts its members (Ashmore, Deaux, and McLaughlin-Volpe 2004). This entwining of fates—which affects the strength of the community—is partly based on a shared history and partly based on the community members' interactions in (and in response to) shared events (McMillan and Chavis 1986). Community

members do not have to directly experience these events, but they must be able to identify with them. Comic book conventions are an occasion for fans of comic books to have face-to-face encounters with one another (Brown 1997; Lopes 2006; Salkowitz 2012) and can serve as an opportunity to solidify the feelings of community for members of the comic book community as these events can increase the shared emotional connection between attending individuals.

METHODS

Despite the usefulness of ethnographic techniques in studying many types of behaviors occurring at comic cons (Bolling and Smith 2014; Kington 2015), one cannot simply observe the attendees at a con in order to examine sense of community. Individuals are not forced to choose among groups with which to identify—they may identify with multiple groups that may or may not overlap with one another (Tyler 2013). Because cons are often designed to appeal to a wide range of fandoms that fans view as more or less distinct from one another (Groene and Hettinger 2015), individuals attending a con may be doing so while identifying with a community other than comics. Indeed, it is probable that individuals identifying *only* with the comic book community are a minority of convention attendees. As cons grow in size, the likelihood of ever more diverse communities interacting also increases. If the collection of all convention attendees is deemed a single community, the idea of increasing diversity holds—as the size of a community increases, so does the multiplicity of interests within that community (Craven and Wellman 1973). In other words, the event community may be conceived of as a community of communities.

With individuals attending comic events potentially members of both a comic book community as well as the comic con community (not to mention any of a number of other communities), the identity that takes precedence for a given individual at a given time is a matter of salience. The most salient sense of community (SOC) becomes an important issue as "SOC has been shown to affect the way in which people perceive their environment, which suggests that SOC may impact the way residents perceive the social implications of festivals within their community" (Van Winkle and Woosnam 2013, 27). In any social context, the most salient aspects of one's self-concept are those that are shared with other members of the same social situation (Brewer 1991). Thus, the most salient identity determines the most relevant SOC, impacting the individual's perceptions of the event.[1]

If SOC cannot be simply observed in an ethnographic fashion, individuals must be asked about it. To this end, a survey was conducted to measure the SOC at comic book events. Research participants self-selected for the study. The survey was made widely available through social media, and targeted invitations were sent by email to past attendees of thirty-one comic cons in five countries. Respondents' subjective identification with both the comic book and comic convention communities were measured using the Sense of Community Index version 2 (SCI-2). Analysis of this tool has found it to be both valid and very reliable across cultures, languages, and settings. The four subscales—membership, influence, reinforcement of needs, and shared emotional connection—have also been found to be reliable, with coefficient alpha scores of 0.79 to 0.86 (Chavis, Lee, and Acosta 2008). The SCI-2 was presented twice to survey respondents: in one, the community was defined as the "comic book community"; in the other, as the "event community." The order of the two presentations was randomized.

In addition to the SCI-2 surveys, respondents were asked to indicate the personal relevance of a number of common behaviors and attitudes (as related to comic books and convention attendance), and some rudimentary demographic information was also collected. The results discussed in this chapter are based on the 246 completed surveys received.

FINDINGS AND DISCUSSION

Comparisons of the SCI-2 results for the two communities reveal a significant difference in how conventiongoers relate to them. Specifically, scores for the event community were significantly higher for SOC ($p<0.001$) and for each of the subscales: membership ($p<0.001$); influence ($p<0.001$); reinforcement of needs ($p=0.001$); and shared emotional connection ($p=0.005$). Interestingly, however, there was no significant difference between the event and comic book communities on the importance individuals placed on feeling a sense of community with other community members. Even people who responded "true of me" or "mostly true of me" to the statements

"I consider myself a fan of comics" ($p<0.001$),

"I consider myself part of a comics community" ($p<0.001$),

"Comics are my favorite entertainment option" ($p<0.001$), and

"My identity is partly informed by my enjoyment of comics" ($p<0.001$)

had statistically significantly higher SCI-2 scores for the event community. These statements were designed to identify people one might expect to have strong attachments to the comic book community, but their SOC with this community was neither more salient, nor even insignificantly different, than with the event community.

We can gain a more nuanced picture of the sense of community by examining survey respondents' reported comics- and fandom-related activities. When examining the reported activities of survey respondents, the tendency for the convention community to have a more salient SOC was found less frequently. Individuals who reported engaging in activities that may be considered solitary or do not require face-to-face contact with other community members tended to have no significant difference between the two SOCs of interest. Specifically, no significant difference between the two SOC scores was found among respondents who reported engaging in the following activities: purchasing comics (61.8% of respondents); reading about comics/comic creators online (55.7%); visiting a physical comic store on a regular basis (46.3%); purchasing or reading comics online (45.5%); discussing comics/creators online (35%); and writing fan fiction (16.3%). Conversely, activities that require traditional social interaction—attending comic book events once a year or more (85.8%) and cosplaying (54.5%)—were associated with significant differences (p=0.001) between the two SOCs. In the former set, preferred ways of engaging with comics and comics culture do not strictly require any face-to-face interactions with other people. While this type of interaction does not necessarily have to take place for SOC to exist, solitary activities seem less likely to lead to any SOC than those activities that lend themselves to in-person encounters, including attendance at comic book conventions.[2] It is also possible that individuals reporting involvement in solitary activities may identify with a community that is more specific and narrowly defined than that of a "comic book community"; the lack of a significant difference between the two SOCs would then be attributable, at least in part, to the fact than an individual can feel as though they belong to a group that is nested within a larger group and simultaneously also feel a sense of belonging to the larger group (Tyler 2003). But in no situation was the SOC score or any of the SCI-2 subscales significantly higher for the comic book community than for the convention community, suggesting that a generic comic book community is never more salient than a convention community. There are a number of potential reasons why this may be the case.

As the participants in this research self-selected based on their interest, if not their direct participation, in comics events, it is reasonable to assume that respondents have an inherent interest in the convention community. That is, the recruitment process itself may have already made one of these communities more salient than the other. Due to the research design, it is impossible to determine if the higher salience of the convention community is due to chronic or situational accessibility. However, it may also be the case that the face-to-face interaction at events makes the community more "real" in the minds of participants. As the community at these events is more "real" than the "imagined" comic book community, it is therefore more salient, leading to a higher SOC.

Another issue complicating analysis is the fact that both the comic book community and the event community may be too broad, thereby confounding an accurate, shared understanding of "community." It has been noted that comic fandom has its own groups (Lopes 2006); therefore, the comic book community may be better conceptualized, too, as a community of communities. The overarching diversity may mean that the identity of "comics fan" may be an ascribed identity—an identity bestowed upon an individual by others, perhaps less knowledgeable others. The individual's achieved identity—the identity selected by oneself—may be much more precise than that of "comics fan," instead belonging to a particular, much more specific and well-defined subgroup. This idea is supported by the fact that this research revealed no significant difference between the statements of importance for each community. That is, at no point was the comic book community the more salient community.

Because of the growing popularity (and therefore increasing acceptability within the larger social sphere) of many of the entertainment properties represented at comic cons, as well as the growth and proliferation of these events themselves, individuals may be more willing to adopt the more positive social identity associated with these events (Ashmore, Deaux, and McLaughlin-Volpe 2004) than that of the "solitary comics fan," which still retains a lingering stigma (Lopes 2006). As people tend to feel more committed to those groups they have selected for themselves over memberships ascribed to them (Ellemers, Kortekaas, and Ouwerkerk 1999), it may be that an individual's identity as a member of a comics-convention community is more salient than that of an ascribed membership in the comic book community. Jenkins (2012) noted this phenomenon, writing, "Comic-Con is a gathering of the tribes, a crossroads for many different communities drawn together by their shared love of popular mythology" (23), and Salkowitz (2012) echoes this sentiment when he reflects upon being "surrounded by people who share a passion for sharing their passions" (166) at Comic-Con.

CONCLUSION

The wandering seniors, the young families, the middle-aged men, the cos-playing girls, and all the myriad other individuals filling the convention halls are joined, then, in sharing a piece of their identity. In some small way, these individuals tend to feel connected to one another. They define a part of themselves in the same way, and there is a shared sense that they all belong to something important, something intangible, and something they can count on.

Although significant differences between the two communities have been identified, it may be much more useful in future research projects to identify more specific comics communities rather than speak of a generic "comic book community." As it stands, individuals are more likely to identify themselves as members of a comics-convention community, the "event community." Even those individuals preferring solitary engagement activities with comics do not clearly identify with the comic book community over the event community. It's not that a comic book community does not exist, but membership in that community is not a highly salient identity. Thus, we should not think of comic conventions as a gathering of the comic book community. Instead, these events constitute a community in and of itself—a community that tends to inform participants' identities.

This study suggests that, in studying comic book fandoms, it is important to consider the context in which these investigations take place, particularly when it comes to examining the role of fandoms in identity. In the case of this study, the event community was the more salient identity; as such, investigations into comic book fandom identity could have been confounded without such an understanding. Further, it illustrates that, as communities nest within communities, it is not always obvious which community will give rise to the most salient identity. Studies looking into identity and fandom need to take great care to ensure that they are accessing the identity under study and not a more salient, but unexpected, identity.

Notes

1. It is understood that there may be interplay between the various levels of identity—it is not an either/or situation. This research, however, is only a first step into exploring the issue.

2. Only one activity ran counter to this pattern: respondents reporting they engage in the activity "Purchase graphic novels/comics collected into trade paperbacks" (62.6%) had a significant difference in their SOC scores ($p<0.05$).

References

Anderson, Benedict. 2006. *Imagined Communities: Reflections on the Origin and Spread of Nationalism.* New York: Verso Books.

Ashmore, Richard D., Kay Deaux, and Tracy McLaughlin-Volpe. 2004. "An Organizing Framework for Collective Identity: Articulation and Significance of Multidimensionality." *Psychological Bulletin* 130 (1): 80–114.

Bolling, Ben, and Matthew J. Smith, eds. 2014. *It Happens at Comic-Con: Ethnographic Essays on a Pop Culture Phenomenon.* Jefferson, NC: McFarland.

Brewer, Marilynn B. 1991. "The Social Self: On Being the Same and Different at the Same Time." *Personality and Social Psychology Bulletin* 17 (5): 475–82.

Brodsky, Anne E., and Christine M. Marx. 2001. "Layers of Identity: Multiple Psychological Senses of Community within a Community Setting." *Journal of Community Psychology* 29 (2): 161–78.

Brown, Jeffrey A. 1997. "Comic Book Fandom and Cultural Capital." *Journal of Popular Culture* 30 (4): 13–31.

Burke, Liam. 2015. *The Comic Book Film Adaptation: Exploring Modern Hollywood's Leading Genre.* Jackson: University Press of Mississippi

Busse, Kristina, and Jonathan Gray. 2011. "Fan Cultures and Fan Communities." In *The Handbook of Media Audiences,* edited by Virginia Nightingale, 425–43. Malden, MA: John Wiley & Sons.

Cameron, James E. 2004. "A Three-Factor Model of Social Identity." *Self and Identity* 3 (3): 239–62.

Carlson, Brad D., Tracy A. Suter, and Tom J. Brown. 2008. "Social versus Psychological Brand Community: The Role of Psychological Sense of Brand Community." *Journal of Business Research* 61 (4): 28–291.

Chavis, David M., Kien Lee, and Joie Acosta. 2008. "The Sense of Community (SCI) Revised: The Reliability and Validity of the SCI-2." Paper presented at the 2nd International Community Psychology Conference, Lisboa, Portugal, June 4–6.

Coffman, Donna L., and Rhonda BeLue. 2009. "Disparities in Sense of Community: True Race Differences or Differential Item Functioning?" *Journal of Community Psychology* 37 (5): 547–58.

Cohen, Anthony P. 2002. "Epilogue." In *Realizing Community: Concepts, Social Relationships and Sentiments,* edited by Vered Amit, 165–70. New York: Routledge.

Craven, Paul, and Barry Wellman. 1973. "The Network City." *Sociological Inquiry* 43 (3–4): 57–88.

Ellemers, Naomi, Paulien Kortekaas, and Jaap W. Ouwerkerk. 1999. "Self-categorisation, Commitment to the Group and Group Self-esteem as Related but Distinct Aspects of Social Identity." *European Journal of Social Psychology* 29 (23): 371–89.

Fiske, John. 1992. "The Cultural Economy of Fandom." In *The Adoring Audience: Fan Culture and Popular Media,* edited by Lisa A. Lewis, 30–49. New York: Routledge.

Groene, Samantha L., and Vanessa E. Hettinger. 2015. "Are You 'Fan' Enough? The Role of Identity in Media Fandoms." *Psychology of Popular Media Culture* 5 (4): 324–39.

Hogg, Michael A. 2006. "Social Identity Theory." *Contemporary Social Psychological Theories* 13: 111–36.

Ito, Mizuko, Sonja Baumer, Matteo Bittani, Danah Boyd, Rachel Cody, Becky Herr-Stephenson, Heather Horst, et al. 2010. *Hanging Out, Messing Around and Geeking Out: Kids Living and Learning with New Media*. Cambridge, MA: MIT Press.

Jenkins, Henry. 2012. "Superpowered Fans." *Boom: A Journal of California* 2 (2): 22–36.

Jenkins, Richard. 2008. *Social Identity*, 3rd edition. New York: Routledge.

Kington, Candie Syphrit. 2015. "Con Culture: A Survey of Fans and Fandom." *Journal of Fandom Studies* 3 (2): 211–28.

Kral, Michael J., Jorge I. Ramirez Garia, Mark S. Aber, Nausheen Masood, Urmitapa Dutta, and Nathan R. Todd. 2011. "Culture and Community Psychology: Toward a Renewed and Reimagined Vision." *American Journal of Community Psychology* 47: 46–57.

Laverie, Debra A., and Dennis B. Arnett. 2000. "Factors Affecting Fan Attendance: The Influence of Identity Salience and Satisfaction." *Journal of Leisure Research* 32 (2): 225–46.

Lopes, Paul. 2006. "Culture and Stigma: Popular Culture and the Case of Comic Books." *Sociological Forum* 21 (3): 387–414.

Mannarini, Terri, Alessia Rochira, and Cosimo Talò. 2012. "How Identification Processes and Inter-Community Relationships Affect Sense of Community." *Journal of Community Psychology* 40 (8): 951–67.

Mannarini, Terri, and Angela Fedi. 2009. "Multiple Senses of Community: The Experience and Meaning of Community." *Journal of Community Psychology* 37 (2): 211–27.

McCain, Jessica, Brittany Gentile, and W. Keith Campbell. 2015. "A Psychological Exploration of Engagement in Geek Culture." *PLOS ONE* 10 (11).

McMillan, David W., and David M. Chavis. 1986. "Sense of Community: A Definition and Theory." *Journal of Community Psychology* 14 (1): 6–23.

Muñiz, Albert M., Jr., and Thomas C. O'Guinn. 2001. "Brand Community." *Journal of Consumer Research* 27 (4): 412–32.

Obst, Patricia, Lucy Zinkiewicz, and Sandy G. Smith. 2002. "Sense of Community in Science Fiction Fandom, Part 1: Understanding Sense of Community in an International Community of Interest." *Journal of Community Psychology* 30 (1): 87–103.

Pearson, Roberta. 2007. "Bachies, Bardies, Trekkies, and Sherlockians." In *Fandom: Identities and Communities in a Mediated World*, edited by Johnathan Gray, Cornel Sandvoss, and C. Lee Harrington, 98–109. New York: New York University Press.

Phillips, Tim. 2002. "Imagined Communities and Self-Identity: An Exploratory Quantitative Analysis." *Sociology* 36 (3): 597–617.

Puddifoot, John E. 1995. "Dimensions of Community Identity." *Journal of Community & Applied Social Psychology* 5 (5): 357–70.

Pustz, Matthew J. 1999. *Comic Book Culture: Fanboys and True Believers*. Jackson: University Press of Mississippi.

Reysen, Stephen, and Nyla R. Branscombe. 2010. "Fanship and Fandom: Comparisons Between Sport and Non-sport Fans." *Journal of Sport Behavior* 33 (2): 176–93.

Salkowitz, Rob. 2012. *Comic-Con and the Business of Pop Culture: What the World's Wildest Trade Show Can Tell Us about the Future of Entertainment*. New York: McGraw-Hill Professional.

Sandvoss, Cornel. 2005. *Fans: The Mirror of Consumption*. Malden, MA: Polity.

Terry, Deborah J., Michael A. Hogg, and Katherine M. White. 1999. "The Theory of Planned Behaviour: Self-identity, Social Identity and Group Norms." *The British Journal of Social Psychology* 38: 225–44.

Trempte, Sabine. 2006. "Social Identity Theory." In *Psychology of Entertainment*, edited by Jennings Bryant and Peter Vorderer, 255–71. Mahwah, NJ: Erlbaum.

Tyler, Bruce David. 2013. "Fan Communities and Subgroups: Exploring Individuals' Supporter Group Experiences." PhD diss., University of Massachusetts Amherst.

Wertsch, James V. 2002. *Voices of Collective Remembering*. Cambridge: Cambridge University Press.

Woo, Benjamin. 2011. "The Android's Dungeon: Comic-Bookstores, Cultural Spaces and the Social Practices of Audiences." *Journal of Graphic Novels and Comics* 2: 125–36.

11.

Follow the Readers

LEADERSHIP ELECTIONS IN THE SILVER- AND BRONZE-AGE LEGION OF SUPER-HEROES

Christopher J. Galdieri

Elections do not just choose leaders. A group choosing a leader is also deciding what their group stands for and aspires to. Imagine a recreational sports team electing a captain for its upcoming season. One candidate emphasizes good sportsmanship and fun, while the other wants to improve the team's win-loss record. Either result will reveal a great deal about how the players view the point of the team's existence. When it comes to choosing leaders on larger scales, as in national election campaigns, the choice is not simply between candidates with different policy prescriptions but between competing visions of what the nation, and membership in the nation, really means. This helps explain the reactions we often have to disagreeable election outcomes; yes, the likely policy outcomes are upsetting, but even worse may be the fact that our fellow citizens have chosen someone who does not represent the country as we see it. This is also why elections have such symbolic importance. A victory by a member of a historically excluded or underrepresented group signals a fuller membership for that group in the body politic (Leege 2002).

Leadership contests are thus also battles to define a group's identity, whether the group is large or small. Group identities are, Stern (1995) argues, created in part through political rhetoric; over time, the stories leaders tell unite a group by creating an identity shared by group members. These identities in turn shape whom group members see as potential leaders. Hogg (2001) argues that the members of a group who are seen as its most prototypical members are also those most likely to be seen as having leadership qualities.

In other words, embodying the traits associated with being a good group member is linked to being seen as a good leader.

The importance of leaders and elections presents storytellers with a wealth of dramatic possibilities. Television series like *The West Wing* and *Veep* have made elections the focus of entire seasons; other series, like *Lost*, use the tensions between a group's would-be leaders as an engine for storytelling throughout their runs. Stories about leadership frequently recur in superhero comics as well: Cyclops and Storm fought for the leadership of the X-Men (Claremont, Leonardi, and Portacio 1986); Hawkeye grumbled that he, not Captain America, should lead the Avengers (Lee, Kirby, and Ayers 1965); and Batman used one punch to end a rogue Green Lantern's attempt to claim leadership of the Justice League (Giffen, DeMatteis, Magiure, and Gordon 1987) in memorable stories.

During the Silver and Bronze Ages of American superhero comics, the creators behind the Legion of Super-Heroes, a long-running DC Comics feature, went so far as to hold elections in which readers cast ballots to choose the team's leaders. I examine these elections with particular attention to how leadership contests can become conflicts over or expressions of group identity. The results of the Legion's elections suggest that the readers often advanced an expansive conception of heroism by electing characters who did not necessarily fit the heroic mold that was prevalent in superhero comics at the time. Legion fans in many cases ensured that the team was led by characters who were female, underestimated, or identified by readers (if not depicted by creators) as gay. In doing so, these fans challenged existing conceptions of what heroes—super and otherwise—truly are.

THE LEGION AND ITS FANS

The Legion of Super-Heroes debuted in April 1958's *Adventure Comics* #247, as a variation on the trope of Superboy encountering other super-teenagers. In this story, Superboy meets three teenagers—Cosmic Boy, Lightning Lad, and Saturn Girl—who belong to a club of super-teens in the thirtieth century who were inspired by his example. They invite Superboy to travel with them to the future to try out for their team. After Superboy appears to fail a series of tests, the Legionnaires reveal that they had engineered these failures as an initiation prank, and the story ends with Superboy inducted into their ranks as the Legionnaires cheer.

There matters might have ended, with the Legionnaires taking their place alongside Krypton Kid (Binder, Swan, and Kaye 1957), Marsboy (Woolfolk,

Swan, and Fischetti 1951), and other forgotten, one-shot heroes. But the volume of letters sent in response to this story was so strong that Superboy began traveling to the future for adventures with the Legion on a regular basis. As each story introduced new members of the group, the three heroes from that first story were quickly joined by many more. The Legion soon became the lead feature of *Adventure Comics*, and the readers whose letters convinced DC to bring back the Legionnaires grew into a devoted fanbase.

Several aspects of the Legion made it uniquely appealing to readers. First, the team was a club made up of teenagers who just happened to have superhuman powers. Many early stories opened with the team holding tryouts for prospective members. Others ended with characters exclaiming that an exciting development was par for the course for their extraordinary club. Some stories focused on rituals of membership, like the oath sworn by members (Siegel and Forte 1964a), or made the rules of the team into plot points (Siegel and Forte 1963; Hamilton, Swan, Moldoff, and Klein 1966). Later stories dealt with the need to limit the team to twenty-five members to maintain a tax exemption (Bridwell, Mortimer, and Abel 1970) or used a team meeting as a framework for a story (Levitz, Giffen and Mahlstedt 1983). This ongoing emphasis on the team's history and operations appealed to readers who only dreamed of joining a club of superheroes. Being privy to the Legion's history and traditions was the next best thing to being a Legionnaire.

The Legion also benefitted from its ties to the mythology of Silver Age Superman comics, such as the Phantom Zone and the many colors of kryptonite. The Legion's setting in the future of DC's universe also kept these ties to Superman at enough distance that they did not overwhelm the team's adventures. The Legion developed its universe of characters and settings and tropes in relative isolation from the rest of DC's superhero comics. In-story declarations that the Legionnaires were the premiere superheroes of their future could not be challenged by rival features with higher circulation figures, as was the case at Marvel in the 1980s when the *X-Men* outsold and outshone *The Fantastic Four* and *The Avengers*.

The nature of the team's membership also helped a robust fandom develop. Previous teen heroes had tended to be sidekicks, as Robin was to Batman and Bucky was to Captain America, for example. Sidekicks deferred to their adult mentor, received and delivered exposition, and imagined someday becoming full-fledged superheroes. The Legionnaires, in contrast, were heroes in their own right whom government and police officials treated as respected peers and equals.

The Legion's hazy and indistinct history further encouraged fans. Readers first encountered the team from Superboy's perspective as a mystery to be unraveled. The team lacked an origin story for a decade after their first appearance (Bridwell and Costanza 1968), and many stories mentioned unseen past adventures and missions undertaken off-panel by absent members. Many fans tried to "solve" mysteries like the identities of the members, visible only in silhouette, who cheered Superboy's initiation to the team or the precise order in which members had joined in much the same way that Sherlock Holmes enthusiasts debate the location of Watson's war wound. The gaps in the team's history invited readers to elaborate upon the stories that they read every month, and the world beyond those stories.

Additionally, the Legion was the largest superhero team of them all. Many writers and artists, exasperated by juggling dozens of heroes, used charts to keep track of the characters (O'Neil 2001; Swan 1975). But what frustrated creators was part of the team's appeal to readers. As sometime Legion editor and writer Mark Waid (1998, 23) noted, "with that many members to choose from, any reader could find a favorite." While superhero comics of the 1950s and early 1960s lacked in-depth characterization, this paradoxically may have helped the Legion attract fans. Enthusiastic readers looked at the tiniest action or bit of dialogue or character design—for instance, Ultra Boy's ducktail haircut—and extrapolated entire backstories—concluding that Ultra Boy had been a futuristic rebel without a cause before he became a hero. Over time, many of these speculations found their way into the pages of the comics.

While the Legion's membership never achieved gender parity, it offered more female heroes than teams like the X-Men or the Avengers, whose early rosters included exactly one woman. This, as writer Mike Madrid notes, led to a very different gender dynamic among the Legionnaires. Whenever the lone female on other teams—the Invisible Girl, the Wasp, Marvel Girl—expressed an interest in fashion or romance or another stereotypically "feminine" subject, her male teammates would roll their eyes and dismiss her. But the female Legionnaires' "strength in numbers" headed off that kind of storytelling (Madrid 2009, 143). And while a panel in which Brainiac 5 tries to exclude Saturn Girl from a mission on the grounds that "It's too dangerous for a girl!" remains notorious decades later, in that same panel Saturn Girl pushes back and accompanies her teammates on their mission (Hamilton, Forte, and Oksner 1964, 4/1). The Legion's gender breakdown helped attract girls as well as boys in an era where female superheroes were rare.

It also helped that the members themselves represented a wide variety of heroic types. Some, like Superboy and Mon-El, possessed a full suite of powers. Others, like Chameleon Boy or Phantom Girl, possessed one superability. And a handful, like Bouncing Boy (with his power of superbouncing), Matter-Eater Lad (who could consume any form of matter) and Triplicate

Girl (who could split herself into three identical teenage girls), had delightfully bonkers powers that were played absolutely straight. As a result, no matter what a reader thought a good superhero "should" be like, there would almost certainly be someone in the Legion who met those criteria. This diversity of types on the team's roster helps clarify the appeal and significance of the Legion's readership elections: In many cases, the readers were not simply voting for characters based on popularity; they were also voting for particular models of heroism. The origins of these elections are rooted in one of the grand institutions of twentieth-century comics, the letter column.

THE LEGION OUTPOST

The Legion's close ties to its readership date back to the letters that led DC Comics to bring back the Legion after their first appearance. By the time the Legion took over *Adventure Comics*, the letter-writing readership had grown, and the comic's letter column was soon renamed the Legion Outpost. In the pre-internet era, letters pages served as a forum where readers offered critiques, suggestions, and comments on characters and stories, and creators and editors responded. They also facilitated interaction between readers, as enterprising fans could write letters to the readers whose letters—and addresses—were included in letter columns. At times, they turned to broader issues, as when *Captain America* hosted a debate on patriotism in the context and shadow of Vietnam from 1969 to 1976 (Stevens 2011).

For Legion fans, the letter column was the origin point for a participatory ethos that grew to greatly influence the series. A feature—itself suggested by a letter in *Adventure Comics* #301—called Bits of Legionnaire Business was a forum for readers' suggestions for new characters, many of whom—Spider-Girl, Color Kid, Polar Boy—ultimately appeared in the comic (Flynn 2004). This practice was encouraged by Edmond Hamilton, writer of many early Legion stories, in a letter printed in *Adventure* #310 that reinforced the idea of two-way communication and exchange between readers and creators. This collaborative dialogue between fans and creators made the Legion's future "more realistic and three-dimensional" (Pustz 1999). The letters page became the nexus of what Gordon (2012) terms a "discursive community" where readers helped shape the Legion's world through questions and speculation that influenced creators' stories and characterizations. As Pustz notes, this influence was mediated through DC's editors; readers could not force their letters to be printed, and creators had no obligation to address readers' concerns or incorporate their suggestions. But the letters fostered a sense of fan involvement and investment, and enough fan ideas made it into stories to make letter-writing worthwhile. Any reader, after all, might create the next Color Kid.

During the *Adventure Comics* run, a contest was held to determine the most popular Legionnaire. After months of letters making cases for various Legionnaires, Mon-El won, receiving one more vote than Lightning Lad (Weisinger 1966). Andrew Zysman of Hillside, New York, bemoaned his failure to vote in a letter, because his vote for Lightning Lad would have tied the vote. The editorial response admonished Zysman to remember that a ballot "can be as powerful in its own way as Lightning Lad's bolts!" (Weisinger [and Bridwell] 1966).

Not long after, Tredgar Waller of Rosemount, Minnesota, suggested that since the Legion's constitution (printed in text pieces periodically during the Legion's run) required a new leader be chosen every year, readers should do the choosing (Weisinger [and Bridwell], 1968). The editorial response agreed and gave readers a deadline of December 26, 1967, to submit ballots. With this, the Legion tradition of reader elections was born. This first election did not simply spring into being; it emerged from years of back-and-forth in the letter column. The following sections examine the results of these elections and what they show about how the Legion's fans viewed heroism.

LEADING THE LEGION

Team leadership had been a factor in stories even before the reader elections. In the Legion's earliest appearances, the team was led by Cosmic Boy. Subsequently, Saturn Girl was twice chosen as leader, followed by Brainiac 5 and then Invisible Kid. All three had relatively undramatic powers: telepathy, superintelligence, and invisibility, respectively. Their selection may have helped keep these characters from being overshadowed by members with flashier powers. And it should be noted that putting Saturn Girl in charge of the team was a very progressive move in the early 1960s.

In the first few reader elections, however, readers displayed little progressivism or imagination: Ultra Boy and Mon-El, two of the team's more standard superheroic types, won four of the first five reader elections. The one exception was Karate Kid, elected to a term in November 1969's *Action Comics* #382—not long before the martial arts craze that swept popular culture in the early 1970s. However, only one of these elections took place during the team's run as the lead feature in *Adventure Comics*. The others took place when the Legion was a back-up feature in *Action Comics* or appeared on an occasional basis in *Superboy*. In other words, the voters in most of these elections consisted, at least in part, of people for whom the Legion was not the main attraction in the comic they were reading.

A similar issue complicates Wildfire's election in *Superboy and the Legion of Super-Heroes* #225. In that case, rather than having readers choose a leader by mailing in ballots, the attendees at DC's "Super-Celebration" held in New York City during the winter of 1977 had the chance to pick the leader. Superboy—by far the most recognizable character on the team—received the most votes, but in-story was deemed ineligible thanks to his temporal commuter status. Wildfire, the runner-up, became the team's leader. And Wildfire, as a relatively new character with a dynamic costume and a mysterious-looking plate of black glass where his face would be, may have appealed to casual readers and convention attendees in a way that the other Legionnaires did not. Further indicating that this election was decided by people other than the team's most active fans was the fact that Tyroc—who was listed on the ballot but had not yet appeared in the comic—placed fifth.

This first wave of elections received little attention in the Legion's stories, beyond the fact of their taking place. A lack of serialization from issue to issue meant that one issue's election might have little impact on the next. And the elections' timing was irregular; Ultra Boy won an election in *Superboy and the Legion* #184, and just six issues later, Mon-El was elected to a second term of his own. Nearly five years then passed until the next election. So, while elections happened and readers voted in them, these elections were not yet vehicles for collaboration between readers and creators.

The second phase of reader elections, beginning in January 1977's *Superboy and the Legion* #247, demonstrated a greater role on the part of Legion readers. It is likely not coincidental that these elections took place during two lengthy runs by writer Paul Levitz, one of several Legion fans who became comics professionals and spent part of their careers creating Legion comics. Levitz saw the reader elections as a tradition worth upholding and as a method of fostering an ongoing, interactive relationship with readers (Cadigan 2003). Levitz's writing was also informed by the same sorts of speculative extrapolation found in many fan letters. For instance, he noted in one story that Colossal Boy was Jewish, largely because Levitz realized that the hero shared a surname with an Israeli cabinet minister (Kaplan 2008, 192–93).

The results of the first election of Levitz's tenure were announced in *Superboy and the Legion* #247. Because it shared an issue number with the team's first appearance in *Adventure Comics*, the comic was treated as an anniversary. Its cover contrasted the founders' contemporary disco-styled costumes with their original Eisenhower-era looks, while the election story was full of references to the team's history and, obliquely, to the readers themselves. Levitz's story sets up an electioneering rivalry between Brainiac 5 and Wildfire, who focus on each other and ignore Lightning Lad. When the votes are tallied, however, Brainiac 5 exclaims, "The others remembered! And they chose the one charter member who has never been a leader before!" (Levitz, Staton, and Abel 1979). The word "others" here has dual meanings. Within the story, they are the Legionnaires who voted for Lightning Lad. For readers, the "others" are the fans who chose Lightning Lad in what that issue's letter column described as a "landslide." The pseudoanniversary may have encouraged readers to vote for Lightning Lad as a nod to the team's history. These readers thus created an opportunity for Levitz to write a story in which a tour through team history ended with Lightning Lad's election; without those votes, this particular story could not have been told.

Levitz left the book for a time after this story, and no reader elections were held in his absence. Levitz's successors were content to leave Lightning Lad in place indefinitely. When Levitz returned to the book in 1982, the first election in nearly four years was held. The letters column in issue #282 "cordially invited" readers to vote, in accordance with team bylaws (Barr 1981), and #286 announced that well-known fan Rex Joyner had cast the election's first ballot (Barr 1982). An announcement in #288 said that over 700 ballots had already been received and that the clock was ticking for any last-minute votes to be received (Sutton 1982).

The result, announced in #291, was a surprise to many, including the creative team on the book. The winner—with 109 of the 784 votes cast—was Dream Girl. This was a shocking outcome because Dream Girl had often been relegated to the background of stories. Her codename referred both to her appearance—she was drawn from her first appearance to look like a pin-up girl—and her power to see the future through prophetic visions. In her earliest appearances, she had to be literally asleep and dreaming in order to use her powers, which was a poor fit for a visual medium like comics. Subsequently, she had been defined mostly by her appearance (less Marilyn Monroe than Heather Locklear by the 1980s) and her relationship with Star Boy. As a largely blank slate, her election was particularly challenging for the book's creators. Indeed, that may have been the point of her election. Years later, Levitz suggested that some fans had tried to stuff the ballot box in her favor (Rogers 2008). The evidence for this effort is ambiguous; the 784 votes cast in 1982's election exceeded the 538 that would be cast in 1984's election but were roughly similar to the 815 votes in 1985. But the mere prospect of such an effort indicates how passionate fans had come to view the leader elections as their opportunity to influence the content of the Legion's stories, in this case by giving the creative team the difficult task of turning an oft-dismissed character into the team's leader. The Dream Girl election demonstrates that many readers saw their relationship to the comics' creators as a push-pull arrangement, rather than one in which they passively and obligingly consumed each month's new issue.

The creators' response to the readers' challenge was to develop aspects of Dream Girl's personality that had received little attention previously. During her tenure, she was shown to be a capable leader, one of the team's stronger scientists, and increasingly creative in using her powers—for instance, by foreseeing and preemptively responding to an opponent's moves during combat. None of these newfound characteristics contradicted anything established previously. Dream Girl was still an attractive young woman, still involved in a stable relationship, and still flirtatious; at the same time, she was revealed to be a strong, intelligent, and effective leader. Whatever their motives, the readers who elected Dream Girl caused a reinvention of a character who had for years been thought of, when she was thought of at all, in terms of her physical appearance. These readers' ballots also gave the Legion its first female leader since Saturn Girl. The Legion's creators' depiction of Dream Girl in her term as leader shows that they were willing to accept the readers' challenge and demonstrates the interactive effect of the reader elections. Had readers chosen another Legionnaire, the transformation in Dream Girl's characterization might never have happened.

The outcomes of the next two elections demonstrate Legion fandom's tenacity. The winner of each was Element Lad, whose private life had long been a subject of fan speculation. Recall how early fans of the Legion often latched onto tiny details or moments and extrapolated from them entire backgrounds and personality traits. Few characters were the object of as much elaboration as Element Lad. In an early appearance, Element Lad thinks to himself that he is "out of [his] element when it comes to romancing girls" (Siegel and Forte 1964b). This thought, plus the character's predominantly pink costume and his bachelorhood in flash-forward stories about the Legion as adults, led some fans to speculate that Element Lad was uncomfortable with girls because he was gay (Companik 2001; Darius 2014). Even Element Lad's hesitation to become involved with a (female) romantic interest, whom Levitz introduced to subvert reader expectations, could be read by fans who saw him as gay as consistent with their extracanonical characterization.

This ongoing speculation may have helped Element Lad in reader elections. As Levitz noted when Element Lad was finally elected leader, he enjoyed remarkably consistent support in each election; after placing third in the first two, he then won second place in each election until winning in 1983 (Berger 1983). Element Lad consistently won between 10 and 14 percent of the votes cast through the end of the team's 1980s run. For comparison, Mon-El, who received over 28% of the votes cast in 1969's election, never won more than 8.3% of the vote after that. This dedicated support kept Element Lad prominent in the team's adventures. For fans who were themselves gay or lesbian, votes for Element Lad were votes to keep someone like themselves in the spotlight and votes affirming the idea that the best example of heroism among a team of two dozen members could very well be gay. Element Lad was also the only leader elected by readers to two consecutive terms.

In that second election story, Levitz again cast the election in light of the team's history and fandom. The story ignores the candidates' electioneering and instead focuses mainly on people outside of the team—newscasters, police officers, young heroes aspiring to join the Legion—as they speculate about the results. The story returns in its final scene to Legion headquarters, where Element Lad watches the returns with the team's three founders. The final page of the story breaks the fourth wall twice. When Element Lad realizes he's won, he looks directly at the reader as he expresses his surprise and accepts the founders' congratulations. And in the final panels of the story, Flynt Brojj—a Legion fan who first appeared in *Superboy* #209 and was named for two real-world Legion fans—waits outside to learn the results. As Element Lad leaves to tell Flynt the news, he muses, "Guys like him stick by us ... they really care, don't they?" (Levitz, Colón, and Mahlstedt 1985, 11/3–4). This story salutes its readers and their role in helping to shape the Legion's adventures; had five more people cast ballots for Brainiac 5, he, rather than Element Lad, would have been the one to tell Flynt the results.

The next election involved the victory of a character who, like Flynt Brojj, was in many ways a stand-in for fans. In 1987's *Legion of Super-Heroes* #36, readers elected Polar Boy leader. Polar Boy was a longstanding character who had only recently become a Legionnaire; introduced during the *Adventure Comics* era, he was a member not of the Legion of Super-Heroes but of the Legion of Substitute Heroes. The Subs were a group of heroes who had auditioned for the Legion, been rejected, and formed a team of their own to fill in when the Legionnaires were away on a mission. In September 1985's *Legion of Super-Heroes* #14, however, Polar Boy disbanded the Subs and again tried out for the Legion, this time successfully.

Polar Boy's candidacy was not met with open arms from all of his teammates. Phantom Girl cautions him that he's too enthusiastic, and Saturn Girl and Brainiac 5 appoint themselves Element Lad's campaign managers—despite his firm statement that he is not interested—to stop Polar Boy. On the other hand, Ultra Boy tells teammates he'll vote for "the little guy," and Invisible Kid says, "I support the underdog ... always" (Levitz, LaRocque, and DeCarlo 1987, 11/1, 18/6). The announcement of Polar Boy's victory is met with mixed results: some Legionnaires are pleased for him and see his win as legitimating the team's newer members; others see it as humorous, given that he was once rejected as a member; and some grit their teeth and predict disaster. A final scene in which Polar Boy formally takes office echoes in many ways the sorts of scenes that closed many early Legion stories, with members reflecting on how a given adventure added to the club's history.

Polar Boy's election becomes an opportunity for reflection on the complicated relationship between fandom and tradition. For Polar Boy, becoming leader fulfills his lifelong adoration of the Legion as he becomes part of a line of leaders that stretches back to the team's founders. For other members, his election threatens the tradition he has become part of. This is a classic conundrum that faces organizations and communities in the real world as surely as it does in long-running fictional narratives: As history rolls on, can we preserve the traditions and institutions that have led us to the present day? Change is necessary for survival, but the wrong changes can undo decades of work and dedication. This is heady subject matter for any work of art; in a comic as tightly tied to its own history as the Legion, it made for fitting subtext.

The final Legion election of this period took place in 1989's *Legion of Super-Heroes* #60. Unlike the previous elections, this one took place off-panel, with the first page of the story delivering via exposition the news that Sensor Girl has been elected leader and Timber Wolf deputy leader. Sensor Girl is reluctant to serve, and Timber Wolf is confused by his own election, but he talks her into accepting the position because their teammates have placed their trust in them. Despite once again choosing a female leader for the team, this was in retrospect a minor note to end the tradition on. The results were announced at the start of Levitz's final four-part story as the Legion's writer, and not long afterwards, the Legion began a long series of relaunches and reboots, during which the election tradition fell by the wayside. Readers continued to agitate for its return, and it did (along with Levitz) in 2010, when a leader election was conducted with online votes. Soon after that, the Legion found itself canceled during a period of editorial tumult at DC Comics. But when it comes to the Legion, two things are, in the fullness of time, inevitable: the book will return, and once it does, readers will clamor for the chance to elect the team's leader.

CONCLUSION

The people we choose to lead us say something about how we view ourselves. This is part of why elections are so tempestuous and can provoke such strong emotions. We are not simply choosing someone to perform a task. We are also, in concert with our fellow citizens, making a choice about what our community stands for, and we know we stand a good chance of losing the argument. When it came to readers' choices about who should lead the Legion of Super-Heroes, the stakes were not as high as they are in a national or even a local election. No one would live or die as a result, no one's taxes would go up or down, no one's daily life would be seriously affected. But these elections were not meaningless.

As the tradition of reader elections became established, readers appear to have made their decisions about the team's leadership in a way that at least in part reflected concerns with diversity and representation and helped make them more than mere popularity contests or random outcomes. A reader who voted for a particular Legionnaire—a traditionally powered hero like Mon-El, an overlooked character like Dream Girl, comic relief like Bouncing Boy, or someone else—did so because something about that character represented something about heroism to that reader. The size and diversity of the Legion's membership gave readers more opportunity to find a favorite member who truly spoke to them than any other superhero team did, along with the ability to choose among many different models of heroism. As the Legion's readers continued to select the team's leaders, time and again they chose leaders from among the team's more unusual and overlooked members. In an era when there were no more than two women serving in the US Senate, readers twice elected women to lead the team. In an era when positive depictions of gay characters in media were few and far between, readers twice elected a hero many of them identified (or identified with) as gay. And many of the winners and runners-up in the Legion's elections were characters who were underestimated and overlooked by many of the team's creators and readers. While it is impossible to say that all of the readers who voted in Legion elections had representational concerns in mind, taken in the aggregate, these results suggest that the Legion's fandom was challenging traditional depictions of superheroes. The interactive culture that started in the letter columns of *Adventure Comics* helped create a fandom that embraced the diversity inherent in the Legion and sought to elevate that diversity in its choices of leaders. For a long period in the 1970s and 1980s, the readers who voted in the Legion's leadership elections made a sustained push that argued for an expanded conception of who can be a hero. In this regard, these readers were, like the Legionnaires themselves, ahead of their time.

Acknowledgments

Thanks to Russell Burbage, Ian Gordon, and Steven Thompson for generously sharing digital copies of various letter columns; to Paul Levitz, for recollections on the results of the Dream Girl election; and to my parents, James and Donna Galdieri.

References

Barr, Mike W., ed. 1981. Legion Outpost. *Legion of Super-Heroes*, vol. 2, no. 282. DC Comics.

Barr, Mike W., ed. 1982. Legion Outpost. *Legion of Super-Heroes*, vol. 2, no. 286. DC Comics.

Berger, Karen, ed. 1983. Legion Outpost. *Legion of Super-Heroes*, vol. 2, no. 306. DC Comics.

Binder, Otto, Curt Swan, and Stan Kaye. 1957. "The Kid from Krypton." *Adventure Comics*, vol. 1, no. 242. DC Comics.

Bridwell, E. Nelson, and Pete Costanza. 1968. "The Origin of the Legion!" *Superboy*, vol. 1, no. 147. DC Comics.

Bridwell, E. Nelson, Win Mortimer, and Jack Abel. 1970. "One Hero Too Many!" *Action Comics*, vol. 1, no. 387. DC Comics.

Cadigan, Glen. 2003. "Paul Levitz Interview, Part Two." In *The Legion Companion*, edited by Glen Cadigan, 145–52. Raleigh, NC: TwoMorrows Publishing.

Carlson, K. C. 1999. Introduction to *Legion of Super-Heroes Archives*, vol. 9, 5–7. New York: DC Comics.

Claremont, Chris, Rick Leonardi, and Whilce Portacio. 1986. "Duel." *Uncanny X-Men*, no. 201. Marvel Comics.

Companik, Chris. 2001. "The Confusing Sexuality History of Element Lad." FANZING: The Independent Online DC Comics Fanzine, June. http://www.fanzing.com/mag/fanzing35/feature10.shtml.

Darius, Julian. 2014. "On 'The Elements of Heartbreak': A Special Valentine's Day Post." Sequart, February 14. http://sequart.org/magazine/35039/on-the-elements-of-heartbreak/.

Flynn, Mike. 2004. "Xanthusian Eyes and Trommite Hearts." In *The Best of the Legion Outpost*, edited by Glen Cadigan, 101–4. Raleigh, NC: TwoMorrows Publishing.

Giffen, Keith, J.M. DeMatteis, Kevin Magiure, and Al Gordon. 1987. "Gray Life, Gray Dreams." *Justice League*, vol. 1, no. 5. DC Comics.

Gordon, Ian. 2012. "Writing to Superman: Towards an Understanding of the Social Networks of Comic-Book Fans." *Participations: Journal of Audience & Reception Studies* 9 (2): 120–32.

Hamilton, Edmond, Curt Swan, Sheldon Moldoff, and George Klein. 1966. "The Legionnaire Who Killed!" *Adventure Comics*, vol. 1, no. 324. DC Comics.

Hamilton, Edmond, John Forte, and Bob Oksner. 1964. "The Legion's Suicide Squad!" *Adventure Comics*, vol. 1, no. 319. DC Comics.

Hogg, Michael. 2001. "A Social Identity Theory of Leadership." *Personality and Social Psychology Review* 5 (3): 184–200.

Kaplan, Arie. 2008. *From Krakow to Krypton: Jews and Comic Books*. Philadelphia: The Jewish Publication Society.

Lee, Stan, Jack Kirby, and Dick Ayers. 1965. "The Old Order Changeth!" *The Avengers*, vol. 1, no. 16. Marvel Comics.

Leege, David C., Kenneth D. Wald, Brian S. Kreuger, and Paul D. Mueller. 2002. *The Politics of Cultural Differences: Social Change and Voter Mobilization Strategies in the Post-New Deal Period*. Princeton: Princeton University Press.

Levitz, Paul, Ernie Colón, and Larry Mahlstedt. 1985. "The More Things Stay the Same." *Legion of Super-Heroes*, vol. 3, no. 12. DC Comics.

Levitz, Paul, Greg LaRocque, and Mike DeCarlo. 1987. "Peace, Quiet and Impending Doom." *Legion of Super-Heroes*, vol. 3, no. 36. DC Comics.

Levitz, Paul, Joe Staton, and Jack Abel. 1979. "Celebration! A 247th Anniversary Special!" *Superboy and the Legion of Super-Heroes*, no. 247. DC Comics.

Levitz, Paul, Keith Giffen, and Larry Mahlstedt. 1983. "Siege Perilous." *Legion of Super-Heroes* vol. 2, no. 304. DC Comics.

Madrid, Mike. 2009. *The Supergirls: Fashion, Feminism, Fantasy, and the History of the Comic Book Heroines*. Minneapolis: Exterminating Angel Press.

O'Neil, Dennis. 2001. *The DC Comics Guide to Writing Comics*. New York: Watson-Guptill.

Pustz, Matthew J. 2000. *Comic Book Culture: Fanboys and True Believers (Studies in Popular Culture)*. Jackson: University Press of Mississippi.

Rogers, Vaneta. 2008. "The Legion of Super-Heroes at 50: Talking to Paul Levitz." Newsarama. com, August 20. http://www.newsarama.com/830-the-legion-of-super-heroes-at-50-talking-to-paul-levitz.html.

Siegel, Jerry, and John Forte. 1963. "The Stolen Super-Powers!" *Adventure Comics*, vol. 1, no. 304. DC Comics.

Siegel, Jerry, and John Forte. 1964a. "The Eight Impossible Missions!" *Adventure Comics*, vol. 1, no. 323. DC Comics.

Siegel, Jerry, and John Forte. 1964b. "The Revolt of the Girl Legionnaires." *Adventure Comics*, vol. 1, no. 326. DC Comics.

Stern, Paul C. 1995. "Why Do People Sacrifice for Their Nations?" *Political Psychology* 16 (2): 217–35.

Stevens, Richard J. 2011. "Let's Rap with Cap: Redefining American Patriotism through Popular Discourse and Letters." *Journal of Popular Culture* 44 (3): 606–32.

Sutton, Laurie, ed. 1982. Legion Outpost. *Legion of Super-Heroes*, vol. 2, no. 288. DC Comics.

Swan, Curt. 1975. *Amazing World of DC Comics*, no. 9. DC Comics.

Waid, Mark. 1998. "Staying Power." In *Comic-Con International: San Diego Souvenir Program Book*, 23–24. San Diego: Comic-Con International.

Woolfolk, William, Curt Swan, and John Fischetti. 1951. "The Boy from Mars!" *Superboy*, vol. 1, no. 14. DC Comics.

Weisinger, Mort, ed. 1966. Legion Outpost. *Adventure Comics*, vol. 1, no. 341. DC Comics.

Weisinger, Mort, and [E. Nelson Bridwell], eds. 1966. Legion Outpost. *Adventure Comics*, vol. 1, no. 345. DC Comics.

Weisinger, Mort, and [E. Nelson Bridwell], eds. 1968. Legion Outpost. *Adventure Comics*, vol. 1, no. 364. DC Comics.

12.

Not Just Superhero Stories

COMIC BOOK FANDOM AS A RESOURCE IN THE CULTURAL TOOLKIT OF LIFE

Adriana Estrada Wilson

The first time I walked into a comic book store I was twenty-nine years old, but I felt like a kid her first time at Disneyland. I was excited, overwhelmed, mystified, and intimidated. I knew I had discovered a magical place but, at the same time, I had no idea what that meant. I was instantly bombarded with curiosity, and the sociologist in me knew that there must be a deep meaning to this place for those who frequented it. From that first moment, I wanted to know what it was that gave this place meaning. My curiosity about the store soon expanded to a curiosity about comic book culture. As I began talking to patrons and employees of the store, I discovered that comics were more than just stories to these people. For many, comics had become an integral part of their life. It was from these initial conversations that I decided to explore further the role that comics held for the members of this unique, thriving subculture.

Academic interest in comics is nothing new. Studies relating to comics have come from an array of disciplines such as literature, communications, sociology, anthropology, gender studies, philosophy, education, and even business (Adkinson 2008; Beaty 2004; Gray 2010; Peterson and Gerstein 2005; Singer 2002; Taylor 2007). These studies have explored topics such as cultural criminology and the development of the Comics Code; influences of comics on art and art on comics; business structure in the comics community; comics as a means of cultural resistance; and content issues of race, gender, inequality, authority, and body image. Yet, even with all this interest, there is still little information available about how people engage with comic books. Several studies have looked at how fans use their cultural resources within the subculture as a way of gaining acceptance and cultural capital (Brown 2001; Pustz 1999; Woo 2011; Wright 2001). Few, however, have ventured to explore how insiders make use of these unique cultural resources in their everyday lives. I address this oversight by focusing on the ways social actors transform cultural resources gained from subcultures or personal interests into universal resources applicable to various aspects of their life based on a qualitative study of a comic book store. What I observed were not just the practices of a subculture but also how individuals use comics and their interest in them as a cultural resource for navigating through the broader social world.

CULTURE INFLUENCING ACTION

Sociologists have long been interested in how cultural context influences individual interests and behavior (Bourdieu 1984; Csikszentmihalyi and Rochberg-Halton 1981; Dittmar 1992; Featherstone 1987). Early understandings of cultural analysis as outlined by Weber (1946) and Parsons (1937) assumed that culture provides values and end goals that direct individual action. According to this view, values learned through culture are the main causal element of social action. Consider, for example, the "culture of poverty" argument that suggests those raised in poverty do not learn the same values and aspirations as those from working- or middle-class backgrounds. People from a culture of poverty are believed to have no motivation to live a different type of life because their culture has not instilled these values in them. By contrast, those who learn the values associated with upward social mobility will engage in actions that will lead toward the end goal of financial success. Thus, action is influenced by culture. Today, the culture of poverty argument is considered by many to be weak and outdated. In most cases, lack of upward mobility is due to extenuating circumstances, not a lack of values or desire to move up. People living in poverty are often some of the hardest working, holding multiple jobs with the hope of attaining a better life. The culture of poverty argument may be flawed, but it is a perfect example of how values are seen as directing action in cultural analysis.

Swidler (1986) believes the values paradigm is too one-dimensional and provides an alternative method of analysis for the causal significance of culture. This study employs Swidler's (1986) culture in action approach as a means for investigating how comic books and the culture surrounding them influence action. Swidler (1986) explains that action is not a solitary act with one end goal in mind but is composed of larger assemblages she refers to as "strategies of action." As people have various end goals, each act is not chosen to meet a singular, given end. Instead, people construct chains of actions with various different links. It is through the organization of these links, through strategies of action, that culture influences action. This approach removes many of the assumptions made in values-driven cultural analysis and allows more freedom for the data to present themes that may otherwise be overlooked. Since real cultures often have conflicting symbols, rituals, stories, and guides to action, there is no constant direction for action. Therefore, culture becomes a "toolkit" or repertoire that actors can use to justify and construct lines of action. This being the case, social actors are not "cultural dupes" (Garfinkel 1967; Wrong 1961) but "active, sometimes skilled users of culture" (Swidler 1986, 277). This theory allows for a deeper exploration of the variety of ways actors use culture by allowing one to focus on the motivations of an individual actor rather that of the group as a whole.

In her later work, *Talk of Love*, Swidler (2001) expands on this idea by exploring how social actors draw on narratives that align with their various ideologies surrounding the concept of love to explain or justify the actions they take. A classic Swidler analysis of fans would have considered the ways in which fans draw from cultural narratives that exist in society to explain or create value for their comic book fandom. Take for example the cultural narrative that reading is an enriching activity and viewed positively in society. Individuals can give value to their fandom using this cultural narrative since comic book fandom involves reading. This approach again makes assumptions—notably, that fans are in need of a way to validate their fandom. However, my data told a different story.

To better understand the various ways social actors are influenced by culture, I apply Swindler's culture in action theory in a new way. It is still the case that social actors use culture as a toolkit to create strategies of action but in a different way than Swidler suggests. Rather than utilizing existing social narratives to validate action, social actors use their fandom as a resource in their cultural toolkit to create narratives that address their personal needs in other domains of life. When fans want to be better at their jobs, they draw on their fandom as a unique cultural resource that can be used to their advantage. In this example, comics fandom serves as a source of inspiration or as a helpful tool in the workplace. My focus is not on identity formation itself but rather on the use of comic book fandom in this process. I use the construction of self as a lens for interpreting some ways that social actors are influenced by culture. For this group, comic fandom can provide a cultural repertoire that is useful in the construction of a desired kind of self. Rather than limiting themselves to the construction of a subcultural identity, fans find ways to use their fandom in the construction of their overall identity and the kind of self that they are attempting to portray in the broader social world as well.

COMIC BOOK FANDOM IN ACTION

This chapter discusses the findings of a qualitative study employing ethnographic methods in a comic book store, "Metropolis,"[1] located in a large city. Fieldwork consisted of participant observation of the site as well as participation in activities based around the store, including meetings of a comic book readers' club, game nights, author signings, and other events sponsored by the store. I also conducted eighteen formal qualitative interviews off-site with employees and patrons of the store. Data were analyzed using a grounded theory approach (Glaser and Strauss 1967) and established coding procedures and techniques (Emerson, Fretz, and Shaw 1995). Questions that framed the process of coding were provided by Emerson, Fretz, and Shaw (1995, 146) and focused the analysis on processes instead of causes and motives. During analysis of the data, three strong themes emerged: finding community, sense of comfort, and use in the workplace. These themes are not viewed as motivating factors for being a fan but rather benefits gained from their existing fandom. They exemplify some of the ways comic book readers engage with comics and find use for them in their everyday lives.

Finding Community

The obvious reason for going to a comic book store is to purchase comic books and other related paraphernalia. However, many patrons seemed to have multiple motivations for visiting the store. For example, social encounters with others that have similar interests were a clear motivator that became evident during both observation and interviews. Many store regulars were on a first-name basis with the clerks who worked there and often engaged them in conversations as lengthy as the employees would allow. After general greetings and pleasantries were exchanged, almost every conversation became focused on some aspect of popular culture, including movies, television, video games, tabletop games, and of course comics. The social attraction of the store is also communicated by the frequency that some patrons visited. Although new comics are only released once a week (on Wednesdays), several respondents admitted to visiting the store more than once a week. Many patrons do not view the store purely as a place of commerce where one goes to buy products. It is also viewed as a social environment with a ready supply of enthusiasts with similar interests.

The comic book store often operates as a "locale" for the social interaction that takes place within this subculture. Woo (2011) suggests that this locale acts as a sanctuary from outsiders and as an arena to showcase knowledge. The findings presented here reinforce these ideas but also present another less complex explanation. The comic book store is a locale that offers a ready-made community with a stockpile of people who hold common interests. Modern American society is becoming increasingly individualistic, causing a general decline in the strength of traditional communities that one is born into such as ethnicity, religion, class, and so on. Some argue that this is a detriment to society, causing a general breakdown of the concept of community (Putnam 2001). Another argument that has gained popularity is that this phenomenon has created a situation where individuals are more free to pick and choose which communities they want to be a part of (Bauman 1998; Beck 1992; Featherstone 1987; Giddens 1991). Locales such as the comic book store make the search for a desired community much easier.

Comic book readers can draw from their cultural toolkit and use their interest in comics as a means for connecting with a like-minded community. During routine visits to the store to buy comics, patrons James and Tim were able to establish personal connections with store employees, which were described using the phrases "got really cool with" and "They all know me by name; I know them by name." James explained that as connections with those employees with whom he had "a lot of similar interests" grew, so did his time at the store. When *his* employees left, his time at the store diminished, reinforcing the idea that he had learned to use the store as a site for connecting with like-minded people. Similarly, Tim showed his use of the store as a connection site by distinguishing between visits that were for buying comics and visits that were for socializing, which he described as "entertaining" and "fun." Dick, a fairly new comic book fan, described a similar connection to the community at the store, saying, "It's fun to find a bunch of people that have similar interests. It seems like people that are into comics generally like music and like films and stuff like that too. It's a nice subset of people, and it's something I'm glad I'm a part of now."

In some cases, comic book readers (like those above) exemplify social actors in search of a community that fits their needs and aligns with their sense of self. By accessing their cultural toolkit, in this case their interest in comics, the search for a desired community becomes much easier. Comic book fans were able to use their fandom to locate and connect with people that not only shared their interest in comics but also were generally like-minded. As seen here, readers may not necessarily be looking to adhere to a predefined fan identity or find a stage to display their knowledge; they may be exploring a new outlet to make friends. Being able to connect with people that are like-minded and share similar worldviews enables the individual to fortify their personal worldview and sense of self through the support of others.

Sense of Comfort

Comics are often discussed as being a tool used to escape from the world through the act of reading and engaging in an imaginary world (Botzakis 2009; Brown 2001; Wright 2001). In the course of this study, the data provided a way that comic fandom can also be used indirectly for escape in an entirely different facet. Several respondents who visit the store frequently described a supplemental motivation for visiting the store, the feeling of happiness that comes from being there. For many, this feeling alone was enough to entice them to visit the store. Here comic book fandom offers an escape but not through the venture into a story or direct use of the medium itself. The escape offered by the experience of visiting the store is one that brings peace and comfort.

The ways in which this feeling of comfort was attained varied among respondents. Several respondents explained that while in the store it was not necessarily the comic book or story itself that was important at the moment; it was the act of searching and the "thrill of discovery." For example, Allison had become bored with the monotony of life and was looking for a new form of entertainment when she rediscovered comics. Here Allison describes how the store makes her feel:

> **Allison:** I realized I feel a little bit better when I hang out at the comic book store. I realized that no matter how bad of a day that I am having, no matter how depressed or sad or angry I might be, I go to the comic book store, and I feel so much better. It's a little bit of an escape. I spend twenty-five bucks in one day, but I figured, okay, it is better to spend twenty-five dollars in one day than to spend twenty-five hundred in therapy or running up a bar tab or going to a liquor store.
>
> **Adriana:** What do you do at the comic book store that makes you feel better?
>
> **Allison:** Just trying to discover new stories, trying to get whatever the current issue is of whatever I've been reading . . . I kind of get the thrill of discovering; it's like looking for treasure in a way.

Comic books and the comic book store provided respondents like Allison with a unique outlet that they could be excited about. It allowed fans to momentarily escape their day-to-day lives and focus on something that provided thrills, surprises, and rewards.

Another pattern that emerged among respondents was the view of the store as a "happy place" with the ability to stimulate a good mood. For some, visiting the store was about more than just buying comic books, engaging with interesting people, or the thrill of discovery; they felt a connection to the comics and the store itself. For patrons like this, being able to walk into a physical environment that was built entirely of comics was in and of itself enough to stimulate feelings of happiness. When asked about how often he visits the store and what he does there, Mark responded:

> I generally go a lot. I'm there at least once a week. I will be there on Wednesdays when the new issues come out. Then I will typically stop back in just because the comic shop makes me happy. Not so much the buying things truthfully . . . I really enjoy walking through the shop and looking at numerous toys and t-shirts and posters and stuff.

Visiting the store allowed him to literally step into a world that was wondrous and engaging. Even though he had been there many times, Mark expressed that he is still enchanted by the items in the store. He described the store as a place that he could go to momentarily escape his troubles and feel at peace. This sentiment about the store was not exclusive to Mark. Other respondents expressed similar feelings, and regulars in the store displayed actions that indicate they may have felt the same way.

By using the store as a means of escape and to induce feelings of comfort, these fans were engaging in active cultural work in which comic book fandom served as a key tool. When visiting the store and engaging with comics, these social actors were using their cultural toolkit to change their mood to one that better aligned with the kind of self they wished to construct, someone satisfied with life and in control of their emotions. Here we see that fans can use their fandom to avert their personal problems by shifting their focus from the problem at hand to something that brings them joy and induces feelings of comfort. Engaging with comics in the store setting can provide people with the capacity to assert their ideal self when faced with an emotional state that is counter to the kind of self they wish to construct.

Use in the Workplace

A common use of comic fandom that emerged among respondents was the incorporation of comic book culture into professional life. Unlike the previous themes discussed, the use of fandom in the workplace often resulted from the acknowledgment by fans that their interest in comics was not just a hobby but also a resource that could be useful in other parts of their life. Viewing comics or any hobby as mere entertainment greatly limits its potential for other uses. For some, changing the way they viewed their connection to comics was a revelation. When discussing his decision to leave his job as a graphic designer and go back to school to study sculpture and create art influenced by comic book culture, Brandon said: "For me it was making a decision of this is important to me in a way that's not just a hobby, that I want to use it as a vocabulary to do work." Once Brandon saw comics as having the potential to be something other than just a hobby, he was able to use them as a tool to help him figure out what he *wanted* to do. Not all fans expressed experiencing such an "ah-ha" moment. However, those who approached their fandom with an open mind were able to find ways it could be useful in their work life.

Among those respondents who pursued creative work in cultural industries, comic books sometimes served as a source of inspiration. Many respondents admitted that the inspiration from comics was very direct, leaving them with the artistic desire to create comic-related material. Some were successful in achieving this goal. For example, after years of dedication, Blake, an established comic book artist who does freelance work for various companies, is now in the process of signing a contract to draw for DC Comics. Blake's story, however, is not the norm. For most respondents, creating comic books was merely a childhood dream that eventually became more of a pastime to work on in their spare time.

In spite of this, several respondents found that comics could be used as a source of inspiration in other ways. For example, Harold, an aspiring musician, explained that the artistic ability and craft of storytelling that goes into creating comics inspired him to create things on his own. He admits that, while he is no good at drawing and is not a writer, he is still able to draw inspiration from comics:

> I think in that way maybe it influences me 'cause, just that, respect for being able to do something so long and do a good job at it, and to be above a mediocre storyteller but be a really good storyteller. Again, I don't write, but it's just that respect of life like where wow, 'cause I do

things like artwork and music and photography just to say well if I'm gonna do it let me do it well. This guy can do it well for twenty years and this guy can do it well, why can't I do what I do well? But you know I think that would apply to, if I were a fisherman, well this guy can write comic books well, why can't I be a good fisherman?

Here, Harold is discussing his favorite comic book writer who has been able to produce quality work for over twenty years. For Harold, being able to create something that well for that amount of time is itself an inspirational act. Having comics in his life gave Harold the attitude that he too could be good at what he does, that he too can create beautiful things. Harold provides an example of how viewing comic book fandom as something other than just a hobby or entertainment can be useful in the development of a worldview that aligns with the attainment of a certain kind of self. Here, the fan uses comic books to develop the worldview that anyone can achieve greatness and uses that to foster his creative endeavors.

Comics were not only useful to those engaged in creative work. More than a few respondents who engaged in more traditional work shared that they too had found ways their fandom was useful in the workplace. Tim, who works for the public library system, openly admits that comics "impact how I approach my job, they influence some of the things I do within my job." Using his comics knowledge and connections, Tim was able to organize a panel discussion with local comic book writers and artists hosted by the public library; the event was a success. Rather than leaving his interest in comics at home, Tim found a way to make use of his knowledge at work, making himself an asset with insight to offer on a medium that is rising in popularity. His knowledge of comics provided him with a specialized skill set that he was able to use at work to set himself apart and gain the esteem of his superiors.

Among other respondents who used comics at work were two youth pastors who both found comics helpful in their jobs. The two did not know each other, but both described their use of comics in very similar ways. Working with kids, the pastors found that comics provide relatable stories that children can understand much easier than complex religious abstractions:

It's easier for a child to relate to a superhero and our need for some-body to save us than it is for some to try and help them to relate to a prophet. A prophet is something that's a language that they can grasp but for them to understand, a superhero is a lot easier for them to understand. Somebody who comes in and saves them from whatever evil villain or something like that versus if you say a prophet who is trying to lead you back to God. It's easy for a kid to understand superheroes, so using that as the language I'd have to say is very helpful.

In this example, the pastors were able to take their personal use of comics and apply it to their work. Each of the pastors read comics from a young age, and when they began to study and become deeply invested in religion, they both found comics to be a very useful tool for understanding religion. Having that personal experience, they were able to incorporate comics into their teachings in ways that were beneficial to the learning process rather than distracting from it.

Fans who changed their perception of comics from just entertainment to a possible resource found various ways comics and their fandom could be useful in the workplace. At work, fans accessed their cultural toolkit in ways that become useful not only on the job but also in the construction of a kind of self. Some draw inspiration from comics as part of their cultural toolkit to help build a worldview that aligns with the kind of professional self that they want to construct. This is achieved, not by drawing on content, but rather by changing the way they view their relation to comics. Once fans changed the way they viewed their connection with comics, they were able to proactively reap the professional advantages afforded to them from utilizing their fandom. Some fans referenced their cultural toolkit in the development of skills that assisted them in the process of doing their job. This aided in the construction of a kind of self by providing them with helpful tools that gave them the capacity to portray a certain kind of self to those they work with. In all cases described above, the social actors utilize their fandom in the construction of a certain kind of self either through the creation of a worldview or the development of a skill set.

DISCUSSION AND CONCLUSION

Previous studies of comic books and comic book fans have focused on concrete uses of comics within the subculture and the meanings that readers derive from comic book content. Initially, I set out to examine how social actors draw from their cultural resources to construct a subcultural identity. This assumed that social actors were using their cultural toolkit mainly to establish themselves as insiders. Perhaps this assumption was made because the majority of subculture studies work within the parameters of constructions of insiders and outsiders: Who is an insider? How do insiders interact with other insiders? How are insiders viewed by outsiders? Given what I have observed, I question whether this is the best approach to understanding unique social groups. There is definitely a distinct culture present here, but I'm not sure it can be defined and fully understood under a model of insiders and outsiders. According to many respondents (whom I as an observer would categorize as insiders) the construction of a subcultural identity was neither the most important nor the most beneficial use of comics. Many of these social actors do not use their fandom as an identifier of who they are, so who are we as observers to come in and place that label on them?

My initial misconception was that the cultural toolkit afforded by comic book fandom was only beneficial within the social world directly based around this cultural object. What I observed, however, was that, rather than limiting themselves to the construction of a subcultural identity, fans were also finding ways to use their fandom in the construction of their overall identity and the kind of self that they were attempting to portray in the broader social world. As the data show, insiders have learned to transcend the social barriers of the subculture and use their fandom in ways that allow them to meet like-minded people, find comfort through escapism, and strengthen their position in the workplace. These are very different examples, but each showcases a way that social actors are able to apply their cultural toolkit in ways that are beneficial to their everyday lives. The kind of self one is constructing varies from fan to fan, but the use of the cultural repertoire acquired from fandom appears to be a somewhat common practice in the process.

Through application of Swidler's (1986) culture in action theory, a unique understanding of the influence of comic book culture was able to emerge. Here, culture does not *dictate* action by providing values and end goals but rather *influences* action by providing social actors with resources to construct lines of action. In *Talk of Love*, Swidler (2001, 5) focuses on the culture of love to explore various ways culture is "appropriated, mobilized and linked to experience." She does this specifically by focusing on a strategy of action where social actors use various existing cultural understandings and narratives of love to justify and explain their actions. This study expands on Swidler's work by exploring another possible strategy of action—namely, that social actors use their interests as a resource in their cultural toolkit to create unique narratives that fit their personal needs. For many in this group, comics fandom motivates action in the construction of self not only by providing an identity that they can adhere to but also by providing a cultural repertoire that is useful in the construction of a desired kind of self. Comparing these examples, we can begin to understand that the ways in which culture influences action may still have many complexities that have yet to be explored.

During the course of this study, I gained insight into the complex bonds that comic book fans form with this subculture. I observed that social actors are able to utilize the cultural resources they gain from being a fan both inside and outside of that subculture community. This being the case, we can no longer approach practices of fans, audiences, and subcultures as relevant only to their subculture. Future research should investigate further whether the utilization of subculture resources in the broader social world is something that is unique to certain fan bases and subcultures or if it is a common practice. By considering how social actors transform the cultural resources gained from subcultures or personal interests into universal resources in their cultural toolkit, we can gain a better understanding of the significance of culture and cultural objects in the socialization process.

Notes

1. All subjects and locations have been given fictitious names to ensure confidentiality.

References

Adkinson, Cary D. 2008. "*The Amazing Spider-Man* and the Evolution of the Comics Code: A Case Study in Cultural Criminology." *Journal of Criminal Justice and Popular Culture* 15: 240–61.

Bauman, Zygmunt. 1988. *Freedom*. Milton Keynes: Open University Press.

Beaty, Bart. 2004. "Roy Lichtenstein's Tears: Art vs. Pop in American Culture." *Canadian Review of American Studies* 34: 249–68.

Beck, Ulrich. 1992. *Risk Society: Towards a New Modernity*. London: Sage.

Botzakis, Stergios. 2009. "Adult Fans of Comic Books: What They Get Out of Reading." *Journal of Adolescent & Adult Literacy* 53: 50–59.

Bourdieu, Pierre. 1984. *Distinction: A Social Critique of the Judgement of Taste*. Cambridge: MIT Press.

Brown, Jeffrey A. 2001. *Black Superheroes, Milestone Comics, and Their Fans*. Jackson: University Press of Mississippi.

Csikszentmihalyi, Mihaly, and Eugene Rochberg-Halton. 1981. *The Meaning of Things: Domestic Symbols and the Self*. Cambridge: Cambridge University Press.

Dittmar, Helga. 1992. *The Social Psychology of Material Possession: To Have Is to Be*. Hemel, Hempstead: Harvester Wheatsheaf.

Emerson, Robert M., Rachel I. Fretz, and Linda L. Shaw. 1995. *Writing Ethnographic Fieldnotes*. Chicago: University of Chicago Press.

Featherstone, Mike. 1987. "Lifestyle and Consumer Culture." *Theory, Culture and Society* 4: 55–70.

Garfinkel, Harold. 1967. *Studies in Ethnomethodology*. Englewood Cliffs, NJ: Prentice-Hall.

Giddens, Anthony. 1991. *Modernity and Self-Identity: Self and Society in the Late Modern Age*. Cambridge: Polity.

Glaser, Barney G., and Anselm L. Strauss. 1967. *The Discovery of Grounded Theory: Strategies for Qualitative Research*. Chicago: Aldine.

Gray, Maggie. 2010. "'A Fistful of Dead Roses . . .': Comics as Cultural Resistance: Alan Moore and David Lloyd's *V for Vendetta*." *Journal of Graphic Novels and Comics* 1: 31–49.

Parsons, Talcott. 1937. *The Structure of Social Action*. New York: Free Press.

Peterson, Bill E., and Emily D. Gerstein. 2005. "Fighting and Flying: Archival Analysis of Threat, Authoritarianism, and the North American Comic Book." *Political Psychology* 26: 887–904.

Pustz, Matthew J. 1999. *Comic Book Culture: Fanboys and True Believers*. Jackson: University Press of Mississippi.

Putnam, Robert D. 2001. *Bowling Alone: The Collapse and Revival of American Community*. New York: Simon & Schuster.

Singer, Marc. 2002. "'Black Skins' and White Masks: Comic Books and the Secret of Race." *African American Review* 36: 107–19.

Swidler, Ann. 1986. "Culture in Action: Symbols and Strategies." *American Sociological Review* 51: 273–86.

Swidler, Ann. 2001. *Talk of Love: How Culture Matters*. Chicago: University of Chicago Press.

Taylor, Aaron. 2007. "'He's Gotta Be Strong, and He's Gotta Be Fast, and He's Gotta Be Larger Than Life': Investigating the Engendered Superhero Body." *The Journal of Popular Culture* 40: 344–60.

Truitt, Brian. 2010. "'Incognito' Powered by Pulp Ethos." *USA TODAY*, November 6. http://www.usatoday.com/life/comics/2010-11-06-incognito_N.htm.

Weber, Max. 1946. "The Social Psychology of the World Religions." In *From Max Weber*, edited by H. H. Gerth and C. Wright Mills, 267–301. New York: Oxford University Press.

Woo, Benjamin. 2011. "The Android's Dungeon: Comic-Bookstores, Cultural Spaces and the Social Practices of Audiences." *Journal of Graphic Novels and Comics* 2: 125–36.

Wright, Bradford W. 2001. *Comic Book Nation: The Transformation of Youth Culture in America*. Baltimore: Johns Hopkins University Press.

Wrong, Dennis. 1961. "The Oversocialized Conception of Man in Modern Sociology." *American Sociological Review* 26: 183–93.

13.

Pirates and Publishers

COMICS SCANNING AND THE AUDIENCE FUNCTION

Kalervo A. Sinervo

In May of 2011, DC Comics announced that beginning that September, all of their major titles would be revamped and relaunched as "The New 52," featuring new number-one issues and "day-and-date digital publishing" (Hyde 2011), wherein digital and paper editions would be released simultaneously. DC was not the first publisher to commit itself to digital distribution, nor the last; Archie Comics beat them to market in April 2011 (Mahadeo 2011), and before the end of the year, both Image and Marvel had pledged to follow suit (Polo 2011; Phegley 2011). These decisions by prominent American comics publishers signified a powerful move toward digital media in the North American comics industry, marking 2011 as a flashpoint for the formalized acknowledgment of digital reading in comics. Their moves to day-and-date digital publishing represented the first widespread institutionalized instance of what Marjorie Perloff calls "differential text production" in the comics industry, texts "that exist in different material forms with no single version being the definitive one" (2006, 146). Adrienne Resha (2017) defines our own moment in comics history as the "Blue Age of Comics," set apart from earlier ages by digital readers, guided reading technology, and social media. Resha identifies the 2007 debut of digital comics retailer comiXology as heralding the dawn of the Blue Age (2017, under "The Medium of Comic Books"), and the 2011 shift to day-and-date concretized the transition. However, we might slightly amend this timeline to include something that went unmentioned in all the publishers' press releases: that an illicit form of differential text production in comics had already existed for over half a decade by the time of day-and-date.

In terms of digital distribution, mainstream publishers lagged behind the prolific activities of a handful of anonymous fans colloquially known as comics pirates or comics scanners (Wershler, Sinervo, and Tien 2013). Since the advent of affordable at-home flatbed scanners and rapid online file-sharing options such as filelockers and BitTorrenting, comics scanners had been distributing both current and older comics free of charge. Official day-and-date strategies tacitly addressed this problem: before 2011, digitizing catalogues wavered somewhere between a sideline and a promotional tool for publishers. Only comics scanners realized the potential of digital distribution to address issues of access and completion, but their work constituted exactly the kind of piracy that initiatives like the Digital Millennium Copyright Act and the Stop Online Piracy Act were ostensibly built to combat. Day-and-date offered a legitimate option for digital comics reading, particularly when paired with advances in material technology (the iPad was released in 2010) that improved the digital reading experience. Since 2011 was also the year in which organized, unauthorized comics scanning began to decline (Wershler, Sinervo, and Tien 2014, 337), recording digital comics scanning history before it erases itself is key to understanding how scanners worked, and how they saw themselves and their place within the larger world of comics culture.

This chapter is derived in part from a larger project that seeks to frame the historical period in which comics scanning was an organized, internally structured practice. Who were the pirates? What ideologies motivated them, and what methods did they employ for both the work of scanning and the organization of their efforts? The project focuses on two of the most active English-language comics scanning groups (or *crews*) of the 2000s, Digital Comics Preservation (DCP) and Minutemen. Coalescing in 2005 and reaching peak productivity in 2010, DCP and Minutemen have since unofficially dissolved, living on only as case studies for a specific moment in the histories of both comics and the internet. The comics scanning project collected torrent packet metadata from BitTorrent tracker sites to trace the productivity of these two groups from 2005 through their decline in activity in 2012. This chapter draws on that data and examines several scanned comics to argue that comics scanners constitute a significant public within comics culture. It also argues that the perspective decoded from their work meaningfully challenges notions of authorship in comics, offering a new take on the infrastructural work of digitization and digital editing as creative contribution.

Framed in terms of author functions (Foucault 2007), audience functions (Johnson 2013), fandom and labor (Scott 2013), and encoding and decoding (Hall 1980), comics scanners alter the authorial signifiers of the comics they digitize and form a node of participatory culture in the comics world. By outlining their practices and examining the objects they produce, we can override the discourse of piracy and recontextualize scanners as users employing complex practice sets, rather than as criminals trading in a shadow economy or as free-speech/open-access evangelists.

CONTEXTUALIZING COMICS SCANNING

Debates about file sharing have been highly polarized. If you ask media industry giants, piracy is a vile scourge that amounts to blatant thievery, but it represents the utopian promise of a truly free internet to file sharers and torrent trackers (Seagrave 2003, 147; Klinger 2010, 106). Comics piracy offers an escape from this discursive binary in a number of ways. First, as Ramon Lobato notes in his book, *Shadow Economies of Cinema*, "the war on piracy needs to be understood as a public relations exercise" on behalf of industries using "inevitably speculative" means of quantifying data (2012, 73–74). Second, although comics publishers' parent companies like Warner Brothers and the Walt Disney Company obviously have a strong lobbying presence, the comics industry does not represent the same magnitude of legal juggernaut as organizations like the MPAA or RIAA, and it must attempt to contain comics piracy through industry practices and digital distribution methods, rather than litigation and prosecution of pirates (Lima 2011). Third, the specifically creative labor (that which is less editorial and more clearly productive) that goes into scanning comics, though unsanctioned, is generally easier to identify than in (for example) an illegally distributed MP3. While information about the provenance of an MP3 is only available in metadata, scanned comics typically include pages indicating the scanner and their affiliation embedded directly into the file; this provides an avenue to identify and discuss what contribution the scanner may make, if any, to the overall work. Finally, the relative newness of comics piracy separates it from the longer history of bootleg music and films. Unlike older forms of media copying like bootleg audio and video (Johns 2010, 498–99), comics piracy barely existed before the mid-2000s, when flatbed scanners became both efficient and affordable enough for American consumers. By that point, the internet had effectively begun to marginalize the profit motive for media piracy in Western culture, and the propiracy rhetoric of free speech and file sharing was on the rise (Beyer 2013). Consequently, there has never been a significant market for pirated comics in North America. Unshackled from the history of for-profit illicit media distribution, as well as the dubious findings of industry-led research into the practices of bootlegging, comics piracy allows us to focus on contemporary piracy as a collaborative and even creative practice.

Although a robust literature addresses fan communities that illicitly scan, translate, and distribute manga for consumption outside Japan (colloquially known as "scanlation"), English-language comics scanning has not been studied extensively and has received only scant journalistic coverage. The scholarship on scanlation approaches both the actors and their products from myriad perspectives. For example, Jeremy Douglass, William Huber, and Lev Manovich (2011) used scanlated manga pages to algorithmically visualize manga motifs, Nicole Nowlin (2010a, 2010b, 2010c) adopted an interpretive social science perspective, examining arguments around fair use, motivations, and justifications for scanlations, and the complicated dynamics of the scanlator/publisher relationship, and linguist Cathy Sell (2011) explored the actual practices and protocols of scanlation, identifying the unique translation challenges posed by the intertextual nature of manga. This literature is not only informative in itself but also enables a comparative approach, in that it tacitly highlights some key differences between manga scanlation and comics scanning. First, scanlators have the added task of translation between Japanese and other languages and cultures. Manga exists in a different milieu than North American comics publishing and fandom, so while understanding scanlation provides a lens on the techniques, communities, and products of English-language comics scanning, it is important not to conflate the two worlds. Second, scanlators employ specific discourses to justify their illicit practices. Rather than cannibalizing a legitimate market for manga, scanlators describe their work as building audiences for manga outside Japan, both as a general form (Koulikov 2010) and for specific series (Lee 2009). But such a justification is absent for English-language comics scanners discussed in this chapter. While scanners do sometimes view themselves as providing a service to the comics industry, their work is quite different from the prelicense audience development that scanlators arguably offer the legitimate publishing industries of manga. Under US copyright regimes, comics scanning is far harder to justify as transformative, making it an easy target for the rhetoric of piracy—not that scanlators stand on especially solid ground in this regard (Nowlin 2010a). The dearth of work on English-language comics scanning makes it an excellent point of entry for a broader discussion of media bootlegging, as political arguments of theft and free speech have had less time to develop.

The rhetoric of piracy as theft is also complicated when scanners are situated as audiences. As later sections of this chapter will demonstrate, scanners view themselves as dedicated fans of not only books they love but the medium, culture, and industry of comics as a whole. Without profit motive, and firmly contextualized as fans, scanners can be positioned as participators. Their activities fall into what Derek Johnson calls the "audience function." Johnson asks us to view audiences as a discursive construct that looks beyond the consumers' interpretations of a text (Johnson 2013, 137). A discursive framework based around hierarchical positions of commercial production and circulation determines how audiences are made meaningful and/or legitimate (138), and audiences subsequently play an important role in generating meaning and value themselves. Essentially, it is impossible to account for author functions without also accounting for the audiences in relation to whom works are continually positioned (Johnson 2014, 50).

In comics, hierarchies between producers and consumers are sometimes difficult to parse. As long as comics has been a business, comics publishers have solicited feedback from readers in the form of letter writing. This practice goes back as far as wartime publishing (Kocmarek 2016, 152) and even predepression newspaper strips (Gardner 2012, 51), but letters columns started to become standard in North American comics during the late 1950s, when publishers such as EC would attempt to mobilize fans to write in suggestions for future storylines. Jared Gardner noted the benefits of this strategy, writing, "EC created a self-referential community, winking at inside jokes and speaking with their readers in a slang likely to mystify new readers. The strategy worked, creating a loyalty to the publisher, especially among young adult readers, and the sense that EC was something apart from the standard fare blanketing the newsstands" (98). Other publishers must have taken notice of this success because before long mainstream backmatter was rife with such inside jokes and lingo (Murray 2013, 339). These tactics helped publishers create a brand mythology around themselves and harnessed the labor of fans themselves to generate content and serve as grassroots marketing.

Part of the intended consequence of this was to imbue audiences with a strong sense of their privileges and rights in offering commentary, critique, and even sometimes determining the course of events within comics publishing, but publishers could not predict what might happen when the feedback loop escaped the control of their editorial authority. Fans' self-image as power brokers has been bolstered by the advent of networked digital culture, blogging, and social media. Today, as before, the decision-making power rests invariably in the hands of publishers, who nevertheless publicly position fans as key decision makers with extensive rights. Discursively, publishers want to construct the audience function of comics fans as high up in the hierarchy; frequently, however, they engage in business practices that might indicate otherwise. The construction of discursive frameworks in which the input of fans is highly valued therefore presents a somewhat schizophrenic hierarchy of discourse power.

The industry itself encourages this position by relying increasingly on the idea of official authors and producers as fans gone pro. In considering the rhetoric of media industries in marketing their creators as auteurs and members of fan communities, Suzanne Scott identifies what she calls the "fanboy auteur," a gendered position held by the superfan with professional expertise (2013, 441). The fanboy auteur effectively melds audience function with author function and reifies the cultural authority of the producers while gesturing towards the power of fans to control the media narrative (whether this gesture is empty or not is difficult to define). To be clear, in no way do scanners qualify as auteurs, nor are they conferred any recognition as validly expressing their fandom. What's important about the fanboy auteur to a consideration of scanners is that they do indeed blur the line between producer and consumer. The appearance of sharing control and power over cultural properties with fans can be seen as implicitly encouraging fans to aspirationally participate in the production and circulation of texts. A mixed message is sent when unauthorized fan interventions such as fanfic or fanfilm can lead to a career in the media industries working on the same subject as the fan text. As Scott writes, "the fanboy auteur can simultaneously signify reader, author, and (fannish inter)text" (443); as the next section of this chapter will demonstrate, scanners can simultaneously signify reader, author, and fannish community member performing a service.

Scott also distinguishes between "affirmational" fans (who decode the "correct" reading of the text) and "transformative" fans (who appropriate and interpret in order to express their connection to the text) (2013, 441–42). As fans, comic scanners are decidedly affirmational: the quality of a scan is heavily determined by its ability to polish the quality of the original book without excising any materials. The most dedicated scanners will ensure that splash pages are joined and advertisements and back matter accounted for without qualification or judgment. To perform any transformation of the content (by remixing pages, offering commentary, or otherwise judiciously editing) is unheard of in comics scanning. This is similar to the affirmational fandom performed by scanlators, who are sometimes driven by a need to produce a more faithful or nuanced translation of the original manga than that offered by officially licensed English translations (Deppey 2005; Nowlin 2010b). While the interpretive act of translating is fundamentally transformative, the motivations of scanlators overlap with English-language comics scanners here: a successful product is one that blends into the remediated language.

Scott's arguments about how fans are increasingly framed as producers of media extends past film and beyond the boundaries of auteurs. Across pop culture industries, producers invoke a rhetoric of connecting with fans *as* fans in order to sell their products and themselves. In video games, studios like Bethesda Softworks position themselves first and foremost as lovers of the genres they focus on, both as a marketing tool and in order to justify the necessity of fans taking an active role, using feedback channels to help correct initial release bugs and glitches without losing patience in the product (Gallagher et al. 2017). The political economy of mainstream comics is likewise infused with stories of elite executives and superstar creators being discovered as convention attendees shopping their portfolios to publishers (Lee and Baker 2010, 8–10; Beatty 2017). One of the central markers of participatory culture is the blurring of lines between producers and consumers. It's therefore reasonable, and to some extent predictable, that some consumers expect a measure of sovereignty over the objects they consume that defies permissible bounds and infringes on the grasp of commercial control.

Finally, the retail culture of comics has also contributed to a climate where scanners might view their work as an audience function. The direct market in comics allowed for the development of back bins as an integral aspect of comic collecting (Wright 2008). Back bins lay the groundwork for both a drive towards (and expectation of) completionism for fans and an expectation that comics as objects truly *belong* to the fans to be used as they please. As comics migrate to the digital milieu, it's natural that fans would hope for similar levels of availability and completion and hold similar expectations of ownership (Stevens and Bell 2012, 764). The failure of publishers to predict these assumptions created a gap that scanners filled by offering more selection than online stores and a promise of permanent ownership and portability (756–57). Taking these factors into account, it's increasingly complicated to convince comics consumers that scanners hurt the comics industry or culture with any degree of malice—rather, they appear more and more to be natural outcomes of technological developments and cultural protocols.

THE METHODOLOGY AND IDEOLOGY OF COMICS SCANNING

Regardless of how their practices escape the reach of piracy discourse, comics scanners are necessarily anonymous and, consequently, perform little explicit and public self-reflection on their practices and ideological viewpoints. However, we can contextualize them within the framework of the audience function by looking at the existence of small makeshift subcommunities called "crews." Most comics scanners take on an alias (or a variety of aliases) and operate casually within crews such as the aforementioned DCP and Minutemen. While detailed histories of these groups exist elsewhere (cf. St Claire 2004; Shelley 2009; Wershler, Sinervo, and Tien 2014), a general overview will be helpful here.

Of the many crews operating in English-language comics scanning since the practice began, the two largest, most prolific, and most stable groups by far were DCP and Minutemen. DCP was perhaps the first crew in operation: its work stretches back to early 2000, when the idea of preserving the content of comics digitally for online distribution was a novel concept among both publishers and readers of mainstream North American comics. Minutemen began to form in 2006 under the crew name MMS (presumably "Minutemen Scans"), though in the beginning they were not nearly as formal or large a community. The original torrent file packets in the early days of comics piracy tended to be labeled by the distributor as "DCP & Friends." Some files were attributed to Minutemen, but usually only one or two among several dozen clear DCP releases and a few unaffiliated scanners. This, however, is exactly how a crew forms: by pulling together independent scanners with talent under one workflow process and a set of common editing sensibilities and quality standards. As reported by an individual called CCA_Scanner, talent recruitment can be both informal and self-selective:

> I started doing some research to see if any of the modern groups had done up a tutorial on scanning and editing comics . . . [w]ithout having any luck finding one online, I decided to try to find someone from one of the groups to see if they had an editing guide put together so that I might be able to start using new methods to make the scans look even better. I met someone from one of the groups and was eventually shown their methods and tools used. So I started scanning and eventually I released a few books using that group's tag since I was now a "member." (As cited in Johnston 2012b)

Although there were many independent scanners and smaller release groups producing occasional scans, the bulk of the activity between 2005 and 2011 was performed by DCP and Minutemen. The data collected as part of the larger project upon which this chapter is based shows that each crew tended to focus on certain types of comics. For example, true to the preservationist ethos implied by their name, the majority of DCP's scans from 2005–2013 were comics originally published more than five years before the time of scanning, while Minutemen focused more on newer publications, even exhibiting a certain level of preoccupation with "zero-day" releases (comics scanned and released the same day they became available for purchase in comic book stores).

The workflow process of scanning is hardly monolithic, but clearly three separate operations are necessary: each comic needs to be scanned, edited, and distributed. Scanning is a time-consuming and expensive process. Before day-and-date, the majority of scanning operated along similar lines: the scanner would buy the comic, bring it home, cut it apart, and scan. This means that most comics scanners are either regular customers or employees of comic shops—a hypothesis supported by interviews with comics scanners (though some scanners even position *all* scanners as fans, contesting the idea that any member of the community exists anywhere along the distribution chain other than at the end, as a consumer) (Johnston 2012a; Mroczkowski 2011c)—and that they are effectively buying physical books to destroy them in the digitization process. Broadly speaking, the technical steps outlined here are similar to those performed by manga scanlation groups, with the added tasks of actually translating the manga and editing the new text into the image files (Leavitt 2010; Valero-Porras and Cassany 2015; Fabbretti 2016).

Once the book is scanned, the individual image files need to be edited and compiled into one document. Editing is usually performed by the scanner, but frequently the scanner will send the "raw" image files to an editor to work on (constituting what scanners refer to as "team-ups"). Evidently, team-ups usually occur in the interest of allowing the scanner to process more books in a given week (Mroczkowski 2011c). Any number of graphic editing software suites can be used for this, from Gimp to Autodesk to Adobe Photoshop, but what's important is that orientations are fixed, splash pages are joined and aligned, colors are corrected and touched up for digital display, and pages are collated. It's during this stage that scanners also add their own signatures to the comic (an aspect this chapter will account for at length in the next two sections). Finally, the complete file can easily be saved as a RAR or ZIP, then have the suffix altered manually to CBR or CBZ (respectively), to be readable in any number of "comic reader" applications designed especially for pirated comics.

In this way, comics scanning holds to claims made by Jonathan Sterne in discussing how the MP3 came to be developed and taken as a standard audio format. Technologies are innovated as ways to address needs, not create them. Standardization, meanwhile, operates to create a common language, nonetheless one "bound up with the politics of nations, cultures, and industries." (2012, 136) In distributing copies of digital comic book files that could be readable on both personal computers and mobile devices like tablets, software developers on the fringe of the comics piracy community took it upon themselves to create applications that would offer simple and clear interfaces for formats that were easily extractable. While the first bootlegged comics were PDF files, it wasn't long before applications like Jomic or Comic Book Reader came along, and subsequently almost all pirated comics moved over to a .CBZ or .CBR standard format. In this way, comics piracy catalyzed the formation of a creative commons in a niche online public.

Returning to scanning workflows, the trail goes cold here for a while, as no public documentation exists of how much overlap occurs between the roles of scanners/editors and distributors. But what is clear is that "distribution" consists of four key roles: collecting, uploading, publicizing, and recruiting (Mroczkowski 2011b). Scanners and editors send their files to one centralized distribution hub managed by an individual, who then builds one file and disseminates links for it to various torrent tracker sites and on Twitter. While different sites have different usernames, just like the scanner aliases, they are usually all plays on a theme indicating one actor across multiple sites (Wershler, Sinervo, and Tien 2014). Distributors also seem to act as communication hubs for the crews and often initiate first contact with potential new recruits. However informal their internal ties, for the majority of DCP and Minutemen's existences, they were consistent enough that weekly packets were uploaded fairly regularly, following the same descriptive formatting each week, with the same announcement structure. Uploads from crews customarily contained multiple details listed on tracker site pages, including book titles, issue and volume numbers, publication years, scanner(s), crew(s), whether ads and back matter had been included in the scan (indicated by the notation "c2c" or cover-to-cover), and language. These editorial decisions over what was included and how demonstrate a meaning-making audience function on the part of the pirates: c2c scans, for example, implicitly argue for the value of presenting ephemeral publications in their full context. In creating a category for the preservation of advertisements and editorials, comics pirates do archival work for the public that comic publishers rarely bother with.

For all three aspects of the process, quality varies wildly. Sometimes comics are sloppily scanned at a low resolution, with an obvious tilt to the images. Sometimes splash pages are joined together poorly or not at all, and no touchups to orientation or color are noticeable. And sometimes scan packages are uploaded with accidental redundancies or released only to sites with low traffic where packets are unlikely to be made available for long or to ever have enough seeders at once. The norm, however, is a clear and legible product where the care taken in scanning, editing, and distributing is obvious in the final file. Among scanning communities, the masculinized and lionized version of affirmational fandom is associated with faithfully reproducing print materials digitally. This is true to the extent that competition between crews, in the form of one crew scanning a book already released by another, usually only occurs when scanners take issue with the quality and fidelity of the scan (the other main reason is tied up with speed—who can get their scan distributed fastest after release of the book) (Wershler, Sinervo, and Tien 2014).

SCANNERS VS. BOOTLEGGERS

Removed from any kind of profit motive or economic pursuit, pirated comics as a media form facilitates community creation not unlike the distributional networks built out of video or music piracy in today's digital milieu (Andrade et al. 2005, 111). The main difference is that any instances of profit being derived directly from comics piracy are marginal outliers at most, while other forms of bootleg media have had economic networks built up around them over time and are thus deeply entrenched in a history of exploitation and profiteering (Lobato 2012, 86). This history aside, the same kinds of file-sharing practices performed by comics scanners are increasingly used in other forms of piracy. While the black market for film and music is by no means a bygone economy (Crisp 2015), the derivation of profit from pirated media is increasingly marginalized—especially in North America (Crisp 2014, 45). Furthermore, there may be some question of just how much the corporations are victimized: as with anime dubbing and manga scanlation (Sell 2011; Koulikov 2010), it may be that comics piracy lays the groundwork for expanded markets.

The concept of piracy laying the groundwork for new types of communities and marketplaces is not new or particular to comics scanning. In Nigeria, an entire film industry and cinema culture has risen up around the infrastructure built by pirated video cassette networks in the 1980s. Originally made to serve as a network for bootleg tapes of illicitly imported Hollywood and Bollywood films, the former sellers of copyright-infringing merchandise in Lagos and Kano are now film financiers and distributors (Larkin 2008; Lobato 2012). In North America, the market for anime and manga has its roots in foundational work performed by subtitlers and scanlation groups (Sell 2011). By distributing bootleg tapes or popular anime programs across the United States and Canada (with English subtitles embedded into the tapes by the bootleggers themselves), this pirate community created a demand that showed the Japanese culture industry it could profitably export its media abroad (Leonard 2005; Koulikov 2010; Lee 2011).

That said, to apply these historical cases to English-language comics scanning is utopian thinking at best. No research exists that shows digital piracy of American comics has expanded the spread of English comics into previously untapped global markets, and it's difficult to argue that Superman or Captain America need the publicity overseas that scanlation or fansubbing provided for Japanese cultural products in the West. However, it is clear from interviews that many comics scanners see themselves as supporting the industry rather than subverting it. Former DCP scanner Archangel, for example, mentioned in interview that comic pirates often wait on releasing their scans to minimize impact on official distribution networks:

> When I was scanning, there were times when we did get books really early, for example, Action #900. We had that two weeks before its release date. But we didn't release it until its actual release date. I used to have subscriptions to several Marvel titles, they would arrive the day before to 3 days before the release date usually. They would be scanned and edited but not released until their scheduled release date. (As cited in Johnston 2012a)

Archangel goes on to explain that in addition to respecting the release dates set by publishers, comics scanners have in the past publicized works by smaller presses and independent creators, going as far to say that some books succeeded *because* they were pirated (not only in a foreign market, but at all). Regardless of the accuracy of these remarks, it speaks to a self-perception among scanners that before they are comic pirates, they are comic *fans*—a perspective backed by any detailed breakdown of the visual intertextual signifiers present on signature pages (Delwiche 2014). Examples include extra material appended to comic book files mourning the recent passing of a beloved creator (figure 13.1), or urging readers to support the comics industry by treating the digital file as a sample and going out to purchase the book in print form (figure 13.2). The contradictory gesture of offering a reader a product for free and then pleading with them to pay someone for it notwithstanding, the rhetoric of additional material like this solidifies the argument that comic pirates see themselves as members of a greater cooperative community, viewing their audience function through a particular lens and authorizing their behavior as affirmational fans.

Figure 13.1. When artist Dave Cockrum passed away in 2006, some DCP scans were accompanied by this memoriam page of the penciler's likeness and drawings.

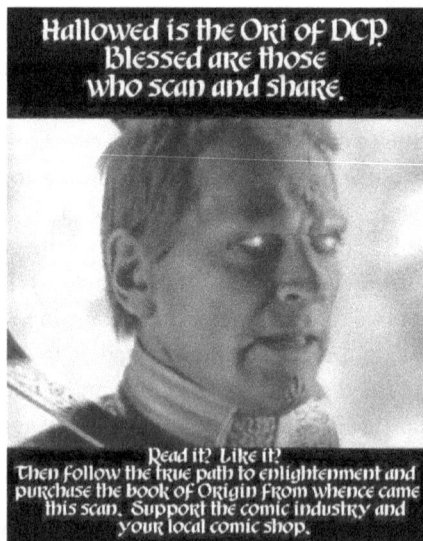

Figure 13.2. This scan tag page directs readers to buy a print copy of the comic it is appended to.

THE PIRATE AUTHOR

Beyond the affirmational aspects of their fandom, comics pirates also engage in a degree of transformational fandom as well. Like DJs, comics pirates sample, remix, and rerelease previously published content. This is where the question of authorship arises in comics piracy; where pirate practices begin to challenge notions of creative labor and contribution; and where Michel Foucault's poststructuralist theories on authorship come into play. Foucault approaches the author as inseparable from institutions and power hierarchies, rather than as a sovereign expressive agent (2007, 910). This demands interpretations of authorship contextualized by systems of control. The next logical step from here lets us posit authorship not as origin, but as creative contribution. In many cases, pirated comics constitute new creative contributions, however unsanctioned the efforts may be. On a fundamental level, for example, most pirated comics are presented in an entirely unique context—that is, in a portable digital form rather than print. Even after comics publishers began to adopt widespread digital distribution methods for their products, their efforts to digitize backlogs remain less prominent than those to promptly recapitulate new and recent titles, or capitalize on opportunities for transmedial synergy. This means that many comics discoverable through pirated sources are unavailable through legitimate digital channels. The aesthetic practices of scanning and editing have also evolved within crews to the extent that pirates usually tweak color and contrast levels so that the comic displays ideally on a backlit, glowing computer monitor, constituting an argument for pirates as artistically minded designers offering medium-specific and style-sensitive creative labor. Their work could be related to airbrushing in photography or digital effects and matchmoving in film post-production. But the issue of authorship is most explicitly reframed by the original artwork pirates produce for their releases.

Comics scanners and their crew allegiances are usually identifiable by the signatures they affix to comics, which we can refer to as tags. Most scanners operate using aliases that frequently change by degrees, and when more than one scanner is involved in one comic, they will sometimes combine their names into shifting portmanteaus. For example, DCP scanners GreenGiant and Hatful of Hollow have each gone by multiple aliases alone and as a team, including GiantHawk, GiantRobot, GG, GreenEngine, GreenVillain, Madvillain, Green Hat, Steamy Hollow, HatfulofWind, and Hollow Knight. Whatever the name, the use of tags for identification inscribes the work of the scanner on the comic file itself, rather than just the metadata. Usually, tags amount to an extra splash page appended to the end of the scanned comic, where the

Figure 13.3. These tags display some of the mixed-media collaging techniques frequently used for scanner signature images.

pirate has edited together multiple images to create a unique signature. The sources for this imagery range from pages from other comics, to photographs, to screen captures from films or television shows, to wholly original art. In most cases, the scanner has laid their alias across this image prominently, with the insignia of the associated crew present as well.

All of this content—aliases, tags, additional signature or message pages—is often bound up with the content of the comics themselves: monikers like BigBlue or RacerX accompany images in the comics files of Superman or a *Speed Racer* character, respectively (figure 13.4). This moves these images closer to the realm of remix culture, where there are just as many questions about intellectual property (Lessig 2008; Diakopoulos et al. 2007; Chang 2009). In the context of music sampling, for example, a sample's origin can no longer predetermine the valency of the original or creative gesture (Chang 2009, 145). This means that to the reader of a remixed work, it is unproductive to look to the original author when attempting to extract meaning from the text. Chang develops this claim into an argument that in terms of sampling and remixing, the notion of creativity must be parsed through the parameters of a project of recombination and recontextualization (146). In comic scans, the translation from print to digital offers a recontextualization in all its

Figure 13.4. Aliases and tag imagery are often inspired by or sampled from recognizable comic content.

material protocols, while the remixed tags are rife with recombinations and intertexts ranging from obvious to oblique. Just how much a pirated comic has been subject to remix, however, remains a question that can only be addressed on a case-by-case basis. To be certain, no practices can be regarded as monolithic, but all constitute forms of originality, hewing closer to Scott's interpretation of transformative fandom.

Of course, not all scanner tags are so flashy or obvious; many attempt to blend in with the rest of the comic in question. For example, a scanner may forego the extra splash page in favor of subtly superimposing his or her alias over the numbers below the bar code on the front cover or embed it within the publication information on the first page of the story (figure 13.5) (a gesture that, in itself, nods to the notion of comic as commodity). Placements like these draw further attention to the distinctions between the sensibilities of pirated comics and commercially digitized comics in that they raise the question of why the scanner left material like publication information or barcodes on the comics in the first place. If the scanner had the opportunity to leave his or her tag in these areas, it's reasonable to imagine that the scanner might also have considered erasing the areas. To leave publication information or barcodes speaks to the preservationist ethos of scanning; as a gesture, it acknowledges that this was once a print object that occupied a specific space in our culture and appeared in a specific way. This contrasts with the majority of commercial digitized comics, which frequently place black bars over such content or (if the publisher has copies of the colored pages from before the content was added) erases it entirely.

Even more intriguingly, the scanner will sometimes embed the tag right above or below the names of the comic's creators, formally and aesthetically challenging the authorship of the title (figure 13.6). Adapting an analytical perspective from Stuart Hall's concept of encoding and decoding (1980, 56) allows the use of an open-text model of authorship. We are free to disregard what we believe we know about the text, that these particular people wrote or illustrated it or this particular company published it. Unmoored from traditional authorship, scanned comics drift in a sea of textual possibilities, dependent upon observable signs of provenance. The scanners encode their perspectives about their audience function and leave readers to draw their own conclusions. Without an insider's understanding of the conventions of scanning, tags like the one in figure 13.6 can easily be decoded as part of the overall artwork or textual information of the cover.

Figure 13.5. Tags embedded subtly in the publication and sales information, highlighted in red.

Figure 13.6. On this issue of *Hellblazer*, DCP scanner Obi's tag is visible right above the names of the comic's creators. Note the effort that has been put into blending the tag in with the cover art.

CONCLUSION

Today, the "scanning" process is harder to parse, as day-and-date has shifted the landscape of availabilities and actors as well as ideologies. Shortly after the industry transition to widespread digital distribution, journalists David Brothers and David Uzumeri postulated that there might be a leak from within Marvel making PDFs available to scanners, who then reverse-engineered the files into CBRs and CBZs (2012). Brothers and Uzumeri based this theory on visual analysis of some of the comic scans being released around the time, noting that in some cases various markers of print-publication scans were absent (such as barcodes or minute artefacts from the scanner) and that the dimensions of images were too uniform to have been scanned. Whether they emerge from within publishers or not, it seems clear that most newer comics scans now appear to begin life online rather than at the local comic shop. By this point, the visual indicators that Brothers and Uzumeri noted are commonplace, and c2c scans have become rarer.

However, tracing the provenance of these original files is as difficult a task as pinpointing specific brick-and-mortar shops would have been. Common sense would indicate that online marketplaces like comiXology probably provide a good deal of fodder for scanners now, and likely some leakages do occur. Regardless, the tasks of the comics scanner have now shifted. Scanning would now better be called webripping—a term that first comes up as a format notation in 2006, but only crops up occasionally until publishers started investing in digital distribution. Between 2005 and 2011, of the more than 47,000 comics scanned by DCP and Minutemen, only 203 were listed as webrips (the vast majority appearing after 2009). In 2010, a new format notation appears: "digital." By the end of 2012, both DCP and Minutemen are in severe decline in terms of productivity, and it becomes impossible to tally annual totals of the two groups because they no longer dominate their own organized weekly packet uploads. Instead, their work appears in packets alongside scans by new crews such as Empire, CPS, and TheGroup. A changing of the guard has taken place and, with, it a change of methods. Of these more intermittent packets, on average more than 50% of the scans are now listed as "digital." The era of digitization is coming to a close for comics as the born-digital age solidifies.

So where did DCP and Minutemen go? It's possible that in a milieu where the product is already available digitally, these crews saw a decline in their own usefulness. There's an argument to be made that the up-to-the-minute aspect of Minutemen's apparent mandate falls away when publishers now make their output immediately available to anyone with a broadband

connection and $1.99 to pay for a new issue. The preservationist aspect of
DCP's work is thornier to sort out. Publishers are now clearly preserving
their comics electronically, but not publicly: individual issues disappear
and reappear from digital storefronts continually, and paratextual content
like ads and back matter are no more present in official digital comics than
they are in collected trade paperbacks. Of course, all of this is speculative;
it could very well be that the crews receded due to internal feuding, closure
of access points, or just boredom. Regardless, while some aspects of pirated
comics today are consistent with those of a decade past—tags, distribution
methods, file formatting—others such as c2c, color correction, and internal
organization seem to be all but extinct.

Whatever their economic and historical ties, some areas of media piracy
are now operating in a new moment where the issue is not who does or does
not own what content or material product, but rather how media objects
are encoded along the production and distribution chain. Using comics
scanning as a case study makes this much clear. This brings us back once
more to decoding and, consequently, questions of how bootlegged media
files connect to both readers and companies. Comics pirates are at once at
odds with and intrinsically tied to the comics industry—at least in their own
view. Today, just as publishers have shifted their methods and embraced new
technologies, newer pirated comics demonstrate a shift in self-perception
on the part of the pirates. Their audience function has changed, and the
transformational aspects of their labor are less necessary when the files they
pirate are already optimized for digital reading. Scanlators continue to be
crucial cultural intermediaries due the intercultures they create through
unique translation (Sell 2011, 95), but English-language comics scanning
and the forms of access it afforded have essentially been eclipsed by official
channels that offer a similar reading experience in a more cleanly packaged
way. Thomas Lamarre reminds us of Innis's points about the promiscuity
of certain media types within an empire when he discusses how the same
tools used by empire to consolidate its power are simultaneously available to
consumers: "Capital must harness the power of labour to achieve its ends,"
writes Lamarre, "but can never control it entirely. Something of labour's
power always exceeds of the grasp of abstract labour." It is thus necessary
to "think about labour in terms of a constituent power of pure or radical
immanence, as an uncontainable power, infinitely protean and continually
creative" (2006, 360). Regardless of the ways that capital would channel labor,
some inevitably explodes outward in creative and unpredictable directions.
This is reflected well in the commentary of former comic pirate CCA_Scan-
ner: "Look at the product the pirates put out compared to yours AND look at

the distribution methods pirates use compared to yours," writes the scanner, imploring the industry to use piracy as a learning opportunity. "The pirates' product is as good as if not better than yours in many cases, especially so in digital comics, and ease of acquisition of said pirated product is better than your method of distribution. We live in the zero second age. I want it and I want it now. And many times I can get it NOW" (as cited in Johnston 2012b). It seems that in several regards, the mainstream American comics industry has taken CCA_Scanner's sentiments to heart. But while day-and-date addresses some of the concerns inherent in comics piracy, the continued practice indicates that these fans still view themselves as both affirmational and transformative. If and when the history of the Blue Age of Comics is written, it should include the work of these niche actors as performing a specific kind of audience function and perhaps even for performing a specific kind of preservation.

Acknowledgments

This chapter would not exist if not for the leadership of Darren Wershler in initiating the Comics Piracy Research Project. Both Darren and our collaborator, Shannon Tien, deserve much of the credit for the research presented here. I must also express my gratitude to my editor, Benjamin Woo, who directed me to excellent resources many times over, and Amanda Dunbar, who provided invaluable feedback.

References

Andrade, Nazareno, Miranda Mowbray, Aliandro Lima, Gustavo Wagner, and Matei Ripeanu. 2005. "Influences on Cooperation in BitTorrent Communities." In *Proceedings of the 2005 ACM SIGCOMM Workshop on Economics of Peer-to-Peer Systems, Philadelphia, 2005*, 111–15. New York: ACM.

Beatty, Gary Scott. 2017. "Breaking into Comics." Comic Artists Direct. Accessed July 11. http://www.comicartistsdirect.com/articles/breaking.html.

Beyer, Jessica L. 2014. "The Emergence of a Freedom of Information Movement: Anonymous, WikiLeaks, the Pirate Party, and Iceland." *Journal of Computer-Mediated Communication* 19: 141–54.

Bogost, Ian, and Nick Montfort. 2009. "Platform Studies: Frequently Questioned Answers." In *Proceedings of the Digital Arts and Culture Conference, Irvine, 2009*. http://www.escholarship.org/uc/item/01rok9br.

Brothers, David, and David Uzumeri. 2012. "Are They Scanning Marvel's Comics from Inside the House of Ideas?!" 4thletter! February 15. http://4thletter.net/2012/02/are-they-scanning-marvels-comics-from-inside-the-house-of-ideas/.

Chang, Vanessa. 2009. "Records That Play: The Present Past in Sampling Practice." *Popular Music* 28 (2): 143–59.

Crisp, Virginia. 2014. "To Name a Thief: Constructing the Deviant Pirate." In *Piracy: Leakages from Modernity*, edited by Martin Fredriksson and James Arvanitakis, 39–53. Sacramento: Litwin Books.

Crisp, Virginia. 2015. *Film Distribution in the Digital Age: Pirates and Professionals*. London: Palgrave Macmillan.

Delwiche, Aaron. 2014. "Scanner Tags, Comic Book Piracy and Participatory Culture." *First Monday* 19 (5). https://firstmonday.org/ojs/index.php/fm/article/view/5247/4086.

Deppey, Dirk. 2005 "Scanlation Nation: Amateur Manga Translators Tell Their Stories." *The Comics Journal* 269. http://archives.tcj.com/269/n_scan.html.

Diakopoulos, Nicholas, Kurt Luther, Yevgeniy "Eugene" Medynskiy, and Irfan Essa. 2007. "The Evolution of Authorship in a Remix Society." In *Proceedings of the 18th Conference on Hypertext and Hypermedia, Manchester, 2007*. doi:10.1145/1286240.1286272.

Douglass, Jeremy, William Huber, and Lev Manovich. 2011. "Understanding Scanlation: How to Read One Million Fan-Translated Pages." *Image and Narrative* 12 (1): 206–28. http://www.imageandnarrative.be/index.php/imagenarrative/article/view/133.

Fabbretti, Matteo. 2016. "The Use of Translation Notes in Manga Scanlation." *TranscUlturAl: A Journal of Translation and Cultural Studies* 8 (6): 86–104.

Foucault, Michel. 2007. "What Is an Author?" Translated by Josué Harari. In *The Critical Tradition: Classic Texts and Contemporary Trends*, 3rd ed., edited by David H. Richter, 904–14. Boston: Bedford/St. Martin's.

Gallagher, Rob, Carolyn Jong, and Kalervo A. Sinervo. 2017. "Who Wrote the Elder Scrolls? Modders, Developers, and the Mythology of Bethesda Softworks." *Loading . . .* 10 (16): 32–52.

Gardner, Jared. 2012. *Projections: Comics and the History of Twenty-First Century Storytelling*. Stanford: Stanford University Press.

Gitelman, Lisa. 2002. "'Materiality Has Always Been in Play': An Interview with N. Katherine Hayles." *Iowa Journal of Cultural Studies* 2. http://ir.uiowa.edu/cgi/viewcontent.cgi?article=1014&context=ijcs.

Hall, Stuart. 1980. "Encoding/Decoding." In *Culture, Media, Language*, edited by Stuart Hall, Dorothy Hobson, Andrew Love, and Paul Willis, 128–38. London: Hutchinson.

Hayles, N. Katherine. 2008. *Electronic Literature: New Horizons for the Literary*. South Bend: University of Notre Dame Press.

Hyde, David. 2011. "DC Comic Announces Historic Renumbering of All Superhero Titles and Landmark Day-and-Date Digital Distribution." The Source, May 31. http://dcu.blog.dccomics.com/2011/05/31/dc-comics-announces-historic-renumbering-of-all-superhero-titles-and-landmark-day-and-date-digital-distribution/.

Johns, Adrian. 2010. *Piracy: The Intellectual Property Wars from Gutenberg to Gates*. Chicago: University of Chicago Press.

Johnson, Derek. 2013. "Participation Is Magic: Collaboration, Authorial Legitimacy, and the Audience Function." In *A Companion to Media Authorship*, edited by Jonathan Gray and Derek Johnson, 135–57. Oxford: Wiley-Blackwell.

Johnson, Derek. 2014. "After the Industry Turn: Can Production Studies Make an Audience Turn?" *Creative Industries Journal* 7 (1): 50–53.

Johnston, Rich. 2012a. "An Interview with a Comic Book Pirate." Bleeding Cool. Accessed May 24 2017. https://www.bleedingcool.com/2012/04/12/pirate/.

Johnston, Rich. 2012b. "Another Comic Book Pirate Writes." Bleeding Cool. Accessed May 24 2017. https://www.bleedingcool.com/2012/04/16/anothr-comic-book-pirate-writes-2/.

Klinger, Barbara. 2010. "Contraband Cinema: Piracy, *Titanic*, and Central Asia." *Cinema Journal* 49 (2): 106–24.

Kocmarek, Ivan. 2016. "Truth, Justice, and the Canadian Way: The War-Time Comics of Bell Features Publications." *Canadian Review of Comparative Literature* 43 (1): 148–65.

Koulikov, Mikhail. 2010. "Fighting the Fan Sub War: Conflicts between Media Rights Holders and Unauthorized Creator/Distributor Networks." *Transformative Works and Cultures* 5. http://journal.transformativeworks.org/index.php/twc/article/view/115.

Lamarre, Thomas. 2006. "Otaku Movement." In *Japan after Japan: Social and Cultural Life from the Recessionary 1990s to the Present*, edited by Tomiko Yoda and Harry Harootunian. Durham: Duke University Press.

Larkin, Brian. 2008. *Signal and Noise: Media, Infrastructure, and Urban Culture in Nigeria.* Durham: Duke University Press.

Leavitt, Alex. 2010. "Inside Scanlation." *Transformative Works and Cultures* 5. https://doi .org/10.3983/twc.2010.0215.

Lee, Hye-Kyung. 2009. "Between Fan Culture and Copyright Infringement: Manga Scanlation." *Media, Culture & Society* 31 (6): 1011–1022. doi: 10.1177/0163443709344251.

Lee, Hye-Kyung. 2011. "Participatory Media Fandom: A Case Study of Anime Fansubbing." *Media, Culture & Society* 33: 1131–47.

Lee, Jim, and Bill Baker. 2010. *Icons: The DC Comics and Wildstorm Art of Jim Lee.* London: Titan Books.

Leonard, Sean. 2005. "Celebrating Two Decades of Unlawful Progress: Fan Distribution, Proselytization Commons, and the Explosive Growth of Japanese Animation." *UCLA Entertainment Law Review* 12: 189–266.

Lessig, Lawrence. 2008. *Remix: Making Art and Commerce Thrive in the Hybrid Economy.* New York: Penguin Press.

Lima, Sara. 2011. "The Sad State of Comics Piracy—It's Worse Than You Think." Comic Vine, June 30. https://comicvine.gamespot.com/articles/the-sad-state-of-comics-piracyits -worse-than-you-t/1100-143281/.

Lobato, Ramon. 2012. *Shadow Economies of Cinema: Mapping Informal Film Distribution.* London: Palgrave Macmillan.

Mahadeo, Kevin. 2011. "Archie Comics Goes Day-and-Date Digital." Comic Book Resources, January 12. http://www.cbr.com/archie-comics-goes-day-and-date-digital/.

Mroczkowski, Jim. 2011a. "Ahoy, Comic Book Pirate!" iFanboy, October 3. http://ifanboy .com/articles/ahoy-pirate/.

Mroczkowski, Jim. 2011b. "The Comic Book Pirate Interviews, Part 1." iFanboy, October 1. http://ifanboy.com/articles/the-pirate-interviews-part-i/.

Mroczkowski, Jim. 2011c. "The Comic Book Pirate Interviews, Part II." iFanboy, October 17. http://ifanboy.com/articles/the-comic-book-pirate-interviews-part-ii/.

Mroczkowski, Jim. 2011d. "The Comic Book Pirate Interviews, Part III." iFanboy, October 24. http://ifanboy.com/articles/the-comic-book-pirate-interviews-part-iii/.

Murray, Padmini Ray. 2013. "Behind the Panel: Examining Invisible Labour in the Comics Publishing Industry." *Publishing Research Quarterly* 29: 336–43.

Nowlin, Nicole. 2010a. "Scanlations: Copyright Infringement for Literature and Art Fans Brought to You by the Internet." *Interface: The Journal of Education, Community, and Values* 10 (1). http://bcis.pacificu.edu/journal/2010/01/article.php?id=633.

Nowlin, Nicole. 2010b. "Scanlations: Copyright Infringement for Literature and Art Fans Brought to You by the Internet, Part II." *Interface: The Journal of Education, Community, and Values* 10 (8). http://bcis.pacificu.edu/journal/article.php?id=729.

Nowlin, Nicole. 2010c. "Scanlations: Copyright Infringement for Literature and Art Fans Brought to You by the Internet, Part III." *Interface: The Journal of Education, Community, and Values* 10 (9). http://bcis.pacificu.edu/journal/article.php?id=737.

Perloff, Marjorie. 2006. "Screening the Page/Paging the Screen: Digital Poetics and the Differential Text." In *New Media Poetics: Contexts, Technotexts, and Theories*, edited by Adalaide Morris and Thomas Swiss, 143–64. Cambridge: MIT Press.

Phegley, Kiel. 2011. "Marvel Goes Day and Date Digital." Comic Book Resources, November 3. http://www.cbr.com/marvel-goes-day-and-date-digital/.

Polo, Susana. 2011. "Image Comics Go for Day and Date Digital Distribution." The Mary Sue, October 4. https://www.themarysue.com/digital-image-comics/.

Resha, Adrienne. 2017. "The Blue Age of Comics." http://scalar.usc.edu/works/blue-age-of-comic-books/index.

Scott, Suzanne. 2013. "Dawn of the Undead Author: Fanboy Auteurism and Zack Snyder's 'Vision.'" In *A Companion to Media Authorship*, edited by Jonathan Gray and Derek Johnson, 440–62. Oxford: Wiley-Blackwell.

Seagrave, Kerry. 2003. *Piracy in the Motion Picture Industry*. Jefferson: McFarland & Company, Inc.

Sell, Cathy. 2011. "Manga Translation and Interculture." *Mechademia* 6: 93–108.

Shelley, Jim. 2009. "Is Illegal Comic Downloading Passe?" *Flashback Universe Blog*, September 25. http://flashbackuniverse.blogspot.ca/2009/09/is-illegal-comic-downloading-passe.html.

St. Claire, Jason. 2004. "Free Comic Book Day 24/7/365: The Scurvy Dogs of Comics Piracy." Comic Book Galaxy. Accessed July 11 2017. http://www.comicbookgalaxy.com/commentary_piracy_111504.html.

Sterne, Jonathan. 2012. *MP3: The Meaning of a Format*. Durham: Duke University Press.

Stevens, J. Richard, and Christopher Edward Bell. 2012. "Do Fans Own Digital Comic Books? Examining the Copyright and Intellectual Property Attitudes of Comic Book Fans." *International Journal of Communication* 6: 751–72.

Valero-Porras, María-José, and Daniel Cassany. 2015. "Multimodality and Language Learning in a *Scanlation* Community." *Procedia - Social and Behavioral Sciences* 212: 9–15.

Wershler, Darren, Kalervo Sinervo, and Shannon Tien. 2013. "A Network Archaeology of Unauthorized Comic Book Scans." *Amodern* 2. http://amodern.net/article/a-network-archaeology-of-unauthorized-comic-book-scans/.

Wershler, Darren, Kalervo Sinervo, and Shannon Tien. 2014. "Unauthorized Comic Book Scanners." In *Educational, Psychological, and Behavioral Considerations in Niche Online*

Communications, edited by Vivek Venkatesh, Jason Wallin, Juan Carlos Castro, and Jason Edward Lewis, 322–46. Hershey: IGI Global Publishing.

Wright, Frederick. 2008. "How Can 575 Comic Books Weigh Under an Ounce? Comic Book Collecting in the Digital Age." *The Journal of Electronic Publishing* 11 (3). http://quod.lib .umich.edu/j/jep/3336451.0011.304?view=text;rgn=main.

14.

Objectifying the Objectifiers

ACADEMICS IN THE COMICS WORLD

An Interview with Charles Hatfield and Franny Howes

In putting this collection together, we have taken the view that one cannot understand a comic—let alone comics as a whole—without understanding its social context. Thus, the volume seeks to relate comics to (some of) the publics for whom they are meaningful. Contributors have discussed artists and producers, intermediaries, and fans and readers as crucial actors who have and continue to influence the meaning of comic art.

However, as Pierre Bourdieu (2013, 4) would note, researchers are not separate from the worlds they study: "Objectification is always bound to remain partial, and therefore false, so long as it fails to include the point of view from which it speaks and so fails to construct the game as a whole." That is to say, comics scholars—whether faculty, students, or independent fan scholars—also constitute publics for comics, and we bring specific interests to our encounters with comic books and graphic novels that are shaped by our social and institutional location. In this spirit, editors Benjamin Woo (BW) and Jeremy Stoll (JS) sat down with an early career scholar, Franny Howes (FH), and an established scholar, Charles Hatfield (CH), to discuss the institutionalization of comics studies in higher education, the forces that have shaped its growth in particular directions, and the future of the field. In a sense, comics scholars, whatever their training or primary disciplinary affiliation, are professional interpreters of comics, but these interpretations are produced under specific, concrete conditions, and this is what we hope to explore through this interview, which has been condensed for publication.

BW: I'd like to start with a question for Charles. There's a lot of triumphalist rhetoric in comics studies these days—"look at all the learned societies, conferences, journals, and book series we have now"—but I'm wondering if you could tell our readers about your experience embarking on a career in comics studies?

CH: One very simple thing that is different now, I think, is that we talk about comics studies as if it were a thing. We say "comics studies." I just finished an edit on a book foreword yesterday for Matt Smith and Randy Duncan (2017), and one of their edits to me was asking me to capitalize the phrase "comics studies," and I thought, "Okay, we are a thing." Comics Studies. And I don't know that I was kicking around that term casually ten or twelve years ago—certainly not twenty years ago when I finally got into the waters of working on my dissertation in a serious way. So the fact that there's this accepted term is a real sign of change, I think.

A more substantive change is people thinking about teaching, mentoring, and advising others coming into the scene who want to also pursue this thing called comics studies. That's really an institution-building question. It was all I could do to keep myself alive, I think, fifteen or twenty years ago. Fifteen years ago, it was enough for me to think, "Oh wow, my first ever comics-centered course," and focus on just trying to communicate something to that group of students that was working with me for the first time. But now there's a larger set of questions which comes up when I'm asked to review a journal article or a potential book, or when people ask me questions that are career-oriented. I take your point about the sort of triumphalist nature of a lot of conversations, but I don't feel triumphalist at all. I feel like a new set of challenges is what's in front of me now. The fact that I can think about that at all, and not only in terms of self-preservation but also in terms of paying it forward, that's a difference.

BW: How do you think the conditions when you started, that sense of just keeping yourself alive, shaped decisions you and your peers made as scholars?

CH: Well, I suppose at the start there was a sense of *can I do this*? Yes, I can do this. Now, it's not a question of that so much as, *how far can we get this*? What are the serious institutional or pragmatic barriers to the growth and institutionalization of this field?

For my part, I'm an English studies scholar. I came up through both undergrad and grad school with no course work that would say "comics studies" to anyone that was looking at my transcripts, with very little actual course work that addressed comics. I had one teacher at UConn before me, Bill Nericcio, who modeled what it might be like to teach contemporary comics in some courses, but my path certainly couldn't be his path, and Bill was no longer around when I was at the dissertation stage. So, you know, I made a lot of traditional lit choices and developed a sort of scattered but interesting résumé of courses and some conference paper experience in various fields—I did things that would be familiar to language and literature departments, particularly English studies—and found my way almost unexpectedly into comics studies. I had made a lot of traditional lit student decisions, which helped me navigate grad school and think very broadly about this history of literature and literary studies, but that didn't really help me when it came to comics studies, so there was an awful lot of bootstrapping with a few peers to pull together stuff that could be useful to me, in terms of visual culture, art history, and art criticism. That was and remains challenging.

Again, comics studies as a thing wasn't on my radar when as a student I sort of swallowed and said, "I think I want to write my dissertation on comics." Being a utility player and developing teachable things in a lot of other areas of English studies probably helped me. I was actually hired to teach children's literature, and my path came through the children's literature course at the University of Connecticut, the course founded by Francelia Butler, which was historically important in the rise of children's literature studies as an academic field. My dissertation, which became my book on alternative comics, had nothing to do with the core issues in children's literature studies; it was not a children's literature dissertation. But I taught this well-known children's literature course at UConn twice just as I was finishing up. I think that's what led to my hire at Cal State Northridge and determined the balance of my teaching for my first handful of years here. Since then, I've ended up teaching a lot more comics than I would have thought—frankly, a lot more—but that need to be able to fill other curricular needs within a program and find ways, despite a heavy teaching load, to do comics studies, I also feel that.

JS: Franny, can you tell us about your early experiences with academic comics studies and what the field looked like then?

FH: I was able to start thinking about comics scholarship as an undergrad. It was still pretty early, but in my senior year of college I got to take a class—a comics class—at Michigan State, and I was interested in comics in other ways, so I had support to do undergraduate research on comics. I did a paper on comics and disability and found my way onto the comix scholars listserv and did as much reading as I could in stuff that was being published. In the gap between undergrad and grad school, I stayed pretty interested. When I did my master's, the first conference I presented at was the University of Florida comics conference, and that was a really great, supportive experience to see other people doing work that was similar and different to what I was doing. I'm in rhetoric and writing or rhetorical studies, so I was coming from a little bit of a different framework from most of the other people who were in literature, but they were interested in what I had to say—and, you know, being a first-year master's student, showing up to a conference, and having people listening to you and writing things down was a really great place to start. I got a publication out of that, which people sometimes still cite and teach, so that was a really, really fortunate thing to happen early on in my career.

At the same time, even though it's definitely got a lot more traction, there were still conflicts and struggles to explain the significance of the comics I was particularly interested in talking about in a rhetorical context. I remember a conversation during my comprehensive exams oral defense in 2013, struggling to explain Lynda Barry's significance as a theorist of comics through comics—that was at Virginia Tech, where I did my PhD—and now I see that the department I graduated from has invited her as a visiting writer for fall 2016.

So I'm part of a modest cohort of people in rhet/comp who got into comics studies in grad school and are starting to proliferate into the field, and my unscientific observation has been that people have done okay. I got a tenure-track job with a comics dissertation, but like Charles said, I also had to be a utility player. Although my research is on comics and decolonial feminist methodologies for researching comics, I teach technical writing, and I very purposely pursued teaching assistantships to get that experience. I've ended up teaching a bunch of other things in my current position, and being able to incorporate comics meaningfully into a variety of writing pedagogies helped. My teaching demo for my job was a memo writing activity where we role-played as the X-Men, and it went over very well. The thing I'm finding challenging now that I have a really intense teaching position is figuring out where comics *studies* as opposed to just comics pedagogy fits in.

CH: Yeah, Franny, I'm not sure where we first met, but I remember your paper on drawing as a part of classroom practice, and it's the first thing I thought of when Jeremy and Ben said, well, we might be able to bring you and Franny together. The rhet/comp thing was very important in my foundational teaching experience at UConn, and although I didn't have teachers who actually did much with comics, I would be remiss if I didn't mention that I first started teaching with visual texts and sequences of visual images—in a sort of John Berger meets Susan Sontag kind of way—in an introductory composition course, and that led to my first composition conference presentation at the Conference on College Composition and Communication [CCCC], dealing with the concept of visual essays with and without text.

Having done it in the classroom and struggling through that with several cohorts of students, that experience was probably in the back of my mind in terms of embracing comics as a dissertation topic.

FH: My first time presenting at CCCC, which is the big, national rhet/comp conference, I was on a panel about comics and I don't even remember what my paper was on, other than it was about rhetorical approaches to comics and feminist comics. And the first question I got was an audience member asking, "How does your research relate to the works of Alan Moore?" Back then, CCCC would have one comics panel. It was super well-attended, but everybody who had any kind of interest in comics was kind of all together. Now, there's a comics workshop, a pre-conference, and more than one panel. People have been able to differentiate a little bit, and I think that's a great sign of growth in who's doing this stuff in rhet/comp.

JS: Some see comics studies, like much of academia, as being dominated by cisgender straight white men. In your view, how has the history of comics studies shaped who gets to speak for the medium?

CH: My sense of that question and that cluster of issues is changing even now and has changed recently. My colleague here at CSUN, Frances Gateward, is one of the coeditors of *The Blacker the Ink* (Gateward and Jennings 2015), which just won an Eisner award for academic or scholarly publication a few weeks ago. Frances is a scholar of African American film and culture but also of Korean and Asian cinemas and gender and popular culture. She teaches in a totally different college from me, but she and I are part of an ad hoc initiative at CSUN to advance comics studies. When I think of volumes like *The Blacker the Ink* and I think, more than anything, of my conversations with people, with Frances and others, I feel like there's tremendous room for expansion on the grounds of comics addressing diverse identities, not only of ethnicity or race, but also of gender identity and sexual orientation and so on, and there is actually a lot that is happening. It's happening partly because of diversification within comics and fandom culture and the increasing number of diversity conversations facilitated by social media, but I think it also comes from the unique academic vantage point that people who have one foot in fandom and one foot outside of it can have.

I mean, let's face it, comic books have been a niche or marginalized phenomenon in North American culture for a considerable long while, but they've also become the gateway to enormous billion-dollar franchises of megaentertainment, and they seem to have a new lease on life. So, as long as the fan culture was perceived as sort of marginal, dealing with a limited market, as we might put it, it was hard to have conversations about diversity and inclusion because of the nature or perceived nature of fandom. It's a hobby, and hobbies are a niche interest. But I feel like that's exploding right now. I'm not sure I can usefully answer the question about how the origins of the field have limited the conversations people have been having, but the conversations people are having *now* are really fruitful and encouraging.

FH: I think there are a lot of good things happening now, but I didn't find a huge amount of relevant work in comics studies to cite when I was doing my dissertation. I found myself relying theoretically a lot more on feminist rhetorical studies, so Royster and Kirsch's (2012) book *Feminist Rhetorical Practices* had just come out when I was doing my work, which gathers a lot of different theoretical and methodological feminist rhetorics work in rhet/comp, and then citing Linda Tuhiwai Smith's (1999) *Decolonizing Methodologies*, Malea Powell's work, Angela Haas, so a lot of my colleagues doing the kind of work that I wanted to do but on different topics. So, I think the topic of diverse comics or comics by creators from underrepresented groups is coming up a lot more, but it's as much a question of method and relationship to comics and where we direct our attention that whitens and straightens some of what comes out of comics studies.

Here's an example because I was thinking of this before the interview: How many comics do you have to do to be worthy of consideration by comics studies? Who is able to have a full-time career as a comics creator, and who is creating comics as part of a literate lifetime? There's a couple of creators I've been really interested in, Nia King and Suzy Exposito, who are full-time journalists or putting together careers in other places, but queer women of color who have done really cool comics work and still consider themselves cartoonists even though that's not necessarily the thing they do full-time. If we want to address those questions, we need to cast our net more widely and think about who we're even considering worthy of looking at, as well as what we want to get out of doing research on them. I think there's also tensions there in what kind of relationship we as scholars want to have with comics creators. It doesn't always feel good to be under the microscope, so we need to take into consideration, when we study creators who have been historically marginalized or continually facing this kind of hostility or scrutiny or minoritization, that they're going to read it and have feelings about it. Is there a way that, instead of a distanced, close-reading analysis, we can have an open conversation about what creators' needs are, what their interests are in making knowledge about comics, and how we might be able to work with them? That's coming from a decolonial approach to research.

CH: It seems like one of the things you're saying, Franny, is that the corpus of things that we study, the comics we think worthy of study, is affected by the disciplinary questions and methodologies that we bring. My daughter Nami recently published in an online journal, *Queer Cats,* an essay from a library-and-information-studies (LIS) perspective about transgender-themed web-comics and how their creators invite input from the community of readers, so thinking not only of the creators' priorities but also of trans webcomics as an instance of participatory culture. The conclusion that she was drawing is that library and archival practice could take lessons from webcomics creators who are engaging marginalized or, as you said, minoritized communities, that there was possibly a lesson for archiving and community building beyond the sphere of comics that could be found by looking at these webcomics as an instance of participatory culture (Hatfield 2015). Those are not questions I would have been able to understand ten years ago, let alone ask. They are not questions that my teaching has taken up until maybe the last couple of years, and certainly not from an LIS perspective. But there is an instance of a body of work, an emerging trend of LBGTQ and particularly trans-themed webcomics, that's brought to light by a methodological perspective or disciplinary perspective I don't have.

Because I'm a language and lit person, and an English department person particularly, I come from a culture of major author studies and all the things that are embedded in that capital-a notion of the Author: professionaliza-tion, eloquence, expertise, brilliance. I'm glad to see comics studies embrace that sort of thing; I'm glad to be able to teach some classes about particular authors, which I've done a couple of times, but those aren't always the right questions to ask. I remember my teachers in grad school who only wanted to teach the heavy-hitters, they taught the Milton, Shakespeare, and Joyce seminars, and there's a part of literary training that leads you to admire that kind of perspective. For me, that might be Jack Kirby or the Brothers Her-nandez or someone like that, but the kinds of questions that I would want to ask about those "Authors" are not the only questions that need to be asked.

Coming back to your initial question, there are a couple observations I could make. First, the academic beachhead for comics studies in the United States was the Popular Culture Association. Speaking personally, I came up through that experience myself. It was sort of a rebellious offshoot of American studies and of literature departments in the '60s and '70s, right? Second, the continuing dominance of comics studies by English departments, at least in the United States and broadly in North America, may also limit the kinds of questions people ask. So you might look at that kind of disciplinary formation as already setting a template or a set of brackets that could, for a generation, limit some of the conversations that we have. Third, it's histori-cally tied to comics fandom, which in the United States is historically tied to a particular kind of comic book, where it's been sort of monolithically white and male despite the many important exceptions that scholarship has now unearthed. Superhero fandom, despite being much more diverse now than it was twenty years ago, also conduces to a particular kind of focus. Comics fandom of the pre-internet age, particularly, feeds into popular comics scholarship, which is also an important source of theorizing of comics, so to the extent that the academic field partakes of that history it's going to take up some of the demographic limitations of the field as well. On my side, it must be admitted, alternative and underground comics in North America are a largely white phenomenon, more so than superhero comics are, frankly. Superhero comics have done a much better job at being diverse than alternative comics have. It shames me to admit that because when I wrote my book, *Alternative Comics* (Hatfield 2005), I thought that was the future of everything, but that's a particular kind of cultural formation, an *avant garde* cultural formation of a certain kind from which some creators and audiences of color have felt themselves to be excluded. So the very things on which the literary appreciation of comics—whether that be mine or, let's say, Hillary Chute and her generation—is premised come out of a tradition that has not been particularly encouraging, frankly, on the matter of race and ethnicity. We have to go a lot farther afield in comics to find the kinds of attention to diversity that Franny was talking about. Here is something where I feel sort of personally implicated because, in the rearview mirror, alternative comics now looks like a very culturally specific formation to me—unless we take a much broader definition that includes webcomics and other kinds of graphic novel production—but what I was studying in grad school that became my first book is not the most diverse corpus of comics.

What I would want people to remember, though, is that all of those areas, whether it be the Pop Culture Association, English studies, rhetoric and writing studies, or what have you, these are all moving targets. They've all had their own struggles with, as Franny said, decolonization, with diversifying and including—not just tolerating—but including, understanding, and learning from, they've all had their struggles with broadening their footprint. Comics studies comes out of a lot of those things.

BW: So, we've taken a journey through the history of comics studies and talked about trying to understand how it's shifted over time. And you've both raised a lot of really interesting dimensions for us to think about how that field has shifted around different centers of gravity as we've moved through things. Now, it seems to me that we have seen some real growth and some really significant advances, yet, despite them, I often feel as though many comics scholars still act as though or assume they're in a position of weakness in any number of ways. Why is there still so much status anxiety in comics studies? And how does that shape the work that we do?

CH: That's exactly what this book foreword that I was working on is about. Why do we keep pretending that we're new? I'm sure that it has an important identity function for us. We're beleaguered in trying to find our way toward jobs and trying to help other people do the same. To be David with a sling in hand, staring down Goliath, is a kind of heroic identity. It's also self-marginalizing and self-defeating. I guess that's a problem. But rhetorically we sometimes take up a resistive, "can't get no respect" kind of stance because—maybe you just have to. Searching for jobs and positions and advocating through dissertation committees—that's difficult for everybody. My fear is that, in persistently claiming its outsider status and forgetting that it actually does have a history, comics studies will keep shooting itself in the foot. It's nice to display your bona fides as an underdog or an outsider, but it can also be self-marginalizing. Franny, what do you think?

FH: I wrote my master's thesis in 2008 and was writing about this. I remember being really irritated how Groensteen used that kind of approach to comics theory. I think it goes hand in hand with the irritation at people constantly discovering comics—columbusing—thinking they're the first person to ever realize this stuff.

CH: Columbusing—a verb—that's great.

FH: I didn't make that up. So, on one hand, we've got the perception that we are outsiders, and I think that's constantly poked at by the people coming in and not looking at the history of comics studies. That there is a body of work on this. But I try not to perpetuate that by acknowledging the breadth and excitement of comics studies.

Even when I was in graduate school, I was always getting forwarded CFPs for conferences all over the world. I'm like, "Well, it's great that these exist. If the person who forwarded it to me would remember that the department doesn't have funding to send me to Europe twice a year, that would be great, too."

I don't know. I don't have a good answer for why we keep doing this, but I try not to. And it's not like we're the only discipline that has a slight chip on our shoulder for people not giving us enough credit. Computers and Writing has this tension with Digital Humanities of—"well, we've been doing this work since the eighties." And now, people are like, "Oh, I just figured this out." We've got several journals and a huge body of work on these things. So, maybe it's the problem of academia in general that we may be a little siloed from one another and we need to find more ways to be visible and accessible to people who want more information on this.

CH: I almost feel like comics studies can be an antisilo. It's such a multidisciplinary activity, and I will always—for my part—encourage that. I do think that there are some real obstacles. I don't think that this is only a matter of managing perceptions. There are some real obstacles. We've learned that having annual or biennial conferences and having dedicated, peer-reviewed journals are not insurmountable obstacles. We've learned that teaching courses in comics or with a significant emphasis on comics is not an insurmountable obstacle. But the ways that we're used to thinking about success academically have to do with program development. And program development is a very difficult obstacle. It is the one area in which comics studies is weakest currently in my view.

By program development, I mean minors, majors, and graduate concentrations in and certificate programs in comics studies. We find a number of majors in sequential art or comics study in creative art programs within art schools. For example, the Columbus College of Art and Design just announced its Comics and Narrative Practice major, and there are comics concentrations that exist at other schools, such as the Minneapolis College of Art and Design and Savannah College of Art and Design. Of course, there are dedicated schools like the Center for Cartoon Studies in New England. In terms of the study of comics outside of creative programs—social scientific and humanistic studies of comics—there are very few concentrations and degree programs. There have been a few minors adopted literally within the last handful of years. There's a graduate concentration at the University of Florida. There are emergent programs in Canadian higher ed. There are a few things here and there—the University of Oregon and also Portland State both establishing minors and concentrations in comics studies. Building degree programs is hard, and I think a lot of people may not feel as if they've arrived until they have that. I've often thought, and still tend to think, that the model for a degree program in comics is going to be a very delicate thing to set out because there is probably not warrant in most colleges and universities for developing a self-contained comics studies department—I'm not sure it would always be a good thing if there were—but there probably isn't because we're using a bunch of different disciplinary skills, those of rhetoric and communication studies, cultural studies, art history, literature, and so on. We're using these skills that are cultivated by experts in other disciplines. Those experts often do have departments of their own at colleges and at universities. We don't necessarily stand to gain by creating new department cultures that are duplicating some of the skills or methods that are served by existing departments in a time of economic privation and drastic shifts in higher ed. Then there's the business of what would a major in comics studies be worth to a student, and that's something we think about a lot in the age of accountability and metrics and so on and so forth.

FH: In a time of increasing vocationalization of the bachelor's degree, it's a particularly hard time to propose comics as something you could major in. Like really hard. It seems like a perfect minor. "That's something I'm really passionate about, but I'm going to major in something that matches a job description." I teach at a polytechnic school, so that's an even bigger concern. If we were having this conversation in a different decade, we might see more majors pop up, but if it's going to grow in that way, comics people are going to have to be wily about it. For me, I'm looking at the growth of the professional writing major, which has come out of rhet/comp for the most part as a different approach to what an English or English-like major might look like. I'm thinking rhet/comp is something that you could make a bachelor's degree in. I've been involved in trying to write a proposal for one at my school, but not everybody is on board. It's hard to propose a new major. Even if you think it's perfectly self-justified, even if you can point to a gazillion job openings, it still requires a huge amount of justification and argumentation.

CH: I had a conversation with Ben Saunders, the founder of comics studies at the U of Oregon about this. Ben wasn't sure that he wanted to angle for a major, having established a successful minor, and I think partly it had to do with what you called the vocationalization or vocational training aspect of it. He said he maybe could envision a comics major if there were a studio component and it were allied with creative arts instruction: illustration, design, or animation for people who are interested in making comics art. I can see that, because you're developing vocational skills—a battery of skills—in addition to developing critical and historical understandings. I've thought about that. At my school and my department, we've developed a minor in popular culture studies. After several years on the backburner, this minor is finally established. We do have a minor in rhetoric and writing. Recruiting for these minors and pitching the new minor, as you say, Franny, is a lot of work. It's especially daunting if you're a relatively recent hire, but I've been at my school for fifteen years, and I'm still learning. I've proposed courses and gotten those approved—but proposing a program? I would have gone to Cal State Northridge already and proposed a comics studies minor if I knew that I had somebody—say, some colleagues in the Modern Languages and Literatures department, teachers of French and of Japanese, particularly—who had an interest in or were qualified to teach on bandes dessinées and manga, in particular. If we had that, I would go and propose a minor, which is basically what they did at the University of Oregon. They have other language programs and arts programs that can help, so it's not just in the English department, which Ben Saunders calls home. The nature and goal of a program and the process of building it are serious challenges to program development.

It's worth noting that the graduate concentration in Comics and Visual Rhetoric at the University of Florida was founded before any of these liberal arts minors in comics studies. I think that may be because the vocational emphasis, as we imagine it, is in undergraduate instruction. The first program I knew of in the United States that had an announced focus in comics was this graduate track in English in Gainesville. It's only more recently we've seen the development of these more or less liberal arts minors in comics study apart from the studio classes. But comics studies does seem like a difficult sell at the undergraduate level. I anticipate doing it at my school; I anticipate doing, as you said, that minor, Franny. It feels like the logical way to go.

FH: There's also the approach to a major that has specializations. Something like a writing major that had comics as a possible focus is another way I could see it working well, like a writing and publishing or professional writing major. I could see comics and visual rhetoric fitting into that. If I were to try to propose something, it would probably be more like that. That's mostly because minors are really hard to pick up at the school I teach at. Most majors are pretty locked into a series of courses. Though my school just started an arts and humanities minor that has exploded and tons of people are minoring in that, so who knows?

CH: I think what we're talking about here is the difference between excelling or doing well at the things you would do to get a job and excelling or doing well at things that you can only do *in* a job. Once you find yourself in a place, the new frontier for comics studies becomes program development. That is extremely challenging to do because it is never only theoretical. It's always a local issue. It's always a diplomatic issue. It's always an issue with resource implications, and it's an issue that will always have to be resolved differently at every single school that will undertake a comics certificate, minor, major, or focus.

We're talking about something that people are not able to do until they've found themselves in relatively secure institutional footing. Only then will program development become something that you could really undertake. Maybe I just feel this way because it's something I'm thinking about quite locally at my school right now. I've gotten a lot of pats on the back for doing comics-related things, but where's the program? Where's the concentration that will take the load off my one and only introductory comics course, where I try to do so many things, and allow me to spread that workload over multiple courses and provide incentives for students to take multiple courses? Where is that?

Lots of newly established or recently established fields across academia are probably feeling the same thing. Again, it's a time of profound challenge and privation in higher ed, where there's an accountability mandate, which can be to some extent be bent into helping comics studies. But it's always difficult. There's so many different mandates. And you hear so many stories about the nature of the profession—higher ed in general—everybody is soul-searching and reexamining themselves, and comics studies is coming up to the chalk line and getting ready at precisely that moment. So, I do think there are still some things to be done that may account for the sense that we still feel a little bit junior as a field. There still is some institution-building to be done, especially in terms of building programs and serving students. In terms of published scholarship, I think we got that. The other vital piece of the picture still feels a little "becoming" to me.

JS: So, given these kinds of challenges, what do you see as the future of comics studies? Where do you see it going? What kinds of issues do you think we really need to address, including things like programming, as we move forwards?

FH: Public scholarship! My thinking about this is currently tied to the idea of doing comics work in rural areas when comics fandom has been implicitly very urban and metropolitan. I was inspired to think about this by going to the Alaska Robotics Comics Camp and hanging out with a bunch of creators and talking about this.[1] There was a panel about rural comics that had Crystal Worl, who is an artist in Juneau, and Kate Beaton talking about her work, and I was like, "Oh, god, I do this." Because I'm a faculty member at a pretty rural university, and I've been involved with putting on a comic con here. My partner and I showed up a month before the first one was held, and it's run by our public library. My partner works at the library, and I'm involved in doing stuff for teens and kids. I teach comics workshops at the library. I did a Free Comic Book Day workshop, and I did a panel on women in comics. So, thinking about what we can give to comics and to fans, showing that comics are teachable and learnable.

For me, as a teacher of writing, my field assumes that writing is teachable and learnable. That's a grounding assumption of what we do, and I bring that to comics. I spread it as far as I can. This is something that people can do. It's not like magical, uniquely gifted artists are the only people allowed to use this technology to communicate. Or if it's presenting models of criticism—for fandom maybe—what do we do? What makes that similar or different to fandom meta? What are the goals? Could we triangulate between fan criticism and scholarly criticism into something that might be a really interesting combination of both?

CH: I think one of the really interesting implications of what you're saying, Franny, is that comics studies has the potential to challenge the very terms of advancement or recognition—what counts as scholarship. Right?

FH: Yes.

CH: We have a particularly interesting and informed approach to public scholarship in comics studies. So much of the scholarship has its roots in the conversation of fans and the activity of fans. This is a fraught relationship for comics studies because there's a need—in terms of academic institutions—to assert one's separateness from fandom as a phenomenon. I myself have felt that need and argued that point, although I've been a fan most of my life and expect to be always, so there's a lot of tension there for me, as there is for a lot of people who try to walk the walk and talk the talk. But we do have this history of fan-based involvement and indeed fan scholarship—without which we would have nothing in comics studies, frankly. Most of the map would be empty. It would be unpopulated. It would be erased. Boy, I'm using a lot of colonial metaphors today: frontiers, maps, the whole territory thing.

FH: Right?

CH: It's a little trite of me to pursue the metaphor, but if not for the people who had charted things earlier coming out of fandom, I think academic comics study would have precious little to build upon.

I do think—and I see this in my colleagues in English as well as across the college generally—that public scholarship is an area of not brand new but growing concern. So, I would agree with Franny in saying that there are opportunities for, as we say on my campus, community engagement and service learning. And that's often the scholarship of teaching and the scholarship of service, which have become buzzwords at a lot of institutions—hopefully at more institutions as they learn to value that.

FH: Or how to do it. It's hard.

CH: But valuing also means being judged. At my school, the mantra is teaching, scholarship, and service. They see your personnel file, and they judge you accordingly. When you introduce a relatively novel concept like the scholarship of service, you're asking people to take on a new set of concepts to recognize and enable public engagement as a kind of scholarship. In these times, again, of privation and challenge in higher ed, I think we see this public intellectual role as both a challenge and an opportunity. We are increasingly called upon to demonstrate the relevance of our work outside of the communities of our work, narrowly conceived, and in that sense comics studies might have a leg up. Most of the people that I know that are engaged in comics studies in a devoted or enthusiastic way have some non-academic piece of it that they like to maintain. Maybe it's a different kind of writing. Maybe it's the organizing of panels for comic con events that are not strictly academic.

FH: Yeah, I think we could be leaders in that if the rest of the university is trying to get in on it.

CH: That said, there are some things that are difficult—there are some academic habits that are difficult to get around. Let me give you a concrete example. Of course, I'm involved with the Comics Studies Society, and we've established *Inks: The Journal of the Comics Studies Society*, with Jared Gardner (and now Qiana Whitted) as editor. I thought, as we were investigating things that the society might provide that would serve the needs of scholars and build the community, that surely we would need an annual or semiannual conference and we would need a journal of record, a journal over which we felt we had some sense of ownership. Well, working at a school where the library has a moratorium on ordering new journals for financial reasons, I'm trying to talk people out of that moratorium when it comes to our newly spawned journal. I had long thought an open-access journal might be the most timely and appropriate thing we could do, but, frankly, that really doesn't support the model of a dues-supported, academic organization. Try as I might, I could not get my mind around how to make that work. Eventually, you have to ask people for money so that you can sustain the work of community-building, and you have to provide a concrete deliverable in return for their money, so we're doing what most groups traditionally do. It's a journal, and it's available either from subscription or through Project Muse for people accessing it electronically. On the one hand, you have the institution-building value of something like the Comics Studies Society and, on the other hand, the public outreach value of doing things in open access. These things don't always jibe together very well. We still operate in a profession where things that must be underwritten or supported either by institutions or members' dues are mission-critical, and that tends to encourage specialization and potentially more of a closing in rather than an opening out. That's not what I would want for comics studies, but I feel like we need a bit of both. We're dealing with a situation where, in order to take the next steps toward professionalization of the field, we have to have these concrete deliverables that we can give to people who are supporting us concretely with their dues, as well as supporting in spirit.

At the same time, so much of what's developing in comics studies is in the realm of public scholarship. In the CSS, we have the Gilbert Seldes Prize, a prize for public comics scholarship published in nonacademic venues, which will probably mostly be online, frankly. We are doing that because it's an important aspect of this field. Historically, that recognition of fan scholarship and essayistic criticism beyond the academy is really important. Likewise, our CSS book prize is open to trade publishers or other publishers, as well as university presses or academic publishers. It sort of has to be. There's too much activity that's meaningful and important in comics studies that's happening outside of academic presses. At the same time, having prizes for books and essays is very much a traditional, dues-supported, academic, learned-society kind of behavior.

FH: We should give way more prizes in comics studies.

CH: Yes. Some of that is outward-looking, and some of it is inward-turning. I think in order to meet the needs of professionalization, we're going to have to do a little bit of both. But I would want to underscore what I take to be Franny's essential point, which is that everything is changing in academia. Comics studies by virtue of its ties to fandom and its historic origins has a potential to embrace some of these changes more readily than other hidebound fields do, and hopefully we can take advantage of that.

Can I say one more thing before we go? If I may say so, I think this is a wonderful time to do this collection. I've seen a lot of emerging disciplinary self-consciousness or self-awareness in recent and forthcoming publications in the field. I think you see a lot of articles and monographs that really question the terms of success. We even started this conversation today thinking about, "Hey, we have success. What does that mean? What constitutes success?" But I'm thinking about people I know, like Marc Singer or Chris Pizzino, who are writing studies now that are really questioning the gentrification of comics underneath the edicts of literary studies. I think there's going to be some nice broadsides fired. That's going to be really useful.

So there is emerging talk about comics studies as a field, not just activity around the study of particular comics but comics studies as a thing. We will see, in the next three to four years, a raft of publications that really take up the idea that, "Okay, comics studies is a thing. What do we do now?" I think that's going to be coming, so I welcome anything that's going to contribute to tipping the apple cart this way or that in order to make interesting conversations about that.

Notes

1. http://minicon.alaskarobotics.com

References

Bourdieu, Pierre. 2013. *Distinction: A Social Critique of the Judgement of Taste*. London: Routledge. First published in English 1984.

Gateward, Frances, and John Jennings. 2015. *The Blacker the Ink: Constructions of Black Identity in Comics and Sequential Art*. New Brunswick, NJ: Rutgers University Press.

Hatfield, Charles. 2005. *Alternative Comics: An Emerging Literature*. Jackson: University Press of Mississippi.

Hatfield, Nami Kitsune. 2015. "TRANSforming Spaces: Transgender Webcomics as a Model for Transgender Empowerment and Representation within Library and Archive Spaces." *Queer Cats Journal of LGBTQ Studies* 1 (1): 57–73. http://escholarship.org/uc/item/3g15q00g.

Royster, Jacqueline Jones, and Gesa E. Kirsch. 2012. *Feminist Rhetorical Practices: New Horizons for Rhetoric, Composition, and Literacy Studies*. Carbondale: Southern Illinois Press.

Smith, Linda Tuhiwai. 1999. *Decolonizing Methodologies: Research and Indigenous Peoples*. London: Zed Books.

Smith, Matthew, and Randy Duncan, eds. 2017. *The Secret Origins of Comics Studies*. New York: Routledge.

Contributors

Bart Beaty is author, editor, and translator of numerous books in comics studies, including *Twelve Cent Archie* and *The Greatest Comic Book of All Time* (with Benjamin Woo). Most recently, he is the coeditor, with Charles Hatfield, of *Comics Studies: A Guidebook*. He is the principal investigator of the SSHRC-funded project What Were Comics?, whose progress can be followed at whatwerecomics.com.

T. Keith Edmunds is an instructor in business administration at postsecondary institutions in Brandon, Manitoba. He earned his PhD from the University of Guelph. While his research interests primarily center around sense of community, he too often can be found reading comics instead of being productive.

Adriana Estrada Wilson received a BA in sociology from the University of California, Santa Barbara, and an MA in sociology from the University of Houston. She has served as an instructor in the Department of Sociology at Santa Barbara City College, where she taught Introduction to Sociology, Media, Culture and Society, and Marriage, Family and Intimacy. She currently serves in the non-profit sector at Project GRAD Houston as the director of programming and innovation. In this role, she is able to apply her knowledge in sociology to help empower learners from underserved communities to access and excel in postsecondary education.

Eike Exner is author of *Comics and the Origins of Manga—A Revisionist History* (Rutgers University Press, 2021).

Christopher J. Galdieri is associate professor in the Department of Politics at Saint Anselm College, where he studies and teaches courses on American politics. He is widely cited as an expert on New Hampshire politics and particularly the state's first-in-the-nation presidential primary. He is the author of *Stranger in a Strange State: The Politics of Carpetbagging from Robert Kennedy to Scott Brown* (State University of New York Press, 2019) and *Donald Trump and New Hampshire Politics* (Palgrave, 2020).

Ivan Lima Gomes is adjunct professor of modern and contemporary/Latin American history at the Federal University of Goiás. He holds a PhD in social history from the Federal Fluminense University, which was supported by funding from the Conselho Nacional de Desenvolvimento Científico e Tecnológico (CNPq). His research interests concern the historiographic study of cultural practices, focused on the aesthetics, history, and theory of comics, publishing history, visual culture, and Latin American history. He is the author of *Os Novos Homens do Amanhã: Projetos e Disputas em Torno dos Quadrinhos na América Latina (Brasil e Chile, anos 1960–1970)* (Prismas, 2018).

Charles Hatfield, professor of English at California State University, Northridge, is the author of *Alternative Comics* (2005) and *Hand of Fire: The Comics Art of Jack Kirby* (2011). He is coeditor (with Bart Beaty) of *Comics Studies: A Guidebook* (2020) and (with Jeet Heer and Kent Worcester) of *The Superhero Reader* (2013). He curated the exhibition *Comic Book Apocalypse: The Graphic World of Jack Kirby* (CSUN Art Galleries, 2015) and coedited (with Ben Saunders) its catalog. His essays have appeared in *Uncanny Bodies: Superhero Comics and Disability, The Secret Origins of Comics Studies, The Oxford Handbook of Children's Literature, Keywords for Children's Literature, The Lion and the Unicorn, Children's Literature Association Quarterly, ImageTexT, SubStance, The Comics Journal,* and other books and periodicals. He has chaired both the International Comic Arts Forum and the MLA Forum on Comics and Graphic Narratives, and he cofounded the Comics Studies Society.

Franny Howes is associate professor of communication at Oregon Tech, where she codirects the Professional Writing program and teaches a variety of classes in writing, digital media, entrepreneurship, and design. She is also a cartoonist with over a decade of independent comics publishing experience. She founded the Lemon Brick Road Studios comics collective in 2016 to share this knowledge with the community.

John A. Lent taught at the college/university level from 1960 through 2011, including stints in the Philippines, Malaysia, Canada, China, and the United States. Professor Lent pioneered in the study of mass communication and popular culture in Asia (since 1964) and the Caribbean (since 1968), comic art and animation, and development communication. He has authored or edited 85 books, published and edited *International Journal of Comic Art* (which he founded 1999–), *Asian Cinema* (1994–2012), and *Berita* (1975–2001), chaired Asian Popular Culture (PCA), Asian Cinema Studies Society (1994–2012), Comic Art Working Group (IAMCR, 1984–2016), Asian-Pacific Animation and Comics Association (2008–), Asian Research Center for Animation and Comics Art (2005–), and Malaysia/Singapore/Brunei Studies Group of the Association for Asian Studies (1976–1983), all of which he founded.

Amy Louise Maynard is a former postgraduate student of the University of Adelaide, where she studied media and communications. She was formerly an undergraduate at the University of South Australia. In 2017, she published her thesis, *A Scene in Sequence: Australian Comics Production as a Creative Industry 1975–2017*. She no longer works in academia.

Shari Sabeti is a reader in arts and humanities education at the University of Edinburgh, United Kingdom. Her research interests focus on arts and cultural heritage education across a variety of sites, including museums, schools, community, and commercial contexts. She has written about creative writing, literary and visual adaptation, and gallery education practices, paying close attention to the perspective of artists and creative practitioners through ethnographic and arts-based methods.

Rob Salkowitz is an author, consultant and educator focused on the media, entertainment, publishing, and events industries. His book *Comic-Con and the Business of Pop Culture* (McGraw-Hill, 2012) looked at how comics moved from the edges to the center of the global entertainment universe in the twenty-first century, represented by the rise of San Diego Comic-Con as a megaevent. He continues to write about the industry in *Forbes*, *Publishers Weekly*, *ICv2* and elsewhere, and works with companies in the media and event space to measure the impact of fandom. Rob is affiliate faculty in the Communication Leadership Graduate Program at the University of Washington in Seattle.

Kalervo A. Sinervo holds a PhD in interdisciplinary humanities from Concordia University, where he wrote his thesis on transmedia strategy, video-game spaces, and Gotham City. He has published and presented widely on digital comics, comics piracy, comics materiality, and the comics industry. In 2019, he began a postdoctoral fellowship at the University of Calgary. He can be found online @kalervideo or at badpanels.com.

Jeremy Stoll is a comics creator, scholar, and assistant professor and head of Science and Social Science at Columbus College of Art and Design. He is committed to ethnographic research on comics and community in India with a focus on artist collectives, independent publishing, and social justice. His scholarship has appeared in *The International Journal of Comic Art; Marg, a Magazine of the Arts; Cultures of Comics Work*; and *The Routledge Companion to Comics*. Stoll is also committed to visual storytelling on the ineffable in life, with recent works in *Rainbow Reflections: Body Image Comics for Queer Men* and *Blocked: Stories from the World of Online Dating*.

Valerie Wieskamp is assistant professor in communication and an affiliate faculty member of gender, women, and sexuality studies at Appalachian State University. She holds a BFA in graphic design from Iowa State University, an MA in multicultural communication from DePaul University, and a PhD in rhetoric and public culture from Indiana University, Bloomington. In her research and teaching, Dr. Wieskamp explores the rhetoric of public advocacy and mediated culture in topics related to gender, race, violence, war, and environmental sustainability through a critical/cultural approach. She has written about sexual violence in US wars, gendered representations of heroism, representations of violence and war in public memory, narratives of trauma, and the use of visual culture to advocate against sexual violence. To support her work on narratives regarding war and military service, she has received grant funding from the National Endowment for the Humanities' Dialogues on the Experience of War program. Her published research has appeared in scholarly journals such as the *Quarterly Journal of Speech, Organization, Western Journal of Communication*, and *Rhetoric & Public Affairs*.

Benjamin Woo is associate professor of communication and media studies and director of the Research on Comics, Con Events, and Transmedia Laboratory at Carleton University (Ottawa, Canada). He is the author of *Getting a Life: The Social Worlds of Geek Culture*, coauthor (with Bart Beaty) of *The Greatest Comic Book of All Time: Symbolic Capital and the Field of American Comic Books*, and coeditor (with Stuart R. Poyntz and Jamie Rennie) of *Scene Thinking: Cultural Studies from the Scenes Perspective*.

Index